LETTING GO

A Parents' Guide to Today's College Experience

GO

LETTING

*A Parents' Guide
to Today's College Experience*

Karen Levin Coburn
and
Madge Lawrence Treeger

ADLER&ADLER

Published in the United States in
1992 by
Adler & Adler, Publishers, Inc.
4550 Montgomery Avenue
Bethesda, Maryland 20814

Library of Congress Cataloging-
in-Publication Data

Coburn, Karen Levin, 1941–
    Letting go : a parent's guide to today's college ex-
perience /   Karen Levin Coburn and Madge Lawrence
Treeger.—2nd ed.
    p. cm.
    Includes bibliographical references and index.
    ISBN 0-917561-7-59
    1. College students—United States—Psychology. 2.
Parenting—United States. 3. Parent and child—
United States. 4. Universities and colleges—
United States. I. Treeger, Madge Lawrence, 1934– .
II. Title.
LA229.C53   1992
378.1'98–dc20   91–46815
                                          CIP

Printed in the United States of
America
Second Edition

*To our loving partners, Stephen
and Tom . . . and Alison, Andrew, Anne, and
Jennie, who continue to teach us about
letting go.*

CONTENTS

Acknowledgements   ix

PART I | The College Experience

Introduction: Letting Go   3

Chapter One   Some Things Never Change:
                The Search for Identity, Independence,
                and Intimacy   11

Chapter Two   Some Things Do Change:
                College Life Today   28

PART II | A Parents' Guide: From Start to Finish

Chapter Three   Great Expectations   71

Chapter Four   Ready, Set, Go: The Departure   97

Chapter Five   Orientation and Disorientation   129

Chapter Six   The Freshman Year: Academic
                Life and the College Scene   151

Chapter Seven   In and Out of Your Life   199

Chapter Eight   Sophomore Slump and
                the Years Beyond   234

Chapter Nine   The End is the Beginnng   274

                Notes   291

                Bibliography   295

                Index   303

ACKNOWLEDGMENTS

We are deeply grateful to all the students, parents, and college faculty and administrators who have shared their insights and experiences with us. We have changed some of the identifying information to protect anonymity but you are the soul of this book.

In addition, we would like to thank the following friends and colleagues who have listened, questioned, critiqued, and continued to give their support during the last few years: Justin Carroll, Robert Easton, Sara Epstein, Heather Feuerhahn, Rosemary Garagnani, Peggy Guest, Julie Jones, Meg Jacobs, Helen Kornblum, Ellen Krout-Levine, Marylen Mann, Marny Muir, Susan Rava, Paul Scheffel, Linda Skrainka, Stephen Skrainka, Bob Sortland, Sally Stein.

We appreciate the active interest of our publishers, Esthy and Jim Adler, who had faith in us from the start. Our editor, Amy Pastan, with tact and care provided suggestions that helped the book take its final shape. And finally we give special thanks to our agent, Elizabeth Kaplan of Sterling Lord Literistics, who saw this project through from the kernel of an idea to its completion. She has been a constant source of good advice, enthusiasm, and encouragement.

PART I
THE COLLEGE EXPERIENCE

Introduction:

LETTING GO

"I'm not getting out."

I sat behind the wheel of the car; Jennie sat beside me with her tattered stuffed teddy bear at her side, and we looked out at the line of young men and women laughing and chatting as they waited for the doors of the freshman dormitory to open.

"I'm not getting out," she repeated.

I panicked. My mind flashed back to the first day of nursery school. "Don't leave me," were her words then.

"But you wanted to get here early to get the best bed," I reminded her.

"I've changed my mind," she replied. That was evident.

We had just traveled for seventeen hours, over two days. Jennie was beginning her freshman year at college—our first child to leave home. Was I going to have to turn around and go back to St. Louis with her still beside me?

"Suppose we get out and just stand next to the car." She agreed reluctantly. I was relieved to see her leave the teddy bear in the car.

Jennie made it to the line of seemingly relaxed, happy freshmen—and was swept along by an over-anxious young woman who handled her anxiety by hyperactivity instead of shyness. I looked over and saw Jennie blending in and looking just as relaxed as the others and let out a sigh of relief.

Within a half hour, I was excess baggage. Now it was my turn to separate. "Why don't you wander around campus and stop back in a few hours," Jennie suggested diplomatically.

(What about all my fantasies of helping you fix up your room, chat with your roommates a bit, and see what coed living looks like?) Of course, I kept these thoughts to myself. I smiled diplomatically in return, said good-bye, and began a somewhat aimless tour of the campus, passing other parents along the way who looked as lost as I felt. When I returned to the dorm, I found out Jennie had arranged for me to have dinner with another parent since she already had plans. I graciously bowed out, returned to the motel, and had a good cry.

Two days earlier, as a part of freshman orientation at Washington University, I had stood on a stage before approximately three hundred parents who had come to hear my professional words of wisdom as a member of the Student Counseling Service. The topic was "Letting Go."

And now *I* had begun.

The process of "letting go" actually starts in the first years of life. As parents, we can remember the struggles of the early years, especially between the ages of one and a half and three, when our children seesawed back and forth between acts of independence—a toddling strut accompanied by a "world is my oyster" smile—and clinging, whining periods of hanging on. Although this separation process continues throughout our children's growing years, it is especially evident as they move through adolescence and begin to leave home, when we once again see their ambivalence acted out in puzzling ways. We were often more patient and understanding of the process when our children were small. We were also better informed. The "terrible twos" may not have been pleasant, but we all knew they were coming, and we knew they would end. Information and reassurance were readily available if we felt uncertain about our children's development or our roles as parents. But when we send our sons and daughters off to college, there are no Dr. Spocks to reassure us, no guidelines for moving through this time of transition.

Some parents don't see this as a time of transition at all. It is simply the end of childrearing for them and of childhood for their sons and daughters. "You're an adult now; start acting like one," they admonish. Others have trouble giving up their role. They still see themselves as necessary protectors and their sons and daughters as immature children rather than self-reliant young adults. "Don't you worry about it, dear. I'll call your Dean and take care of it for you."

Most of us flounder somewhere in between. We send our children off with a mixture of anticipation and anxiety, a sense of loneliness and freedom, fantasy and reality. Our childrearing days are ending. Our children are launched. We anticipate dealing with our own reactions to their leaving—time on our hands, financial belt-tightening, a quiet house—but we are caught off guard by the continuing demands and concerns that we discover as each week and month goes by *after* the launching. As they struggle to be independent and separate once again, as in their toddler years, they venture forth with bravado and periods of new-found confidence and wisdom, only to retreat into times of anxiety and hanging on. They want Mom or Dad to be there *when* they want them. They call and pour out fears and hurts, hoping to be understood, or they withdraw into silence; advice and parental concerns become intrusions.

We shift gears constantly as we meet our offspring in an elusive dance of change. We find ourselves relentlessly retracing old patterns one week and discovering new ways of getting along the next. The temptation to tell our children *how* to be independent is a compelling one. The contradictory, but all too familiar, parental message is, "It's about time you were grown up and on your own, so follow my advice." Translated, this painfully becomes: "It's time for you to be independent, but I don't trust your judgment."

As our sons and daughters enter these college years, we have to come to terms with their strengths *and* their limitations. At the same time we realize that we too are at a watershed, entering into a new phase of our lives—growing older. We may find ourselves taking a new look at our marriage or career—our own limitations. And so as they struggle with a turmoil of conflicting emotions about leaving, we often are flooded with conflicting feelings of our own about being left.

It is common for parents who were eager to see their children leave, to lament their departure later. "Somehow there must be a biological process at work; my son is so impossible this year it makes it easy to see him go—in fact I can't wait," becomes, three months later, "It's so quiet in the house; I have to hold back from wanting to call him and find out how his day went"—the same parent wanting to stay connected and wanting to let go.

Another parent, whose daughter struggled through several rebellious years in high school and emerged at seventeen as a delightful young woman and close companion to her mother, confessed, "I dreaded her leaving; we had just begun to enjoy each other again. But now that she's gone, I have to admit I love the simplicity and freedom of living as a couple again."

We all know intellectually that this is a time for our children to separate and assert their independence. But long after they have become taller or stronger than we are, our primal protective feelings are easily unleashed. We carry images in our heads of the curly haired toddler, the gap-toothed six-year-old, and times when a caress or a hug could make their world all better. As they get older the problems they face have increasingly greater consequences. The stakes get higher. The mature, rational part of us wants them to solve their own problems and believes they can, but another part of us wants to stay connected, be in control, feel needed, and protect them from the pain we know they will have to face.

We tend to see the years of college as the calm before the storm—a time within a safe bastion of learning that will provide a protected environment for our children as they prepare for the "real world." Though college provides a unique opportunity for learning, the college years are no more a "calm" nor a "storm" than all the years that follow. College students are confronted with a host of the pressures and societal constraints that are part of the *ongoing* process of human experience.

Our expectations of college life are often large-scale and grandiose. They are born of many factors: our own hopes and dreams, images from the media, a need to justify the large financial investment we are making. The fire is fanned by the big build-up of years of planning and positioning so that our children can compete in the furor of "getting in." We are courted with a marketing blitz from the institutions themselves, all promising dreams fulfilled, horizons waiting to be discovered, unencumbered bliss. The effect of all this is to raise colleges and universities to a larger than life, once-in-a-lifetime opportunity that will make or break our children's future. Both parents and students feel the pressure and push to make this myth their reality.

Most of us have the same hopes and goals for our children as they have for themselves. We want them to be happy and successful, self-confident and self-reliant. The trouble is that the specific notion of what constitutes success or self-reliance is often very different for a parent than it is for his or her offspring. Although the goal is valued, actual steps toward independence are likely to make parents nervous. Intellectual exploration tends to threaten established family values and ideas about life's meaning. Sudden shifts in behavior and ideas are confusing, and sometimes exasperating, to even the most patient, understanding parents. Too often, parents inhibit their children's growth without realizing how their good intentions are backfiring. It doesn't have to be that way, but as counselors, we've seen it happen again and again, and as parents, we have felt this dilemma ourselves.

Students talk to us about their parents—about pressures and misunderstandings and their longing to be accepted by their parents as separate adults. We listen; we probe; we empathize, and then we talk to our own college-age children who recite variations on the same themes. Only with them, *we're* the ones who "don't understand," who are "putting on too much pressure," who are "overprotective" or "not around" when we're needed. No wonder in the last few years, the family dynamics we hear about from students seem more complicated and more familiar than they used to. Our perspectives have broadened; our experience as parents has brought new insights to our work.

We both have spent much of our adult lives working on college and university campuses. We have listened to countless students as they have struggled with the disparity between their parents' expectations and their own; with broken romances and disappointing grades; with the excitement and the confusion of expanding intellectual horizons and new values. As we look out our windows at the ivy-covered Gothic buildings and the frisbee game in the quad, all may look idyllic, but when we listen to what students have to say it is clear that their lives are complex and often unsettling. No matter how fraught with complications and responsibilities our own adult lives may seem, we can't simply retreat to "the good old college days" refrain sung by many of our peers. Our students give us daily reminders that youth is not synonymous with simplicity or freedom from responsibility.

The college years are a time of transition for young people and their parents. There is no way to move through such an important passage without some feelings of dislocation and loss. But information and insight can help parents negotiate this significant and often neglected phase of their children's lives.

As professionals immersed in the daily routine of life on the college campus, we hope to offer a realistic view of the many facets of this experience—one that reflects the trials and tribulations as well as the excitement, opportunity, and promise of these years. We will focus on the experience of traditional-age college students who go to school away from home. Much of the material will be relevant, however, to parents of commuter students as well.

Part I of this book, "The College Experience," begins with information about late adolescent development, so that our children's behavior can be viewed in the broader context of normal growth. We will explain how *all* college students struggle with developing a sense of their own identity, with becoming independent, and with establishing intimacy. Each young person finds his or her own way to express these struggles, often to the consternation and confusion of concerned parents. But knowing that a certain amount of experimenting and exploring is, in fact, healthy is reassuring. Insight into normal development enables parents to discriminate between the universal problems of college students and those that require parental or professional intervention. With this understanding, parents can respond more appropriately and with more assurance to the signals our children send us.

We will look also at the changes in larger contemporary society, with its proliferation of choices and freedoms, and at its campus reflections in coed dorms, preprofessional pressures, and the paucity of social restrictions. Although we all went through our own versions of young adult confusion and self-discovery, the world in which we grew up was clearly different from the one our children are grappling with today. Perhaps no place is that more evident than on college campuses.

This chapter opened with the story of Jennie, clutching her childhood teddy bear. Her tenuous approach to the freshman dormitory and subsequent dismissal of her mother a few hours later was not an unusual sequence of events. What she needed most at that point was nothing more than her mother's willingness to let go.

Other freshmen find different ways to begin. One departs from his hometown airport, guitar slung casually over his shoulder, barely stopping to wave good-bye as he walks out to the plane. Then he calls his mother every night for two weeks. What does he need? Probably just a reassuring adult voice on the other end of the line who understands and tolerates his temporary need to return to familiar territory while he adjusts to an alien one. A flashback to his toddler years as he rushed off with gusto only to check back and make contact will help us to understand—he is still in the ongoing process of separating.

Another young woman drives off to college only a few hours from home. She doesn't call or come home for weeks. Her parents worry and feel hurt. She too is separating; perhaps she needs to "go cold turkey"—to sever the ties abruptly, at least for a while—so that she isn't pulled back to the close, secure home that is so easily accessible.

The theme of separation is the same for all these young people. The variations are uniquely their own. An understanding of separation, the thematic cornerstone to every chapter of this book, enables parents to engage in that process more productively.

Part II, "A Parents' Guide from Start to Finish," provides a chronological guide to the college experience from senior year in high school through graduation. We'll look at the way the separation process evolves, and the predictable rhythm it takes throughout the first academic year and the years that follow. Above all, we will listen to what college students and their parents have to say as they move through this exciting, sometimes turbulent phase of life. They will tell us what has worked for them and what hasn't.

Understanding what we and our children are going through reduces our fear and validates our reality. It opens our eyes so that we can see what their world is like; it allows us to listen more clearly and communicate more effectively. It frees us to help our children become themselves.

Chapter 1

SOME THINGS NEVER CHANGE: THE SEARCH FOR IDENTITY, INDEPENDENCE, AND INTIMACY

"Who am I, apart from my family, my church, my school?" This question is one young people ask themselves over and over again. It is a question replayed by every generation, each in its own context. We, their parents, struggled with the same question years ago as we tried to carve a niche on our own road to adulthood. The context may have changed, the choices may be different, but the theme is the same—the theme of self-definition. This is the curriculum not spelled out in college catalogues, and yet much of the college experience is devoted to it.

> I'm going to let my hair grow; I'm going to cut out drinking and smoking and be quiet and subdued—the way I was when I came here. They say a girl can't be like that and "get by," but I always loathed the typical college girl anyway. The main trouble is that whenever I am or claim to be different, I'm accused of posing—people can't conceive of how anyone can have any individualism. Damn it all, I'm going to change and be me.
>
> journal entry, sophomore, Smith College, 1924

> I feel like I can't be myself. I try to pretend everything's fine, but who am I kidding? I feel lonely and isolated even from my family and best friends at home. Part of that's my fault, because every time I try to write a letter or talk on the phone, I catch myself trying to impress people with how great things are. I don't want to admit to anyone that I'm having problems adjusting, so I try to overcompensate and act as if everything's wonderful and then I sound fake and I feel fake. I can't be natural—I'm not even sure what that is.
>
> journal entry, sophomore, University of Vermont, 1984

Sixty years passed between the journal entries of this current
college student and her grandmother, and yet both of these
women are grappling with issues of identity, with who they are
and how to integrate this sense of themselves with the world in
which they live.

Becoming a unique and individual person doesn't happen
at any one particular time. Hallmark has yet to design a card
for the universal celebration of "being an adult." Graduation
days, eighteenth birthdays, bar mitzvahs all have been adopted
as marker dates to note entry into so-called adulthood. The fact
that one ritual takes place at thirteen, another at eighteen or
twenty-one tells us that our notion of what adulthood is varies
by religion, culture, and individual family.

Many young men and women leave their homes to work,
marry, or go away to college. But to become separate in a
psychological sense is a lifelong process of becoming—continually building on, reaffirming, refining a sense of self. This
process begins in the first months of life.

Although the seeds of their own identity exist from the start,
infants are totally dependent on the person who cares for them,
usually their mother. Before they can discover their separateness, they must establish the boundaries between their mothers
and themselves. Understanding the complexities of that earlier
time helps put in perspective the often puzzling transitions of
the college years.

Separation in Early Childhood and Adolescence

The separation that begins in the first year of life is a prototype
for later separations, in particular for the turbulent years of
adolescence and young adulthood, when there is once again a
need to diminish the dependency on parents. Separation is not
isolation from others, but is instead a bridge that helps us cross
from dependence to interdependence. Parents' memories and
photograph albums carry images of their children's early attempts at separation: a baby tugging on his mother's nose,
yanking at her hair, peering out from behind chubby spread
fingers to play peekaboo; a seven-month-old, creeping across

the floor, pausing to glance back at her mother before scurrying on; a toddler walking like a drunken sailor, building up speed as he giggles exuberantly running away from his mother; the same toddler, as his mood shifts, waddling along, thumb in mouth, dragging a blanket behind him; a two-year-old throwing herself on the floor of the supermarket, screaming "no" furiously, her face red with rage and frustration, wanting to do it herself one minute and whiningly asking for help the next—all of these are the images of young children struggling with the confusion and ambivalence of separation.[1]

The images of separation in adolescence are as vivid and familiar to all parents as those of our children's early days. They are new images, reminiscent of old struggles. The teenager chafing at his parent's simplest words of advice; the seventeen-year-old, heady with a sense of her own high school success, flying off to college unaccompanied and secure, coming home six weeks later for refueling, her wings clipped with the discovery that she is no longer special; the nineteen-year-old, calling home depressed and frightened; an anxious senior asking her parents for advice one day and snapping, "It's my life" the next. All of these efforts to move away echo earlier times from our children's first three years of life. And they reawaken our own ambivalence about separation and may make it more difficult for us to let go.[2]

Identity

To separate psychologically is to know oneself. The core of identity, of one's uniqueness, is what makes it possible to tolerate the inevitable feeling of aloneness that we all experience. Despite moving across the country or the world, despite dramatic changes in emotions or physical feelings or interactions with a variety of people, we develop a sense of continuity, a consistent sense of who we are. It is this self-knowledge that makes it possible to move into truly intimate relationships with others without the fear of losing oneself or one's own integrity. Indeed, this search for a cohesive and integrated self is one of the major tasks of the college student.

Why now? Why does the concern for identity become so all-consuming during the college years? We know that our children have had distinct personalities for as long as we can remember. We speak of them in phrases that encapsulate characteristics that are so uniquely theirs. "Ellen's our organizer. She's been organized since she was a toddler." Or, "Peter's very easy-going; he's always marched to the beat of a different drummer." Our children have been building since birth an inner core that is exclusively theirs, identifying with significant people in their lives, developing talents, internalizing notions of right and wrong. But puberty arrives and shakes their foundations; bodies shift so that their tall and rounded selves no longer reflect the inner image of themselves as a small and fragile child. Tenors turn into basses and with the change may lose a special singing talent. The "braininess" that was scorned at eight is valued at sixteen, but the feeling of being an outsider—the one who was picked last for the kickball game—lingers. Sexual yearnings are new and unpredictable. With the onslaught of puberty, our children lose the sense of continuity that they had; confusion sets in; change becomes the norm. The spontaneity and creativity of childhood become the self-conscious inhibition of early adolescence.

To assure stability, some illusion of identity, adolescent boys and girls often attach to a group or an idol to show the world who they are—"a jock," "a punk," "a preppie," "a dead-head." And somewhere in the process of discovering who they are, they leave for college. Not all will have reached the same developmental point at the same time or with the same intensity. All the variables that influence development—genetic factors, cultural heritage, gender, societal influences, personal experiences—are brought to bear.

For some the transition to college is a smooth and gradual one; it may be the time for consolidation after a rocky adolescence. For others, the distance in miles that the freshman travels may represent the *only* separation that takes place as the student holds on tightly and brings his parents with him in spirit, if not in body. Their identity is his; he defines himself according to their guidelines. Still another freshman may plunge headfirst into the new environment, cutting loose the ties in an impulsive and sometimes desperate manner, attaching herself quickly in a mutually dependent romance, jumping into a new lifestyle, or running frantically from one new activity to another.[3]

As our children enter college, most of them will be wrestling with the question, "Who am I?" They will be trying to integrate what they've learned about themselves in earlier stages with the demands of the adult world. Some will defer to those demands so completely that they will conform to expectations of family and society at the expense of a sense of self. For others, their identity is so precious that they will ignore social norms entirely and become alienated from the mainstream.

In late adolescence, the time is ripe to focus on self-definition; our children are ready physically, cognitively, and socially. Colleges and universities offer a time-out, a breather after the period of childhood and before the commitments of adulthood. During this time, students may explore, take risks, test and "try on" new ways of being, and make mistakes without drastic consequences. Many of us look back to our own youth and recall such times of uncertainty, excitement, and turmoil.

When our children cast about in search of this sometimes elusive identity, their behavior is often misunderstood. At times, in their exuberant discovery of new worlds, they test extremes and hang on tight to them for a while as their fragile sense of self regains enough equilibrium to settle on a more balanced view. The tighter the psychological knot that ties them to their parents, the more abrasive and rebellious the testing may be. A perplexed mother from New Jersey describes her daughter on her first visit home from college.

> Cindy—she's asked us to call her by her full name, Cynthia—has the most beautiful hair; she's always worn it long to show off its natural thickness and shininess. It was her badge, her emblem—her motions, the way she would peek out from that wavy, raven mop, the way she would toss it around—a sort of exclamation point to emphasize whatever she was saying. It would be both irritating and ingratiating. And now it's gone, at least on one side of her head. She's practically shaved one side and the other is cut in a severe line which falls over one eye—

only she doesn't toss it anymore. It just sort of hangs there. I'm
not sure how she sees, and I'm not sure what it means.

Another exasperated parent from a conservative midwestern community lamented, "I'm still trying to explain to
myself, and to other people, why Brian came home from his
first year at college wearing an earring."

One thing their parents can be sure of, Brian and Cindy are
"trying on" a new identity, one that may or may not fit. They
cling to their new looks, which may be quite different from the
conservative wardrobe they left for school with. Does this mean
Brian is gay? Is this the beginning of a permanent punk look
for Cindy? Perhaps they're both on drugs. The mind of a
worried parent knows no bounds. Parental imagination may run
rampant to explain a new hairstyle or a tiny dot of gold in a
son's ear. But it is best if parents refrain from jumping in and
creating a chasm between themselves and their experimenting
offspring. They might do well to recall themselves or their
peers at eighteen or nineteen as bell-bottomed, encounter group
afficionados of the seventies, peace-loving flower children of
the sixties, or black-stockinged beatniks of the fifties.

One mother commented with amusement:

Every time Maggie came home to visit she had a new "per-
sona." We sent her off freshman year in the proverbial "polo"
shirt and conservative matching shorts. She prided herself on
her neatness, never a hair out of place. We used to laugh about
how long she spent taking showers and joked about finally
being able to use the bathroom again when she went to college.
Her first trip home, we barely recognized her at the airport. She
was wearing a thrift-shop version of a Garbo hat, and a lot of
somebody else's much-too-large and very dirty clothes. She explained that she hadn't done laundry during finals. Actually a
bigger shock came in the Spring when she was wearing men's
boxer shorts and was surprised that we didn't know that they
were the latest thing and wasn't it wonderful how much money
we would save because they were so cheap and she could wear
her father's! Our trips to pick her up at the airport for Winter or
Spring breaks became filled with "what next" jokes between
John and me. She never failed to surprise us.

But these are just the external signs of exploration. Young men and women during their college years are defining everything from their sexual orientation to their place in the world of work. They wrestle with the questions—What do I want to be like as a sexual being? How do I want to define myself as a man or woman? What do I believe in? What will I fight for? What do I want to do with my life? Ideas, values, interests are all arenas open to challenge—discovering what beliefs of parents, church, or ethnic group to hold on to and which ones to discard. The young man who is still so tied to home and places his parents in the center of his thoughts and decisions, who says, "I can't major in Art History; my parents would be so disappointed in me," is struggling with the same dependency as the scientifically talented, but belligerent young woman who proclaims, "I wouldn't consider medicine if it were the last profession on earth. I've had it shoved down my throat all my life. I wouldn't give them the satisfaction." Both are having trouble letting go, unable to make choices based on their own set of values, interests, and talents. Often students find themselves burdened with guilt, wanting to remain loyal to their families' traditional values, but also wanting to chart their own courses.

Intellectual Development: New Ways of Thinking

How do students go about making these important decisions? Along with the dramatic onslaught of hormonal and physical changes, adolescents undergo a more subtle but equally important intellectual growth. During their college years, students develop the capacity to engage in more complex and abstract thinking.[4]

At the time they enter college, many students see the world in black and white, clear-cut, and often rigid terms—a dichotomous view in which answers are simply right or wrong. They view their professors as the source of right answers and assume that their own role is to learn and retain these right answers. For the student who sees the world in this way, absolute truths prevail outside of the classroom as well—right or wrong

answers to moral dilemmas, to career choices—and as a result
they are often seeking *the* right answer and are impatient and
judgmental of compromises: "All jocks are zeros"; "My Dad
sold out when he became a banker"; "I can't seem to find the
right career for me."

As students become exposed to the diversity of ideas and
people at college, their world no longer looks quite so simple.
They gradually move from their clearly defined black-and-
white view of the world to one of stimulating, but often blind-
ing, color—a kaleidoscope of possibilities. Absolute truths no
longer prevail. Many points of view seem to have equal value.

From the day they arrive at their dormitory, they are confronted by the diverse population of their fellow students.
Students who have been brought up in homogenous environments, whether small towns revolving around a single church
or political point of view or sheltered segments of a larger city
bound by social and economic norms, are often overwhelmed
and confused by the variety of people, values, and ideas they
encounter in the first months on a college campus.

An eighteen-year-old freshman from the Bible Belt exclaimed:

> I had never met anyone Jewish before. I always felt kind of
> sorry for them, because they hadn't accepted Jesus and were
> sinners in our church. My roommate's a really observant Jew,
> and we've talked for hours late at night. He believes in his
> religion as much as I do and he's a really great guy. It's confus-
> ing; it's a whole new world here.

In their classrooms too, professors encourage varying opinions and ideas. Students discover that there is no one right
answer or truth, but many perspectives. They see more than one
"authority" with opposing viewpoints. Revered professors disagree with each other. Doing research in the library, students
find sources with different credible answers to the same questions. They can rely no longer simply on the dogma of an
authority. Numerous possibilities become evident. For many,
this is unsettling and often overwhelming. So many choices
may lead to a kind of paralysis. "If all opinions have validity,

how do I decide?" "How do I make sense of my world?" Sophomores, suitably named from the Greek roots for wise and fool, often find themselves at this precarious point, recognizing the complexity of the world and their vulnerability in it.

As they move through their four years, students are increasingly expected to analyze and give evidence to support their opinions, and gradually most of them begin to understand that truth is often relative and depends on the context in which it is viewed. Students are challenged by professors to back up their opinions with cogent arguments and relevant data. The same professor who might have been seen as arbitrary and confusing by a freshman may be valued as a catalyst for individual critical thinking by a junior or senior who has begun to wrestle with the complexity of making personal and intellectual commitments.

Intellectual growth often fosters a new sense of community, as students share ideas in exhilarating late-night debates with friends who hold divergent opinions. The lens that was focused so narrowly when students saw the world in dualist terms and then became wide-angled and expansive begins to focus again. But this time, the so-called authorities are the students themselves. As they see that many dilemmas can't be reduced to simple right or wrong answers, they weigh each situation, let go of the lesser alternatives, and take a personal stance.

Many students leave college before they have made sustained choices of life direction, values, and relationships. Most don't change evenly in their intellectual growth. Some, in fact, pause or retreat or may choose to avoid responsibility altogether by letting the chips fall where they may. But most students will not leave college without making impressive strides in their ability to think critically.

For many parents, the commitments that they made as young adults have become so familiar and so much a part of them that their own beliefs begin to look rigid and arbitrary to their children. Ellen Futter, former president of Barnard College, cautions parents not to support a narrow perspective unwittingly: "When parents impose too much, it communicates that there is a right and a wrong way to do things. This impedes the development of students."

The questions that arise when their children challenge their values often unsettle, even threaten, parents of college students. Parents are forced to look at their earlier decisions in today's context—decisions that may range from the place of sex in relationships to the value of intensive hard work. Through their college years, students confront their parents' values, lifestyles, and relationships. A student's developing identity brings his or her parents face to face with their own.

None of this maturing exists in a vacuum, of course. Growth is nourished by an environment that is both supportive and challenging. Colleges and universities offer students opportunities to stretch themselves, but within safe boundaries. Ellen Futter advises: "College encourages the capacity to take intellectual risks. The idea is to take risks, but not life-threatening ones." Parents can join university personnel as partners in encouraging their children to explore and take those risks, to discover their multifaceted world, and in so doing to discover themselves.

Independence

It is not part of our common parlance to talk about our children's identity formation or intellectual development. We do talk often, however, about their growing independence. Independence is part of our children's vernacular as well, a word bandied about among friends and family. What does it really mean? Probably different things to them than to us, at least initially. For many of our children, it means "I can do it by myself, thank you very much!"—an updated version of earlier attempts at tying shoelaces, crossing streets, and the like. It is the badge of separateness. In high school, the car was the symbol of independence for many students. "I can get away from you—take charge of where I'm going." A car is freedom; it provides an opportunity to explore and experiment with time and space away from home. It is associated with control and power. "I don't need you to drive me" is a metaphor for "I don't need to depend on you anymore."

In addition to the car, many high school students have access to a new financial freedom as they earn their own money working after school or during the summers. Ironically, for those who go away to college to live, these symbols of independence become less accessible. Cars are not permitted for freshmen on many college campuses, and the prohibitive costs of a college education often place students in a dependency bind— reconnected to parents through a powerful monetary umbilical cord.

College students do learn to take care of themselves in important new ways, however. Handling the humdrum details of everyday life that many of us take for granted is an important step on the road to a growing independence. They have to do laundry, to get themselves up in the morning, to decide when to come home at night or if they will come home at all; they manage their money; decide where and if to study, when and what to eat; they take care of their contact lenses, their acne, and their stomach flu. As they move on to become upperclassmen, they may have a car to take care of or may move off-campus and assume the added responsibility of apartment living. To care for themselves as their parents have cared for them brings feelings of confidence and strength, a self-reliance that can't be taught, only learned through experience.

Management of money often becomes an arena for the independence struggle. The reality is that for most students, financial dependence of some sort is a fact of life. In relationships with mutual respect, the conflict should be minimal. But most parents worry about the return on the huge financial investment that they have made in college. The cost seems preposterous—will their child become a successful professional, financially solvent, able to live comfortably on his or her own? Will their investment be worth it? As their worry grows and their resources dwindle, even the most well-intentioned parents may feel the need to take control as they would with any other investment. They may try to direct, to point out how to do it better, to orchestrate their children's college years—which courses to take, how to devote their time, and perhaps even with whom to spend it. In doing so, of course, they deprive their children of the most longlasting knowledge they can gain: the knowledge of how to live independently, form their own opinions, make their own decisions and mistakes, and ultimately make their own commitments to personal and political values, a vocation, and another human being.

The freedom that students enjoy with this sense of independence is often coupled with fears, especially about the change in their relationship with their parents. "Will my parents still care *about* me if they're not caring *for* me?" "Will they still love me even though they don't approve of my choices?" "Will I be abandoning them if I don't need them anymore?" They fear the responsibility inherent in their new self-reliance. The buck stops here.

Part of their discomfort comes from the false notion that independence means never asking for help. Many students, intent on asserting their autonomy, do so with a bravado and insistence that belies the feeling of tenuousness underneath. Teetering on the edge of separation, they turn away help and advice, fearing that they will be pulled back into the safety of the fold. One poised young woman, a Middlebury sophomore from Illinois, looks back at her freshman year:

> I had always prided myself on my independence, so I went to school alone. That was dumb. I was so unfamiliar with the area. I lost all perspective those first few weeks.
>
> I wasn't nervous at all when I went. I took a cab from Burlington—shared a ride with a guy who was also a freshman. I was very friendly, and he was very cold. That started it. People seemed cold in general. The more people seemed turned off to me, the more uptight I became. Then people were really turned off by me. I was very intimidated. I had never had problems meeting people before. I began to think, it must be because I'm from the Midwest. I'm not cool. I'd try to talk to people but I felt so self-conscious and got more and more withdrawn and nervous. People didn't want to be with me. I didn't blame them. I didn't want to be with me either.
>
> My parents didn't know too much about how miserable I was those first few months. I think I was always fighting dependence on my parents so I didn't say much. The one time I

really broke down and called about ten times in one week, my father got angry. For me to be weak was hard for them to see. They counted on me to be strong and independent.

Balancing autonomy and closeness to parents and others is an ongoing theme that intertwines with a developing sense of self. In the comings and goings of vacations and summers during their college years, students often describe a gradual change—a redefinition of their relationship with their parents. One senior at Rice recalls a shift in perspective:

It was winter break of my junior year. I was exhausted from some "all-nighters" to finish up papers and study for finals. In the past, I had often felt mixed emotions about going home. I was usually looking forward to it—anything after the craziness of the end-of-the-semester crunch—but shortly after I got there, my mom and I would be "at it," and I'd just want to get away someplace where I wouldn't be treated like a kid.

But this year was different. I remember saying on the way home from the airport, "I'm really exhausted; I just want to be pampered and taken care of." And I was! My parents were great. I could never let myself admit that that was what I wanted before, but somehow, now I felt different. I knew that I wasn't going to become a baby just because I wanted a little tender loving care. I wasn't fighting it anymore, because I guess I just felt generally more in charge of things.

Intimacy

The issues of identity and intimacy are bound together in a dynamic interplay that encourages the growth of each."[5] Throughout their college years, young men and women experiment with a variety of relationships. These may include intense new friendships with the same or the opposite sex, sexual play and exploration and, for many, "falling in love." As students continue to refine aspects of their own identity through these relationships, they become more self-confident and allow themselves the vulnerability to enter into increasingly open and mature partnerships. Over and over again, students describe their relationships with friends and lovers as critical to the learning and growth that takes place during the college years.

A young woman, in her final year at Washington University, traces the evolution of her developing sexual identity and her increasing capacity to enter into close relationships:

Freshman year I developed some very close friends. We really played a lot. It's kind of hard to describe. Maybe it's easier to describe what it wasn't. It wasn't going out on dates or to parties. It was just two guys and another girl, and we spent a lot of time hanging out talking, going to the zoo and the park. It was a very happy time.

I had a really close relationship with one of the guys. We were together all the time. We even slept in the same room a lot, but it was never sexual. He had a girlfriend at home, and even after I started going with someone, we still spent a lot of time together. This was a big change for me. I wasn't even allowed to have guys come upstairs at home.

Second semester, I started going out with Jim. Our first date was the spring formal. Until then, he was just a guy I knew in the dorm. It was my first real relationship, and it definitely was his. It was a very intense relationship—symbiotic, actually.

We spent about a third of the summer together. He was my life; I was his life—for a whole year. My parents were kind of cool about it. My Dad just said it wouldn't last, and my Mom didn't say much of anything—or if she did, I don't remember.

We spent most of our sophomore year together. We were with each other all the time—slept in each other's rooms. That was never any problem. Our roommates were very flexible. We always worked it out easily. We weren't like the kids who kick their roommates out or leave secret codes on the door that mean "stay out."

We took a couple of classes together, but mostly we were together outside of classes. It was real good for both of us. We both grew a lot, and became a lot more confident. We each began to see each other through the other person's eyes, which I know did incredible things for my self-image, and it did for his also. And it's funny that the basic reason we broke up was that we both needed to spend time with other people, and we couldn't adjust our relationship to do that. We were used to having each other available whenever we wanted. We ended up spending from September to March of junior year breaking up and getting together over and over again. When I think of college, junior year was spent breaking up with Jim. Without us becoming aware of it we had come to expect total availability of the other person. We were an incredible support system to each other. But we just couldn't make the transition to staying together, while moving out to be with other people also.

It was a time of separation from my mother. Up 'til then, my Mom knew everything that happened to me that had any significance, but last summer I decided I didn't want to tell her everything. I didn't want her to know all about us.

My relationship with Jim was an important time of my life; it affects how I am now too. I'm more open. I'm more conscious of what's going on in my relationships, of taking risks and making commitments.

Throughout the college years, the pendulum continues to swing back and forth between separateness and union. Many relationships during these years of learning and experimentation will have the look of intimacy, but may be well-disguised attempts at fulfilling other needs. Often during the freshman year, especially in the first semester, students pair up, substituting new dependent relationships for old ones. As the Washington University senior above related, even though there are difficulties with such a relationship, this kind of bond may serve to help students grow, in the reassurance of their self-worth, in discovering their sexuality, in learning to be open, and in separating from close, perhaps too close, families.

Some students substitute sexual relationships for emotional closeness, a "pseudo-intimacy" that provides temporary release, but often a gnawing emptiness and sense of prevailing isolation as well. Others who do open up and trust before they have a sense of their own identity may become frightened as they begin to feel themselves engulfed by another's demands.

Mutual trust is essential, trust that one's friend or partner will respect and appreciate one's separateness, trust in one's own capacity to "let go" temporarily and remain intact. To be intimate is to expose one's vulnerabilities to another. To be intimate is to balance one's own needs with someone else's and to resolve conflict together. Students learn that to give is not to give in—compromise is part of the partnership.

Change

There is no way to predict exactly how our children will move through the continuing ebb and flow of their growth and development during their college years. For a number of students, college prolongs adolescence and is just the beginning of their search for their identity, independence, and intimacy. For others the progress in these arenas from freshman to senior year is staggering. We *can* predict, however, that change will occur, that it is an inevitable by-product of the college experience. With change, even positive change, adjustment is necessary and stress unavoidable. For most students, many of the disruptions will lead to opportunities for growth, and they will continue to learn how to think more critically and to take responsibility for their own opinions and actions. For these same students, there will be times of stagnation and regression.

Along the way, the road is often a rocky one for parents as well as children. The inconsistencies of a student's behavior may leave parents breathless; how could someone who acted with such mature deliberation one day resort to such ill-conceived impulsiveness the next? Should we respond with amusement or concern?

One mother of a Bates freshman, her first child to go to college, offers a familiar refrain:

> When he was a toddler, I used to worry that Eric would never give up his bottle. I remember my pediatrician telling me with a wry smile to stop worrying, that he would not go to college with it. Now I worry that he will never be organized enough to hold a responsible job. And when I worry, I start barging in on his life and try to tell him once more what he already knows. Won't I ever learn that my perspective as a forty-five-year-old is not his at nineteen? I keep thinking that I will have really matured when I can get that wry smile on *my* face, and stop worrying.

Understanding some of the underpinnings of normal development may alleviate parents' anxiety. It is easier to be supportive when we can see the broader view. Our children may rebuff our advice, but they will appreciate our acknowledgment of their distress—a listening ear that doesn't judge even if we disagree, a sense of confidence that doesn't crumble when they do, an adult anchor who provides perspective on the very predictable but often painful changes that they are bound to go through.

Chapter 2

SOME THINGS DO CHANGE: COLLEGE LIFE TODAY

Strolling onto a college campus, we are struck by a sense of history and continuity. Who walked these paths before? Who will walk them in the years to come? For some of us there is a dizzying nostalgia. For almost all of us there are feelings of respect, even awe.

Imposing rectangular structures of red granite or limestone; Georgian brick residences with symmetrical columns; ivy-covered Gothic lecture halls with leaded windows and vaulted archways announce that this is a place that commands attention. Our eyes glance past the modern glass and steel additions, lighting on the older traditional centers, the quadrangles, the plazas, the courtyards. Giant oaks and elms attest to the passing of time. Latin phrases over doorways remind us of the scholarship that takes place here. This oasis of learning, separated from the cacophony of the workaday world just beyond its gates, lulls us into tranquility, perhaps even reverie.

And so it is with a jolt that we come upon a bulletin board layered with recent posters and notices askew—a collage of ink and paper—a jarring reminder that time has not stood still: "Bulimia Support Group," "Gay and Lesbian Alliance Film Festival," "African-American Studies Department Colloquium," "Networking Workshop," "MacIntosh Users' Group," "Adult Children of Alcoholics Group," "Wanted: Roommate to share apartment. Male or female, non-smoker, no drugs," "AIDS Symposium," "Take Back the Night March," "Women on Wall Street: Alumnae Panel."

Sandwiched between these announcements are notices of recitals and colloquia on more orthodox scholarly topics; of art exhibits and plays and poetry readings; of pep rallies and tailgate parties. But these traditional cultural and social events of the campus scene are overshadowed by the contemporary reflections of today's world.

The social transformations of the past thirty years that have touched all of our lives have invaded the seemingly tranquil campus as well. Changes in curriculum, institutional policies, extracurricular offerings—even the very make-up of the student population—confirm that today's college is neither rarefied nor unaffected by the rapidly changing society of which it is a part.

Who Are Today's Students and What Do They Believe?

Impressionistic portraits of today's students range from conservative, hard-working Babbitts to materialistic, freewheeling Gatsbys—from uncaring, self-involved careerists to statement-making demonstrators who bar the CIA recruiter from the placement office—from fifties style prom lovers to proud and active supporters of gay rights. Personal impressions such as these are important to keep in mind as a backdrop for the profile drawn by specific data and statistics. Both contribute to our understanding of today's college students.

Two major resources provide a storehouse of information about today's undergraduates. One is an ongoing survey of representative samples of college students conducted annually since 1966 by the Cooperative Institutional Research Program and sponsored by the American Council on Education and UCLA. Edited by Alexander Astin and his colleagues, these reports, *The American Freshman: National Norms,* present a vivid picture of changes in the "characteristics, attitudes, values, educational achievements, and future goals of students who enter college in the United States." [1]

Ernest Boyer's book, *College: The Undergraduate Experience in America,* presents the findings of an important three-year study of undergraduate colleges by the Carnegie Foundation for the Advancement of Teaching. Based on surveys, interviews, and observations at thirty public and private institutions, the voices of undergraduates as well as their teachers, deans, and parents provide vivid insight into the current campus scene. Much of the data that follows is culled from these two important research projects.

No longer the elite bastion of affluent, white eighteen- to twenty-two-year-olds, today's college campus is home to students from a diversity of backgrounds. In 1960, 94 percent of college students were white, and 63 percent were men. Colleges and universities first opened their doors to a wider spectrum of students in the sixties and early seventies. The percentage of minorities in entering freshman classes nearly doubled between the mid-sixties and mid-seventies, and minority students became a notable presence on campuses that had formerly excluded them. The growth in minority enrollments came to a halt in the eighties, however. Disillusionment and racial tension have become increasingly prevalent among students, leading schools from the University of California-Santa Barbara in the west to Smith College in the east, to develop programs to promote racial understanding and reduce racial harassment.

The women's movement also has influenced campus demographics. After a steady increase of women's enrollments throughout the seventies there are now more women than men in college. And with the decline in the number of single-sex institutions, women have become an integral part of the most prestigious, formerly all-male Ivys and their small, elite counterparts.

The number of foreign students enrolling in American colleges and universities has reached an all-time high. According to the Institute of International Education, in 1990 there were 386,851 international students enrolled on U.S. campuses—eleven times as many as there were in the mid 1950s. And the "graying" of the campus has become a common phenomenon, particularly at community and other commuter colleges that court older students to fill the gap left by the shrinking pool of eighteen-year-olds.

Today's students come from a broad range of economic backgrounds. An increasing number of them are concerned about having adequate funds for college. Most students have to help finance their education; they spend their college years trying to maintain the delicate balance among part-time jobs, academic demands, extracurricular activities, and time with friends.

Almost 30 percent of the full-time students in Boyer's study worked twenty-one or more hours a week. And as the availability of scholarship and grant money has diminished and college costs have continued to rise, the number of students who will graduate with extensive loans to pay off has been increasing substantially. Educators estimate that at least one-half of today's students will graduate in debt.

The economic polarities on campus are striking. Students whose financial worries are part of their daily consciousness live side by side with those who arrive on campus with a sense of entitlement and an alphabet soup of expensive equipment—TVs, PCs, CDs, and even VCRs.

Reflecting nationwide changing family patterns, more students are coming to college from divorced, single-parent, and so-called "blended families" that are formed through remarriage. In 1955, 60 percent of American households were of the "Leave It to Beaver" genre—working father, stay-at-home mother, and two or more school-age children. By 1985, only 7 percent of the population belonged to this type of family unit, although many people and institutions still think of it as the norm.

The American family is in flux, and a substantial number of today's college students have paid a price. Many come from families that provided them with little structure while they were growing up. It is common to hear students lament the loss of their childhood as they describe taking on the role of friend and confidant to a distraught parent, or the role of surrogate parent to a needy, younger sibling. University personnel are concerned about the high percentage of students who come from families with an alcoholic member. And campus psychologists and counselors serve an increasing number of students who report incidents of childhood physical and sexual abuse.

Some students have struggled with alcohol problems of their own and have participated in residential treatment programs while still in high school. Some arrive on campus with a substantial drug habit or an eating disorder, such as anorexia or bulimia. Many of these students are unable to deal with the stress in their lives; they resort to destructive coping mechanisms that temporarily relieve their pain or provide them with the illusion of control that they desperately seek.

Others enter college with well-developed, constructive coping skills. Many of today's freshmen have a healthy respect for exercise, and they are intent upon enhancing both their physical and emotional well-being. They bike and jog, lift weights and join aerobics classes; they participate in intramural sports, practice t'ai chi, or take dance to keep in shape. These health-conscious students are concerned about eating well and favor salad bars and yogurt over Big Macs and fries. And fewer entering college students smoke than in the past, although the rate of decline over the past twenty years is lower for women than for men.

Today's students enter college with higher high school grades and lower basic skills than ever before. As a result of grade inflation, many are optimistic about their academic performance, but ill-equipped to succeed. They come to college expecting a great deal of themselves, the institution, and the whole academic enterprise.

One way to better appreciate and understand this generation of college students is to view them within the context of the world that has shaped them. To these young men and women, John F. Kennedy and Martin Luther King, Jr. are names in history books, and the Vietnam War is the subject of period piece films. Though the civil rights and women's movements have profoundly affected their own expectations and opportunities, they remain curiously detached from them as impassioned causes. For most of today's students, these are the obsessions of another era—their parents' era. Their realities are the threats of environmental devastation and AIDS, worldwide economic and political upheaval, international terrorism and the fear of nuclear proliferation.

Arthur E. Levine of the Harvard Graduate School of Education speculates that a "Titanic ethic" exists in this generation.

In his keynote address at the 1986 National Conference on the Freshman Year Experience, he elaborated on this Titanic image:

> Students share a sense that the ship, call it the U.S. or the world, is going to sink. Forced to ride on a doomed vessel, students have decided to go first class, seeking all the goodies to make the voyage as luxurious as possible for as long as the ship is still afloat.

There is no doubt that these young people have been affected by the economic and political uncertainties of their formative years. With constant reminders from media that theirs may be the first college generation to face a world of fewer opportunities than their parents had, many of them are seeking a safe route that will lead them to the diminishing number of spots at the top. Whether or not this generation actually will have fewer opportunities for success and career fulfillment remains to be seen. However, students appear to be making decisions about their majors and their futures based on that assumption. Many are turning to courses of study that provide the most obvious and direct connection to the job market. Many are eager to get on the fast track and stay there.

According to Astin, the percentage of freshmen who said they intended to major in business increased steadily throughout the seventies and most of the eighties, peaking in 1987 at 25 percent. Although that figure declined to 18 percent by the fall of 1990, business still remains the most popular major of today's undergraduates.

Other majors that have increased in popularity over the years are economics, engineering, and computer science, although interest in the last two is beginning to wane. Majors in the humanities, the fine and performing arts, and the social sciences witnessed dramatic declines through the seventies and early eighties. Recently, however, numerous universities have reported a trend toward increased enrollments in the liberal arts.

In 1990, more freshmen than ever before in the twenty-five years of the UCLA study, said that an important reason for going to college was "to make more money" and "to get a better job."

Although today's freshmen placed considerably less value than their predecessors did on "developing a meaningful philosophy of life," they stated that it was a "very important" or "essential" goal in life to "influence social values," and to "influence the political structure. " They indicated increasing concern with "promoting racial understanding," and "becoming involved in programs to clean up the environment." As Astin declares in his summary of the 1990 survey, "these trends suggest that there is a rapidly expanding number of American college students who are dissatisfied with the status quo and who want to become personally involved in bringing about change in American society." [2]

Statistical averages come to life when we look at the ways in which increasing numbers of students are devoting themselves to community service. Fund raising and volunteer service projects are part of the tradition of the many fraternities and sororities that are a growing presence on college campuses. Community service organizations such as Phillips Brooks House at Harvard and Student Volunteers Council at Princeton are thriving. About one-half of the students in Boyer's study indicated that they had participated in some kind of service activity, such as tutoring in the inner city, assisting in shelters for the homeless, or canvassing for environmental causes. In 1986, 125 college presidents, including those from George-town, Brown, and Stanford, formed a consortium, Campus Compact, to promote community service. By 1991, the number of member institutions had increased to 266, reflecting the growth of campus interest in community service.

The majority of today's students describe themselves as "middle-of-the-road" politically. The percentage of freshmen who identify their general political position as liberal has declined from 33.5 percent in 1970 to 22.6 percent in 1990. But the data from the UCLA survey indicate that there is still strong student endorsement of traditional, liberal social and political issues. Students support such positions as legal abortion; national health insurance; and greater government involvement in consumer protection, environmental pollution, and gun control. Although their support is quieter than it was in the sixties and seventies, record numbers of freshmen in 1990 reported that they had participated in demonstrations in high school and planned to participate in campus protests in college. Occasionally issues such as military policy on homosexuals in ROTC, abortion rights, or opposition to American foreign policy in the Middle East stir up small but vocal groups of students. Concerns closer to home—an admired professor being turned down for tenure or rising tuition costs—are more likely to mobilize students, even those typically uninterested in political affairs.

There is, however, a widening rift between conservative and liberal students. Isolated ugly incidents shatter an image of harmony on usually peaceful campuses: students signing up for job interviews with the CIA are attacked by picketing protesters; a poster announcing a program sponsored by the university's gay and lesbian alliance is spraypainted with obscenities; the African-American students' center is defaced with graffiti.

Student attitudes toward the roles of men and women have changed dramatically over the last twenty years. When asked whether they supported the traditional notion that "the activities of married women are best confined to the home and family," 30.6 percent of today's male freshmen in the Astin study answered yes as opposed to 66.5 percent in 1970. The support for this view among young women in the freshman class declined from 44.3 percent to 20.5 percent in the same time period. Although only a little over one-third of freshmen women approve of sex between two people who've known each other a short while, 66.3 percent of men support it.

The media have labeled today's youth as materialistic, careerist, conservative, the "me generation," even the "give-me generation." They have been described as impatient, self-indulgent, reluctant to make commitments, desirous of constant stimulation. This is the "Sesame Street" generation that was introduced to education via lively thirty-second segments and to problem solving through popular sitcoms that resolve conflicts in thirty minutes. Many of their teachers comment that they want simple answers to complex questions, that they seek formulas for success rather than opportunities for exploration and risk taking.

Charles Eckert, professor of chemical engineering at the University of Illinois, has been teaching for more than twenty years. His comments are echoed by many of today's faculty:

> In the sixties, engineering and science were somewhat nasty words. Lots of kids who chose those fields had a vision of doing something for humanity. Some wanted to do environmental work; they regarded it as being anticorporate. People used to do science to save the world or win a Nobel Prize. I've gotten a sense from students today that science is a ticket to job security. For them a high paying job is desirable, but security is even more desirable. We've gone overboard on security blankets nationally.Very few students are driven. They appear to be more interested in what's on the test than in learning.

Philip Hallie, a professor at Wesleyan University for over twenty-five years, has a completely different view of students:

> Maybe I've got a very unrepresentative group, but I find a yearning to be compassionate, and almost no concern with careers. They seem to be ready and needing, to have strong feelings....They respond to plot, to narrative, to literature. Ethics becomes a catharsis and an excitement.[3]

Harry Kisker, vice provost at Washington University, like Professor Eckert, is concerned about students' reluctance to take risks:

> Our students are very career-oriented. They worry too much about their grades and about their futures. They are not risk takers, either socially or intellectually. They have a tendency to want structure, to want preestablished agendas, to want a set of directions to their educational experience. Students today seem to have some sort of need for guarantees. They approach their academic work, all too often, with a businesslike "tell me what I need to do" attitude. And like so many collegiate commuters, they treat their studies like work, clocking in and clocking out. They work extremely hard, devoting long hours to course assignments and study for examinations. Yet they remain peculiarly intellectually detached from this constant, herculean academic task.

Paul Ginsberg retired as dean of students at the University of Wisconsin after a thirty-five-year career in student development at the Madison campus. He is a legend among students, proof positive that it is possible to make a personal impact even at the largest of institutions.

Dean Ginsberg bristles at the media's disparaging, throwaway descriptions of today's students. He speaks of them with respect and affection:

> When the media call this an apathetic generation, they misread the lack of marching crowds, protests, and social activism, and assume that there is a return to the apathy of the fifties. This is not an apathetic generation, but the energy level is going toward issues of survival and of academic competency. These young men and women are dealing with options never available to generations of students before, and these choices create tensions and anxieties. They are scared—not uncaring people. They feel they need to taste every morsel on the table of life, because the table may not be there in a few years. This is a generation more tuned in to survival, that is true. But this is not a basis for condemnation.

Listening to faculty and administrators share their perceptions of students, it is sometimes difficult to believe that they are describing the same generation. For in spite of the studies and reports of trends, students differ from campus to campus, as well as within each school. Washington University's Harry Kisker warns about the limitations of sweeping generalizations of any kind:

> For every professional "yuppie" on campus, there are other students who still volunteer to tutor in the ghetto. Student populations, after all, are a lot like real communities; they have their doers and their loafers, their leaders and their followers, their heroes and their low-lifes.

In her 1987 book, *Campus Life*, historian Helen Lefkowitz Horowitz challenges her readers to look beyond the monolithic stereotypes that characterize each generation of college students:

> In any decade since 1920, single images of collegians have dominated the public consciousness; it is implicitly assumed

that no other kinds of students have existed. Thus all students in the 1920s are seen to wear raccoon coats and carry hip flasks, while those of the 1930s march in demonstrations against war. The problem has been the failure to recognize that undergraduates have been divided into contending cultures. In any one era, one of these appears to be dominant and catches the public eye.[4]

Horowitz describes the students that dominate today's campuses as "grim professionals," cramming for tests, more interested in grades than in learning, and driven by a desire for success and security. But sharing the campus with them are political activists, carefree hedonists, and the students she calls "the quiet rebels," who see college, not as a preprofessional hurdle, but as a time to experiment, to struggle with new ideas and take intellectual risks.

What Is Happening on Today's Campus?

Colleges and universities have come under scrutiny recently for everything from athletic scandals, to questions about indirect costs and pricefixing, to debate about the academic canon and the tyranny of the "politically correct." But ask a group of parents what's different about today's campus and the first response inevitably is "coed living." Although residence halls on many campuses have been mixing the sexes since the early seventies, first-time parents of college freshmen often are shocked by the actual sight of young men and women living side by side, brushing their teeth together, mingling in the halls in their bathrobes, casually sprawled on the beds of each others' rooms.

The following tongue-in-cheek comments from the mother of a brand-new freshman at the University of Pennsylvania speak for the anxieties of many parents:

> Initially I was horrified by the fact that the small, squalid bathroom two doors away from Peggy's room was to be shared by students of both sexes. I had been prepared for the coed dorm and even for the coed floor, but the idea of sharing a bathroom with only a torn shower curtain between my naked Peggy and some unshaven lout was an ugly shock.

And from a junior who works for the admissions department at Oberlin:

> Every time I give a tour to parents and prospective students, some parent pops the question about coed dorms, especially coed floors. They really seem hung up about the bathrooms. I try to explain that we just don't think about it, that we're mostly just a group of friends sharing space.

Some things have, indeed, changed.

High-Tech Ivy

Gone are the amenities of genteel college living of the fifties and sixties. Fewer dormitory living rooms contain grand pianos and oriental rugs these days, and the ubiquitous color television in the lounge is likely to be bolted to the table. But college students of this generation are being well taken care of, from their culinary to their counseling needs.

"Retention" is a buzzword on all campuses, and some schools have even hired specialists in "enrollment management" to help them not only attract but also keep students. Consumer-minded students demand services that support their daily living, and colleges and universities have poured their financial resources into out-of-the-classroom facilities—athletic complexes, student unions, and, in institutions such as the University of South Carolina and the University of Michigan, complete underground shopping malls. In recent years, special funds have been earmarked for science and technology laboratories and business departments. But in many colleges and universities, rundown academic offices and buildings stand in sharp contrast to the construction, face lifting, and renovation of centers that enhance student life outside the classroom.

Elaborate sports complexes cater to the health- and fitness-conscious student population with weight rooms, Nautilus equipment, and saunas adjacent to Olympic-size swimming pools. Even small colleges provide students with more sophisticated and extensive facilities than the simple gymnasiums that were standard in the largest universities a generation ago. Translucent bubbles housing indoor tennis courts and skating rinks dot campuses all over the country. It is not unusual, even among some of our most respected institutions, for improvements to athletic facilities to take precedence over additions to the library.

Lavish student centers attest to the fact that today's students take their leisure time as seriously as their grinding academic work. The University of Texas Union houses 575 student-run activities. Wilson Commons of the University of Rochester boasts of three tons of fudge sold annually inside its glass walls. The Aztec Center at San Diego State sits on Mission Bay, a captivating waterfront wonder. An entire community exists under one roof in many of these upscale centers—a bookstore, a bank, a travel agency, theaters and cabarets, video game rooms, computer centers, art galleries, and snack bars catering to an assortment of palates.

In this era of crime consciousness, colleges have appropriated large sums of money for security measures to protect students. Gone are the days when bikes were left unlocked in campus bike racks and dormitories were left open until midnight. Today computerized card systems replace locks on many campuses; special lighting and emergency phones have been installed on pathways to and from dormitories; escort services provide nighttime transportation to libraries, labs, and studios. On a lot of campuses, newly arrived freshmen find an orientation packet that includes information on security, rape prevention tips, and crisis hot line numbers. On city campuses this comes as no surprise, but students who arrive at a halcyon collegiate setting outside of city limits are often skeptical about the message that they too are vulnerable.

Wheelchair ramps and parking spaces for the disabled are welcome campus additions and are evidence of the increased access to college for all potential students. There are more cars on campus and more parking lots than there used to be. But complaints about parking from students, faculty, and staff are more vociferous than ever.

Technology—computerized bank cards, meal cards, and ID cards—has invaded all campuses. Crowded computer centers are filled with students busily writing papers, organizing data, and working with spread sheets. The old oak drawers of library card catalogues share space with sterile computer monitors that call up bibliographic information at the press of a button. And the bleeping noise and flashing lights of video game rooms have replaced the sounds of shuffling cards and campus gossip in the smoke-filled lounges of another generation.

The computer has become an integral part of the lives of most students, whether it is used merely for word processing and e-mail or for sophisticated research. Most residence halls are wired, and students have access to world-wide information exchange via Internet. With a spate of new software developed for higher education, the computer influences not just *what* students learn, but *how* they learn.

At Brown University, Victorian Poetry is taught with the assistance of a software program that provides students with information about writers, including their biographies and comparisons with other writers. The software goes beyond the obvious and includes such possibilities as allowing a student who wonders about a reference to a painting in a poem by Browning to call up information about the painter and the particular painting simply by pushing a button.

At Stanford, computers are used in one course for simulation of economic and social life in seventeenth-century France; in another, for observation of the effects of different treatments on cancer cells.

The computer has become an important writing tool for many students. Some studies even indicate that students who use computers get better grades. It is clear that computers make revision less painful, and most writing instructors agree that students who are motivated to rewrite have the opportunity to learn a great deal about the art of composition.

Beyond the Ivy-Covered Walls: Changing Needs and Services

Beyond the venerable old edifices and dazzling new facilities that pervade the campus there are a legion of services for students that didn't exist thirty years ago: career centers, psychological counseling centers, study skills centers, multi-cultural centers, and women's centers. The business of student development has become an integral part of today's campus scene. Lively and energetic residence hall staff join psychologists and specialists in reading skills, student programming, and alcohol and drug abuse in the daily pursuit of helping students to develop as well as to cope with the stresses and strains of college life. These are the adults who are on the front line and are likely to have the most interaction with students, particularly freshmen and sophomores.

In previous generations, houseparents or proctors who lived in dormitories enforced codes of discipline and provided a haven for "tea and sympathy" as needed. There were clear-cut rules and expectations, and the concept of *in loco parentis*, a Latin phrase meaning "in the place of a parent," was a court-ordered fact of college life. The landmark decision in the 1911 *Gott* v. *Berea College* case stated that college authorities would stand in place of parents to watch out for the welfare of their children while they were under the college's care. Colleges and universities operated according to these guidelines until the late sixties, when *in loco parentis* disappeared altogether on most campuses, along with curfews, stringent rules, and young people's trust in adults over thirty.

In the late sixties and early seventies, students assumed power in all areas of their lives. Along with civil rights and women's rights, students' rights became an issue in itself. In addition to their challenges to the national political status quo, students mobilized changes on campus from the dissolution of parietal rules, to a more open and varied curriculum. They became responsible for monitoring their own behavior in all facets of their lives.

Edward B. Fiske, former education editor of the *New York Times*, recounts the impact of these sweeping changes on large numbers of students and on the colleges and universities them-selves:

The faculty gave away control of the curriculum, and the administration decided it was going to get out of *in loco parentis*. All this freedom worked for some kids, but for lots of others, it didn't. Colleges and universities realized this and began to pick up the pieces with expanded health centers and counseling services and career centers. A whole set of professionals stepped in to serve kids who couldn't handle the freedom. As Ernest Boyer put it, we moved from *in loco parentis* to *in loco clinician*.

The services that emerged in response to the needs and demands of students in the sixties and seventies are now as much a part of college life as the library and the lecture hall. A whole body of research exists about the development of college students, providing theoretical grounding to the work carried out by the student affairs professionals on campus. Students today are searching for more structure. They actively seek out advice from adults and seem more willing to accept restraints. Universities are more concerned about retaining students; they are also more worried about lawsuits in an increasingly litigious society. Almost all schools are reassessing the needs of their students and the role that the institution should play in student development. Although there is virtually no interest in returning to *in loco parentis* as it existed in the fifties or early sixties, colleges are beginning to reevaluate their policies and educational outreach programs within the context of the major social changes that have occurred.

Residential Life

"Some parents are very naive about residential life in college," warns Karen Tidmarsh, dean of the undergraduate college at Bryn Mawr:

Today's dorms are hard places for students to live. The rules and regulations that we used to have gave students something to bump up against. When I went to college, we signed out to where we were going. I felt safe because someone knew where I was.

If Dean Tidmarsh were a student today, chances are that no one would know where she was at any given time. She could spend a day or a week away from school and not be required to check in with anyone. Parents often are horrified by this fact, but, as one director of residence halls at a large university remarked during a parents' orientation meeting, "We haven't lost a student yet!"

Curfews, visitation restrictions, and sign-outs belong to another era. On most campuses today, the rules are minimal. The good news is that residence halls are laboratories for self-development; students have to learn to say no when the university doesn't do it for them. The bad news is that without the boundaries of a stringent code of conduct, the residence halls can be chaotic. Blaring music and spontaneous beer parties make studying in one's room an exercise in frustration. And fines for vandalism are routine additions to some parents' housing bill.

Residence halls range from the small, decrepit, and charming to the high-rise, impersonal, and air conditioned—from the convenient fall-out-of-bed-into-class variety to those located a bike ride or bus ride from the center of campus. Some are single-sex; others are coed and separate the sexes by wing, floor, or room. Many offer choices of quiet floors, no-smoking wings, or suites of students with common majors or interests.

Though they have no intention of returning to the tight reins of earlier decades, increasing numbers of colleges and universities are providing living environments that encourage a sense of pride and commitment to a community. Indiana University now requires that residence hall coordinators and their families live in apartments in the dorms, no longer isolating students in enclaves separate from the adult world. The University of Pennsylvania has broken down the largest freshmen dorms into smaller, manageable units with live-in faculty families and assistant deans. The Sierra Project at the University of California at Irvine is designed to promote character development of freshmen and a sense of community among them. Students in this residential learning program participate in classes and experiences ranging from discussions of race relations to practice in survival skills and community service.

More and more schools are combining living and classroom experience in smaller cohesive units. The Living-Learning Center at the University of Vermont, for example, houses students who study subjects around a common theme of their choice. The University of Michigan, the University of the Pacific, Princeton, Bucknell, and Colby are among schools that have innovative housing systems, which bring the living and learning experience into closer harmony. And the time-honored "house" and "college" systems at Harvard and Yale have remained constant during periods of residential upheaval. With faculty in residence, they have their own libraries and dining facilities and support an active intellectual and cultural life.

Without rules and regulations, who keeps the typical residence halls from deteriorating into total anarchy? The heroes and heroines in the trenches are the resident advisors. The RAs are usually juniors or seniors, who in exchange for room and board, act as the on-site supervisors/counselors/disciplinarians responsible for the day-to-day functioning of a section of a floor or residence hall. On twenty-four hour call, an RA may be found rescuing a student who is locked out of a room, comforting a homesick freshman, admonishing a noisy resident, or counseling someone who is severely depressed.

RA training is often intense and extensive. The best is usually year-long with supervision by graduate student residence directors and student services staff. RAs participate in workshops on everything from suicide and depression to time management; they discuss and develop sensitivity to such issues as racism, homosexuality, and eating disorders. At the very minimum, RA training includes communication skills to help them be alert and reach out to students in need, listen attentively, and learn how and where to refer students to resources and professional help.

Career Centers

Career centers are among the busiest offices on campus these days, and their habitués aren't just second semester seniors dressed in their interview suits. On most campuses, the placement offices of yesteryear have expanded into multifaceted centers. They help students with career development throughout their four years and assist them with their job hunts when they graduate. On many campuses part-time and summer job listings are available at the career center as well.

Students have the chance to meet with career counselors as early as their freshman year to begin the search for knowledge about themselves and the world of work. Through individualized counseling, workshops, computer guidance programs, and career resource libraries, students learn the process of career development—a process that will prove invaluable, since most of them will make at least one career change and an average of six to ten job changes after they land their first position.

Contrary to what many students believe, there is no test that will tell them what their perfect career is or what they *should* be. But counseling and career interest testing can help students begin to focus; to become aware of their interests, skills, and values; and to decide what fields they want to explore. Fortunately, most of today's colleges provide students with a lot of opportunity for exploration. In addition to the written materials housed in career libraries, career panels of local graduates, networks of alumni career advisors, and mentoring programs all serve to bring students together with role models and information sources. Innovative internship and cooperative education programs give students valuable work experience while still in school, helping to solve the age-old dilemma that most recent graduates face—"only the experienced need apply." More and more career centers have reached out into the community to arrange on-the-job apprenticeships, and many of today's upperclassmen, especially those who might have been tempted to desert the humanities, supplement their intellectual nourishment with these pragmatic steppingstones to the work world.

Career centers help with the nuts and bolts of job hunting too. Students learn how to write resumés, target job leads, collect references, and hone their interviewing skills. Today's high-tech centers usually include video tape equipment for practice interviews, computer-generated job listings, and computerized registration systems for on-campus interviews. Most centers serve alumni as well as students, reflecting the contemporary view that career development is ongoing and career change is a common occurrence.

Counseling Services

Counseling centers that were embryonic or nonexistent thirty years ago are now standard fare. Staffed by psychologists, social workers, and counselors, their primary mission is to help students grow and to assist them through the normal developmental hurdles that are so common to late adolescence.

A member of the counseling staff of a private southern university elaborates:

> My role is so varied depending on the student. With some I'm probably not very different from the housemother I had living in my dorm thirty years ago—reassuring, letting a kid know that what he is going through is normal and to be expected. With others I'm an educator, a teacher of a variety of coping skills to deal with the incredible academic and social stresses that are part of their daily lives. And I am, of course, a psychologist, helping students to correct distorted perceptions that cause them to stumble.

"To stumble" often means to suffer from anxiety or depression, the most common problems students bring to counseling services. These can be brought on by anything from a disappointing grade, to a broken romance, to problems at home—the kinds of concerns that have always plagued college students. But the complications of contemporary family life, financial pressures, and the bewildering array of choices facing today's students have brought them in increasing numbers to university counseling centers. A lot more students seem to be willing to ask for help, and it is not unusual for them to recommend counselors to each other. Most students' needs can be met by these centers, but because colleges often place a limit on the number of visits per student, it is common for college counselors to make referrals to professionals in the community for more extended counseling.

Today's counselors are visible on campus, presenting workshops in dormitories, fraternities, sororities, and for other groups on subjects that range from stress management or study skills to sexuality. As trainers and consultants to RA staffs, campus leaders, and peer counselors, they are often well-known to numbers of students on an informal basis. Although much of their work addresses the normal developmental tasks of college students, counselors also present educational outreach programs to deal with some of the critical concerns of contemporary college students such as date rape, eating disorders, drugs and alcohol, and safe sex.

Date Rape

From Stanford to Swarthmore, from Cornell to San Diego State, counselors and public safety officers actively address rape prevention with workshops and self-defense programs. But far more prevalent on college campuses, and more insidious than rape by a stranger, is the crime of date rape, sometimes known as acquaintance rape.

According to a three-year study of seven thousand college students under the direction of Kent State University psychologist, Mary P. Koss, one out of every eight college women indicated that they had been forced to have sexual intercourse against their will through use or threat of force (the minimum legal definition of rape). Almost 90 percent of them knew their assailants. These shocking statistics are not an anomaly. Recent studies at Auburn University and the University of South Dakota reveal that one in five college women were forced against their will to have sexual intercourse by men they knew. Because they are unlikely to use the term "rape" to describe what happened to them, and they often feel guilty and ashamed, most women who are forced to have sex with an acquaintance do not report the incident officially. But the aftermath can be as devastating for them as the consequences of rape by a stranger.

Colleges and universities are focusing attention on the widespread problem. Many campus organizations, such as Stanford's Rape Education Project and the Center for the Study of Campus Violence at Towson State University in Maryland, distribute booklets to students with emergency phone numbers and advice on protection. Programs such as Washington State's "When Sex Becomes a Crime" and the University of Florida's "How Vulnerable Are You?" alert students to the miscommunications and misconceptions that lead to sexual violence. Michigan State even staged a mock trial based on an actual incident of acquaintance rape to sensitize students to the emotional damage the victim suffers, as well as to the legal implications.

Workshops and programs challenge the beliefs of many young men that are rooted in the social fabric of existing sexual myths—"she provoked it," "women say no, but mean yes," "I just lost control; you know how men are."

Counselors and peer educators instruct students about sexual rights and responsibilities and teach women how to say no. They also emphasize that it is essential for both men and women to make active, responsible choices, and point out the role that alcohol plays in increasing the risk of miscommunication and poor judgment.

Since recent research indicates that freshmen are the group most at risk for date rape, many schools now include videotapes or student skits, and peer-led discussions on the topic during orientation. And it's not unusual for fraternities, sororities, and residence hall staffs to follow up with related programs as the year progresses.

Increased awareness about the prevalence of date rape has also produced student demands for more sophisticated campus support services, such as a specifically designated women's counselor, survivors' support groups, more accessible campus reporting mechanisms, and more responsive judicial procedures that take into consideration the special psychological dimensions of sexual assault cases.

Eating Disorders

A mixture of psychological, sociological, and environmental stresses make today's college women particularly vulnerable to eating disorders. Though some students have a history of anorexia or bulimia in high school, others turn early in their college career to the starvation diets that characterize anorexia, or to the binge eating and purging through vomiting, laxatives, diet pills, or fasting of bulimia. The combination of leaving home, coping with the stresses of college life, and the societal obsession with thinness cause some women to engage in these destructive, sometimes deadly, behaviors. College counselors address these issues daily in individual and group counseling. But they also reach out to educate both students and staff about the pitfalls of excessive dieting and the physical and psychological implications of eating disorders.

For example, the George Washington University Counseling Center has strengthened links with other university departments to intervene actively on a variety of fronts. Residence hall advisors receive training during their orientation; the Athletic Department provides a support group for women in sports, a population at high risk for eating disorders, to help them develop alternative strategies for managing stress; the Student Health Service coordinates treatment with the Counseling Center to assure the physical well-being of these students along with attending to their psychological needs.

The University of Georgia has developed a comprehensive, ongoing plan to address the problem of eating disorders on campus: distributing relevant literature; presenting films and discussions as well as educational programs that emphasize responsible nutrition and dieting; offering consultation to faculty and staff, friends, and roommates about how to deal with students struggling with this potentially dangerous problem.

Drugs and Alcohol: Use, Abuse, and Policies

Bathtub gin in the twenties, rum and cola in the fifties—alcohol is certainly not new to the college scene. But its pervasiveness is. On most campuses today, alcohol is everywhere.

According to a 1990 survey by the University of Michigan's Institute for Social Research, 75 percent of college students said that they had consumed alcohol in the past month. This figure is down from a high of 83 percent in 1982. And 41 percent reported drinking five or more drinks in a row within the past two weeks. Though alcohol is the drug of choice for most, the study also reveals that during the prior year 33 percent of college students had used some illicit drug. Approximately 29 percent had used marijuana and 5.6 percent had used cocaine.

Though student use of illicit drugs has declined significantly during the past ten years, temptations and opportunities abound. Students don't have to search very far to find whatever they are looking for. They don't even have to be looking at all. The odor of marijuana wafts down the hall, and vodka bottles and beer cans decorate the windowsills of dorm rooms. On most campuses, hallucinogens and designer drugs, such as Ecstasy, are readily available. Parties erupt spontaneously in residence halls, especially on weekends; alcohol and other drugs are part of the scene that invades students' lives whether they wish to take part in them or not.

When students drink excessively or experiment with drugs, inhibitions fade and young men and women have to come to terms with questions of unplanned sex and irresponsible aggression and vandalism. On Monday mornings deans and residence hall directors routinely review incident reports of the weekend's personal and property damage. The incidents run the gamut from lacerations and chipped teeth to wrecked cars and falls from windows. More private consequences, such as having sex and regretting it later or humiliating oneself in front of friends, rarely show up in official documents, but may produce more permanent scars than the physical damage. Many of the reported cases of date rape involve substance abuse, and most student development professionals agree that on a college campus, it is difficult to address the subjects of substance abuse and sex separately.

Reflecting the heightened national awareness of alcohol as a pervasive societal problem, colleges and universities are now providing educational and support services on a number of related issues. Children of alcoholic groups, AA chapters, and alcohol education programs can be found on many campuses. Chapters of BACCHUS, an acronym for Boost Alcohol Consciousness Concerning the Health of University Students, are active on a number of campuses, led by students advocating responsible drinking. Some schools, such as Tulane, have hired full-time administrators to plan programs, educate and counsel students about substance abuse. Information on drug use and addiction is part of most RA training sessions and has even become part of the curriculum at some schools. Columbia University runs a mandatory drug awareness program for athletes. Fraternities and sororities on many campuses are turning to "dry rush."

The alcohol problem among undergraduates has become increasingly complicated since more states changed their drinking age to twenty-one and George Bush signed The Drug-Free Schools and Communities Act, requiring every institution of higher education to certify that it has implemented a program to prevent the illicit use of drugs and the abuse of alcohol. Colleges and universities have had to come to grips with the fact that for most of their undergraduates it is illegal to drink; thus they have tightened their alcohol policies to protect themselves from legal assault. This poses a dilemma. If they can't drink at public parties, some students simply move the party to the fraternity house or into private quarters. University administrators want to be responsible, but also realistic. Many are ambivalent; they are worried about liability, but don't want to institute policies they can't enforce. Consequently the alcohol policies on a number of campuses are ambiguous and confusing to many students.

"I can drink at a party in a friend's room, and that's legit," said a freshman at a small liberal arts college. "I can get totally smashed upstairs and nobody cares. But if I walk downstairs to an official party in the lounge, it's no beer 'cause I'm underage. It doesn't make a hell of a lot of sense."

Sex: Private Issues and Public Problems

The wide range of behavior that is acceptable to today's college students stands in contrast to the unwritten codes of their parents' generation. Perhaps nowhere is this more dramatic than in the area of sex.

The sexual standards on college campuses thirty years ago were for the most part clear-cut; the double standard operated; nice boys did, nice girls didn't. Women were supposed to ignore sexual longings and, for them, the underlying message was, "Sex is dirty; save it for the one you love." There were accepted stages of courtship and dating, and although many deviated from the norm, the public stance of most college students was to follow the rules. And many rules there were.

Women's dorms above the first floor were off limits to the opposite sex. "Man on the floor" meant a father carrying a heavy suitcase to his daughter's room.

In men's dorms, women might be allowed to visit, but there were parietal hours and rules. The door to the room was to be left open no less than six inches.

At midnight, droves of couples hid behind bushes in front of women's dormitories or dashed from parked cars as house-mothers flashed porch lights to signal the midnight curfew.

And there were notorious rules on many campuses, though hardly anyone can actually remember seeing them written down, that when men and women were together alone in a room, each of them had to keep at least one foot firmly on the floor at all times.

Women didn't have to depend solely on assertive skills to say no. There were rules and boundaries of time and space that helped them fend off the advances of dismal blind dates or their own and their boyfriends' sexual impulses. Codes of conduct, right and wrong, were spelled out, and if one chose to behave differently, the burden of guilt or the label of "fast" would suggest that one had chosen "wrong" over "right."

The social upheaval of the late sixties and early seventies, along with the ready availability of birth control pills, brought about a sexual revolution, which exploded on college campuses. The changes were radical: new freedoms, new notions of right and wrong, and the disappearance of rules, both institutional and personal, which had guided the generations before. Experimentation, spontaneity, and openness became the buzz words of this new era—the celebrated Age of Aquarius. In the fifties "nice girls didn't." In the seventies, women who "didn't" began to feel the pressure to join the sexually active mainstream.

When asked to describe the sexual patterns of today's college students, one college administrator thought for a moment and then said:

> This may seem like a strange analogy, but it's like fashions and hemlines. There used to be a standard. Women in the fifties wouldn't think of wearing skirts above their knees and by the end of the sixties they wouldn't wear them below. But now almost anything goes. People experiment and choose what suits them best. It's the same with sexual attitudes. Kids have no strict guidelines, although they might have parental or religious values that they have internalized. Many experiment, however, until they find their own "right" style. Some are comfortable and have few problems with their sexuality. But for most there is a lot of confusion along the way. And now, of course, the cloud of AIDS is hanging over them.

And a young woman, a junior at Boston University, comments, "I don't think you can say anything is rare or that anything is the norm. I haven't seen anything I can say is the norm."

Today premarital sex is more the rule than the exception, but clearly there is no *one* standard of sexual conduct. Although some students engage in casual sex, a great many are more likely to have a series of relationships that include sex. In the book, *Friends and Lovers in the College Years*, the authors describe "a period of experimental sexual contact that gradually evolves into a pattern of 'serial monogamy.'" [5]

According to health service personnel on many campuses, students know less about sex and birth control than most adults think they do. In spite of generally available sex education courses, students remain surprisingly ignorant about the relative safety and risks of various birth control methods. One dean remarked that on her campus April and May are known as the abortion months; "that's after the spring formals," she explained. At another university, an RA in an all-freshmen dorm called a member of the counseling staff the second week of school requesting a workshop on sexuality immediately; her residents were "bed-hopping" with what seemed to be little regard for the consequences of their behavior.

Most campuses run workshops and seminars on sexuality, and the students and staff at Stanford have even developed a board game called "Sexploration" to help young men and women make more responsible decisions about sex and personal relationships.

The whole subject of sexual practices among young people is changing as the threat of AIDS has reached the ivory tower. College administrators and students debate the format of educational campaigns—should we dispense condoms, should we educate about "safe sex," or should we address abstention as the only responsible solution to this frightening problem? Ethical, moral, and legal questions relating to university policy have brought into the public domain questions usually reserved for private and intimate relationships. And students respond with varying degrees of anxiety. Some toss AIDS off as a problem for gay students, wearing a cloak of invincibility typical of this age and denying the reality of the threat to the heterosexual community. Others have made significant changes in their sexual behavior and are reevaluating this whole arena of their lives.

As a result of the widespread media coverage of AIDS, students have become increasingly aware of the dangers of other sexually-transmitted diseases, such as chlamydia, herpes, and genital warts. Although it is difficult to assess how much influence these developments have had on the intimate relationships and bedroom behavior of college students, there have been some recent developments that suggest major changes may be on the way. As students grapple with what this phenomenon means to them, "safe sex" no longer alludes simply to protection from pregnancy, but protection from disease and even death. And "caution," "abstention," and "monogamy" are becoming part of the sexual idiom of growing numbers of college students.

Making Connections: Campus Groups

Activities fairs, a fall ritual on most campuses, provide a festival-like atmosphere with colorful banners and posters and students distributing leaflets, and invitations to join the Society of Women Engineers, Hispanic Business Students Association, American Indian Students Commission, Organization of United African-American Peoples, Gay and Lesbian Alliance, Islamic Society, Intervarsity Christian Fellowship.

The diversity of the current crop of college students is reflected in this melange of campus organizations. There are more groups than ever before, representing a broad range of backgrounds and beliefs.

Most students thrive on the sense of connection that comes from affiliation with a small group united by a common bond. Interest in large, formal structures such as student government appears to have waned, and there are few rituals or events, except for organized sports and the camaraderie of cheering on a winning team, that foster a feeling of community. But small, informal organizations are a vital part of colleges today. As students choose among this incredible range of campus groups, they are making a statement about who they are or who they want to be.

Minority Student Groups

Anglo students find it hard to believe that minorities are treated differently, but daily episodes belie this reality. African-American and Hispanic students at the University of California at Irvine report that when they go to a local shopping center, they are followed by the security guards; Asian students from Maine to California claim everyone assumes that they are either pre-med or engineering majors, and they feel the thinly veiled hostility of their classmates who are worried about their raising the curve. Students from the Middle East sense the fear and mistrust of their peers whenever there is a widely publicized incident in their part of the world. Hispanic students describe the humiliation of arriving at a fraternity party where the Mexican theme includes Anglos affecting Spanish accents.

Minority student groups, both organized and informal, serve a crucial need as a haven where students of color can be themselves—where they don't have to represent all people of their race or culture, but can speak their own minds.

The cross cultural center at the University of California at Irvine houses student organizations for African-Americans, Native Americans, Asian-Americans, and Chicanos and Latinos. But centers such as these are not without their own internal controversies. Though administrative categories may lump together all Asian-Americans, there are, of course, distinct cultural differences among Vietnamese, Chinese, Korean, and Filipino students—as well as between immigrants and second and third generation students.

Some campuses, such as Berkeley, where white students are now just another minority, foreshadow the American pluralistic society of the not too distant future. Many students at Berkeley report feelings of isolation in the midst of diversity. They use words such as *balkanization* and *tribalism* to describe the break up of the student body into distinctly separate ethnic and racial camps.

Other Berkeley students report that there is more mixing than meets the eye of the casual observer. Though students find support and social comfort by coming together with others from similar backgrounds, many also form bonds across racial and cultural boundaries, as they struggle together with difficult chem labs, or enervating athletic practices, or challenging community service projects. And as they celebrate their own culture, they often enrich the lives of their fellow students. The conventional wisdom from a white student overheard giving a campus tour to a prospective freshman:

> The Asian Students Association has the hottest parties on this campus, especially on the Chinese New Year. Everybody goes. They always have great decorations, good music, and definitely the best food. They even have fireworks.
>
> Black Anthology is the most awesome student production on campus. There's singing, poetry, dance, even a fashion show put on by the Fine Arts students. You have to come early or you don't get a seat.

As the numbers of African-American students at four-year colleges dwindle, those who remain on predominantly white campuses struggle with a sense of alienation and disillusionment of spirit. Many have chosen to attend a school in which African-Americans are likely to represent less than 5 percent of the student body, to "brave it" in an environment more like the real world than the black college alternative. They are received in a climate that is, at best, lukewarm and at worst, hostile, to pursue the rigors of their academic and personal development. There are subtle reminders daily that they are not welcomed by many of their classmates and professors—not recognizing them or confusing them with other black students, failing to respect or acknowledge their insistence on celebrating the life and death of Martin Luther King Jr., suggesting that they accept a mediocre performance rather than reach for higher academic goals, implying that they had been admitted as a result of preferential treatment.

Most African-Americans, both on campus and off, talk of a dual consciousness, of their ability to switch from their black world—a shared language, heritage, and music—to the world of the white majority and its cultural norms. This split is particularly exhausting and confusing at a time when a young adult is sorting out a sense of his or her own identity. Many feel forced to make a choice. A freshman at a prestigious college addresses a dilemma common to many minority students:

> If I join a black sorority or hang out with my friends from BSA [the Black Student Association], the white kids say I'm segregating myself. If I go out with some of the white kids on the floor or a couple of them I knew from high school, then my black friends give me a hard time and say I'm turning my back on my own. I almost went to Howard, and I still think I might transfer. It seems like such a hassle a lot of the time.

Indeed, recent studies show that students attending the top black colleges, such as Morehouse, Spellman, and Howard, have statistically out-performed black students who attend predominantly white colleges. Jacqueline Fleming, a black psychologist who specializes in the field of motivation and is the author of *Blacks in College*, notes the strong influence of the varied supports that black students have on an all-black campus—greater access to friends, relationships with professors who believe in them and support their dreams, and exposure to role models. In a 1987 address to the American College Personnel Association, she challenged black and white faculty and administration at all institutions to take note and to become mentors to students:

> It's relationships first and foremost that seem to make the difference in fostering intellectual development. If I had to choose one category, I would choose informal relationships with teachers and administrators who can serve as mentors.

Religious Revival

Today's students are searching for answers in uncertain times—for rituals and traditions in an era of rapid change and rootlessness. In the sixties, the fervor of anti-war demonstrations or the collective outrage against civil rights violations brought groups of students together in an impassioned community. Today, the lack of a cause, of a central focus to make meaning of their lives, has left a void for many students. And they are returning to religion in droves, looking for answers, for structure, for some stability. Conservative in spirit as well as mind, young men and women attend traditional services, join Bible study groups, and some even live in small enclaves that carry on rituals or traditions of their faith.

Across the country, memberships at the Newman Centers and Hillels, traditional gathering places for Catholic and Jewish students, are flourishing. And alongside these, the numbers of different religious groups are mushrooming continually—the Chinese Christian Fellowship, the Bahai Campus Club, the Moslem Society. The University of Texas has forty-nine different religious groups, two and a half times as many as it had fifteen years ago. At the University of Illinois, almost one-quarter of the students are active members of religious organizations.

Students who join a group with a religious focus find companionship as well as spirituality. Many of these organizations sponsor parties, picnics, or other social events. For some students the identification with their own ethnic group is more important than the spiritual experience or religious ritual. For others, membership provides an oasis of calm in a stressful landscape.

Administrators on many campuses are concerned about students' susceptibility to cults. Seymour Lachman of the City University of New York, speaking at a "Cults on Campus Seminar at CUNY," explained that such groups usually have a "self-appointed, messianic leader claiming divine selection who focuses followers' attentions exclusively on him and exercises autocratic control over them." Cults manipulate, control, and isolate their members. They demand unquestioning loyalty and obedience. And college students who are searching for answers, for an identity, for some stability in their lives, are a target group to fall victim to their lure.

Using sophisticated recruiting techniques, cults seek out students at times that they are most likely to be vulnerable—after midterm grades are posted, during exams, after fraternity and sorority rush. Cult recruiters have been known to position themselves outside the counseling service or in the student center, looking for students who appear depressed or lonely. Numerous organizations around the country monitor the activities of cults. The Cult Awareness Network of the Citizens Freedom Foundation is a nationwide coalition of affiliates concerned about destructive cultism. Based in Chicago, the network maintains a library and hotline and is a resource for both students and parents.[6] Steven Hassan's book, *Combatting Cult Mind Control*, and Marcia Rudin's book, *Cults on Campus*, also provide valuable information on this topic.

Gay and Lesbian Support Groups

Homosexuality has come out into the open on many college campuses. University-sanctioned student organizations commonly include gay and lesbian groups. Most of these support groups offer social and educational programs, and some serve as political action groups as well. They confront overtly discriminatory policies and incidents, and also attempt to sensitize the university community to the more subtle forms of harassment they experience. The University of Pennsylvania has even hired an administrator to work specifically on behalf of lesbian, gay, and bi-sexual students.

Campus recognition has changed the lives of gay men and women, offering them a place to share their concerns with their peers—a far cry from the isolated, guilt-ridden secret lives of those in earlier times. In spite of this improved climate, there has been a recent increase in blatant anti-gay incidents, brought on primarily by anxiety about AIDS. According to Ethan J. Felson, former co-chairman of the Northeast Lesbian and Gay Student Union, gay activists are confronting this new outburst of homophobia: "We have to fight homophobia in the dorms, because people are scared of contacting AIDS by living next door to someone who might not be a carrier of the disease but is in a high-risk population." [7]

In this highly charged atmosphere, gay student groups have taken the lead in dispelling such myths and educating the campus community about AIDS prevention and safe sex.

Greek Revival

Although some colleges such as Colby and Amherst have disbanded their Greek system in recent years, fraternities and sororities are definitely back in vogue on many campuses. New chapters arrive yearly on campuses that spurned them twenty years ago. They provide students with a family of "brothers" and "sisters" and an instant identity advertised by the pins, jackets, and sweatshirts they proudly wear. The Greek system has opened its ranks along with the rest of the university. Most nationals no longer tolerate restricting membership based on race or religion. Some fraternities are even coed. Hazing, and its sometimes tragic consequences, has come under scrutiny, and increasing numbers of states have passed anti-hazing laws.

Present-day Greek life is a study in contradictions. On the one hand, fraternities are typically notorious for their wild parties, excessive alcohol consumption, and drug use. The "Animal House" image is alive and well. On the other hand, an increasing number of fraternities and sororities have taken the lead in campus activities and community service. Though more diverse in membership than they used to be, they still cater mainly to the affluent and exclude individual students, who suffer the pain of rejection. Today's students see "networking" as a plus in the stampede for professional success, and these coteries provide the first stop on the "old boy" express and its "old girl" equivalent. Those who are excluded from membership often feel that they have been exiled permanently from the mainstream.

Today's colleges and universities have acknowledged officially the value of students' extracurricular involvements, whether through Greek life or social, religious, or political groups. Under the aegis of the dean of students, a new cadre of student development professionals advises student groups and provides training in leadership skills. They coach and teach and act as confidants and mentors. Their mission is to help students gain confidence and competence in the world outside their classroom.

In their concern about their child's ability to meet academic demands and maintain a high grade point average (GPA), many parents view student involvement as a frivolous pastime. Yet recent research by Alexander Astin highlights the positive influence of involvement outside the classroom on the way students grow and develop. Charles Schroeder, vice chancellor of student affairs at the University of Missouri, urges parents not to discount the impact that the extracurricular experience can have on their child:

> We try to encourage broad-based student involvement in a variety of settings. The intent is to promote character development and values, leadership skills, and the ability to communicate well. Much of this comes from involvement outside the classroom. Students spend approximately twelve to fifteen hours a week in class. Just think about how many hours kids spend together talking, drinking, playing sports, working together in a host of student activities. The intensity of their relationships is powerful. Part of what we do in Student Development is help students make meaning out of the collegiate experience.

Academic Life

Academics remain at the core of the college experience. And here, too, parents may be in for a surprise.

"Oral Literature? Ethical Issues in Medical Technology? Whatever happened to English Lit and Biology 101?" queried a puzzled father after his son called home to report on the classes he planned to take. Like many parents he was more than a little suspicious of courses with such esoteric titles, courses he wouldn't have found in a college catalogue when he was his son's age.

The course listings in contemporary catalogues include a legacy from the sixties and seventies when universities opened their doors to diverse populations, and the civil rights and women's movements made their mark. "At that time colleges and universities began to give students a variety of lenses through which to view a problem," comments Thomas Ehrlich, president of Indiana University. He adds:

> Western Civilization courses, which were equated with the history of great men, were dropped. We began to ask, what about women and minorities? The structure of the curriculum became more open, and courses began to cut across disciplines. We developed a much more variegated academic set of inquiries.

In recent years many universities have failed to support the black and women's studies programs that were created twenty years ago. Some survive, however, and many have left their impact. Feminist theory and research have changed the face of contemporary psychology, and history departments have incorporated scholarship on women and blacks into the curriculum. The English department no longer divides its courses by centuries and traditional literary periods. "Women Writers in Medieval France" and "The African Folktale" join the more traditional fare of "Chaucer" and "British Renaissance Poetry."

The recent explosion of knowledge in the sciences has altered the curriculum also. Many educators are adamant about the necessity of integrating new technology and the social sciences, stressing that both are essential for the educated person. Science, technology, and society courses, known as

STS programs in academic circles, often are taught by a team of professors from different departments. Interdisciplinary in approach as well as content, these innovative courses are gaining acceptance on hundreds of campuses. Every student at Union College, for example, is required to take coursework in technology and its social applications. Lafayette's STS courses address issues such as "Health Care in a Technological Society," and at Wellesley students can register for "The Politics of World Energy" or "Structure in Music: Experiments in Computer Modeling."

Some courses have made their way into the contemporary curriculum because they meet new marketplace demands— courses such as telecommunications, data processing, computer graphics, and human resources management. Others reflect a growing interest in international affairs and an increasing awareness on the part of students that we are truly members of a global village.

The decline in interest in foreign language study that grew out of the sixties' pleas for relevance now appears to be reversed. The majority of colleges and universities offer opportunities for study abroad. Foreign language courses are in ascendancy, and the number of institutions that require coursework in a foreign language for completion of an undergraduate degree has increased markedly during the last ten years.

Even in schools that don't require foreign language study, students are flocking back to these courses. Language classes are particularly popular at schools that have instituted the Dartmouth method, an active oral approach developed by the charismatic Dartmouth professor John Rassias.

But the language courses today's students are choosing aren't limited to traditional Romance languages and literature sequences. Language study often takes a vocational slant, as students enroll in "German for Business" or "Scientific Russian" or "Computer Portuguese." Students are broadening the choices of languages they are studying too. With an eye on the international job market, they are turning to Russian, Japanese, Chinese, and Arabic.

Students are flocking, also, to courses in Latin American studies. At Notre Dame the demand for courses in Latin American studies tripled between 1979 and 1986. Students at Tulane can choose among three courses in Latin American Studies to fulfill the non-western distribution requirement.

Through a satellite and cable hook-up originated at Columbia University, students at twelve colleges are learning about Russian culture by watching Russian television. Courses in peace studies are also gaining in popularity. More than a dozen colleges and universities, including Tufts, Wesleyan, and UCLA, offer courses in international terrorism.

In an attempt to understand the culture spawned by the sixties, students gravitate to courses about that era. Some courses, such as "The Impact of the Vietnam War on American Values," at the University of California at Santa Barbara, deal not just with the war itself, but the cultural and political movements that grew out of that era in our history as well. There are now more than three hundred such courses on campuses across the country.

Today's students are demonstrating a resurgence of interest in the study of religion and are signing up for courses in religion in record numbers. Harvey Cox's course, "Jesus and the Moral Life," draws as many as nine hundred students per semester at Harvard, and additional students have to be turned away. Today's students don't limit themselves to learning about the Judeo-Christian tradition. Many are studying Eastern religions and are immersing themselves in the thought and faith of distant cultures.

Although enrollments in the liberal arts dropped precipitously in the seventies, there is evidence that the pendulum is starting to swing back. In the late eighties, applications to liberal arts colleges increased at a greater rate than applications to universities and technical schools. Selective, small liberal arts schools, such as Wesleyan and Pomona, report that competition for admissions has been particularly keen in the last few years.

The word is out that employers are interested in liberal arts students. They are sending messages that they value critical thinking and writing skills and the ability to be flexible—that technical training is outdated quickly and today's workforce, above all, has to be adaptable to change. Moreover, students enrolled in undergraduate professional programs such as business and engineering are taking more liberal arts courses than they used to. At the University of Miami students in several of the professional programs such as education, communications, and nursing are required to declare a second major in the liberal arts. And MIT has broadened its engineering program to include more coursework in the arts, humanities, and social sciences. There is more crossover in general, and liberal arts students are also taking advantage of the opportunities to supplement their studies with courses in business or computer technology.

On campuses across America, curriculum reform is the order of the day. Much of the recent criticism about higher education has been leveled from within, beginning with the 1985 report "Integrity in the College Curriculum" by the Association of American Colleges, which used the word "incoherent" to describe the status of undergraduate education. The sixties' concern for egalitarianism has been replaced by today's concern with quality and cohesion. The days of unlimited pass/fail courses, no requirements, and widespread independent study appear to be coming to a close.

Almost all institutions are in the middle of curriculum change. They are looking at ways to introduce students to the ideas and arts of non-western cultures. They are developing new general education requirements and are examining more closely the actual skills that students are learning. They are concerned about competencies in writing and quantitative analysis. They are grappling with questions of assessment, and are discussing methods to measure their effectiveness with an eye toward using that information in planning for the future.

Edward Fiske, former education editor of the *New York Times* thinks the roots of much of this academic self-analysis are political:

The faculty is taking back the control that it gave away in the '60s, reinstituting requirements and establishing a core. This trend started at Harvard in the late '70s, which spurred lots of other schools to do the same. In the beginning it was a political rather than an academic event. The primary issue was control, not content.

More and more faculty and academic deans are expressing concern about academic overspecialization, the rise of pre-professionalism, and lack of common goals that are all too common on today's campuses. They are claiming that it is not enough merely to reinstate a hodgepodge of distribution requirements, but that it is essential to come to some cohesive view of what should constitute the core experience of education today.

Some schools such as Princeton and Columbia are quick to point out that they never gave up their general education programs in the first place. Others, such as Skidmore, which went through major changes in the sixties and seventies, have introduced a whole new core curriculum. Gustavus Adolphus re-evaluated and essentially redid its catalogue from scratch. The trend is definitely toward more control, toward establishment of a core academic experience for undergraduates. Just what should be included in this core curriculum is the subject of endless debate among deans and faculty, but there is no doubt that the content of college catalogues is changing again.

Some critics equate this core curriculum movement with the back-to-basics trend in primary and secondary education. Others say the motivation comes from concern about declining enrollments and the need to be able to justify what a college is doing.

Educator Ernest Boyer sees the widespread reexamination of curriculum and goals as part of a desire for national cohesion after a period of confrontation:

> As a nation we go through periods of ambivalence and disintegration about values and purposes. Then there is a follow-up period in which we look for cohesion. Reform movements followed World War I and II. The case can be made that the

search for general education on the college campus reflects the larger national mood for integration after conflict and confrontation—a national desire to reaffirm values and structures.[8]

It is clear that in spite of the timeless image they often project, the colleges and universities our children attend are not the same institutions they were twenty or thirty years ago. Reports and studies about today's students and campuses give us insight into the changes that have taken place. They confront the assumptions we tend to make based on our own experience and views, but they are by their very nature limited when it comes to understanding what our children are going through. College students have much to tell us about themselves and their generation. The challenge for parents is to listen to what they have to say; to encourage and advise; and, without resorting to stereotyping and labels, to try to understand them within the context of today's college experience.

PART II
A PARENTS' GUIDE:
FROM START TO FINISH

Chapter 3

GREAT EXPECTATIONS

"Thank God the best years of my life are almost over!" a college senior yelled into the phone, leaving her parents stunned at the other end of the line. That all too common phrase, "These are the best years of your life" had been uttered once too often and at just the wrong moment. She walked back to her room and slammed the door in frustration.

The phrase, "these are the best years of your life" is familiar to most of us. We probably have heard it or said it, often with an added phrase, "so make the best of them" or "enjoy them while you can." As parents we transmit to our children countless images and expectations of college life. Whether or not we are explicit in our comments, we are likely to herald the college years as a golden time.

The Big Build-Up

Although we are all well aware that no one is continually happy in any period of life, we and our children tend to develop great expectations about the next four years as we get caught in the big build-up that precedes entrance to college. The build-up culminates during the senior year of high school, but for many families, expectations about college begin when our children are infants, that wonderful time when they seem flawless and filled with infinite possibilities.

College admissions officers tell tales of parents of newborns calling for advice about preschools. Horror stories abound, especially in New York City, about three-year-olds being prepped for preschool interviews and parents hiring stretch limos so the family can arrive in impressive style. Applications to private schools have been increasing each year. In high schools all over the country, there is more interest than ever in the so-called hot colleges, such as Brown, Duke, and Virginia. There is tremendous pressure on students to pursue admissions to one of these prestigious schools.

The number of applications to selective colleges has increased dramatically in the last two decades, and with the opening up of formerly white male bastions to women and minorities, the composition of the whole admissions scene is very different from what it was twenty-five years ago. Schools such as Stanford claim that they could more than fill their freshman class with straight-A applicants. The lower the percentage of applicants a college accepts, the more desirable it appears, perpetuating the cycle of anxiety and rejection of highly qualified applicants. Prep schools throughout the country report that cheating is widespread and that many students seek counseling and medical care for stress-induced symptoms. One psychiatrist has coined the phrase "the valedictorian syndrome" to describe the condition of his steady stream of anxious, highly capable high school patients. It is not unusual for parents of college preparatory students to hire tutors when grades slip from A's to B's, as the jockeying takes place for top class ranks.

Other families may begin in a less frenzied manner, but find themselves caught up in the whirlwind as classmates of their sons and daughters take prep courses for the SATS, go to private college counselors, and build their resumés with unique and interesting summer experiences, all with an eye toward becoming more marketable commodities. Are we letting our children down? we ask ourselves. Will they be left behind if we don't join the race, even if we find the race distasteful? And so we get caught up in the intensity of the pursuit, and in doing so promote the unspoken expectation that college is the be-all and end-all, the magical answer to all these years of preparation, as well as the ticket to continued success. We imply to our children that these will be four wonderful years, but that it's also important to keep the motor running, to keep up, to stay on track.

In spite of the increased competition for admission to a small number of selective schools, the pool of potential college students has declined and competition for the best and the brightest is fierce. According to the National Center for Education Statistics, the number of traditional college-aged students, aged eighteen to twenty-four, will continue to decline through the mid-nineties. Paradoxically, colleges have never been more worried about enrollments, and students have never been more anxious about admissions. The atmosphere is highly charged on both sides.

College admissions staffs, therefore, play their parts in heightening expectations as they vie for position in the competitive scramble to keep their schools alive and well in financially shaky times. Twenty years ago a student inquiry to a college admissions office produced simply a catalogue and an application form. Today there are an ever increasing number of slick viewbooks and video tapes to lure youngsters to the goodies that their schools can provide.

Even the most selective schools employ large staffs who monitor their admissions techniques and formulate strategies to increase their yield of accepted students. Many colleges compete for academic superstars by offering them lucrative, merit-based financial packages. College admissions departments do sophisticated marketing studies, and phrases such as "prospect lists" and "overlap schools" are part of the jargon spoken by admissions officers in every school in the country. We are in collusion—parents and high schools and college admissions staffs—in setting up unrealistic images of the college experience. We are not doing this intentionally; we don't mean to be deceitful. Most of us believe that a good college experience is important—a once in a lifetime opportunity. The unspoken message that often permeates the frantic years leading up to admission, however, is that college is also a haven of constant intellectual stimulation and wonderful friendships, camaraderie, and young love.

In actuality the college experience can be rich with stimulation, wondrous new experiences, and relationships, a unique and special time that is never repeated in quite the same way. It is also a time of enormous stresses, confusion, loneliness, and uncertainty; and this too has its own uniqueness, never to be experienced again from the vantage point of a young adult whose perspective is clouded by his or her own inexperience, insecurity, and the struggles of discovering a separate identity.

Where do parents get their idealized views of college? For some who have never been to college themselves, this may be a dream of what they never had, a fantasy of something special they missed. They form images from television and the movies, pictures of ivy-covered paradises, settings for romance, care-free romping among the stacks, wild fraternity antics, and intense discussions about esoteric topics. Or perhaps they remember idealistic young men and women of the sixties marching for civil rights and devoting themselves to causes that broke the boundaries of the gothic quadrangles of their college lives. Rarely do the media images include the relentless every-day stresses of the classroom or dormitory living, and many of our frozen images are outdated.

Parents learn of college life from friends. Dinner party conversation is often sprinkled with happy news about their successful offspring: "Alice is premed, getting straight A's and immersed in her tutoring work in the inner city"; "Jack's an accounting major and is already being sought after by com-panies at phenomenal starting salaries." Occasionally we hear the war stories: "My daughter has spent the whole first semester miserable, trying to figure out how to get her roommate's boyfriend to move out. He's been living there since the semester began." But often when we hear about some of the more difficult times, they are mentioned with humor, after the fact, with the sleepless nights of parental worry omitted.

Many parents know about college because they went there. They often look back, however, with rose-colored glasses and selective memories of the good times: the football games, first loves, an inspiring professor, immersion in fascinating studies. They tend to forget the all-nighters with No-Doz and countless cups of coffee, the periods of loneliness, the anxiety before midterms or dates, the boring lectures and tedious assignments, the times when first loves were no more. They also forget that today's college experience is very different from the ex-perience of twenty or thirty years ago. Although parents know things have changed, they don't really believe it—or, they don't want to believe it. It is difficult to separate the fantasies, memories, and myths from the reality, and it takes a conscious effort for us and our children to develop realistic expectations about college, especially when we have become so caught up in the race for admissions.

The Admissions Marathon

The admissions marathon usually begins in earnest during the spring of junior year in high school with college visits and fairs and the inevitable onslaught of unsolicited viewbooks. A veritable courtship between college and student has begun. SAT scores become a new identification tag, and the question—to coach or not to coach—is the topic of discussion among parents and counselors alike. There is even a game called "College Pursuit" to help students prepare for SATs. Set up like its more famous counterpart, "Trivial Pursuit," it features sample math and verbal questions. Players can convert their scores in the game to equivalent SAT scores, so on any day they can get a reading of just where they stand in this aspect of the admissions race. Of course there are also the books. Some bookstores now have a whole section devoted to college admissions. There are SAT and ACT and achievement test preparation books and college guides, as well as handbooks of the "how-to-get-in" genre.

Many parents and high school juniors start the college exploration process with a sense of excitement. It is a time of possibilities and dreams and an incredible number of options. Parents may enjoy looking at the college viewbooks and videotapes, and visiting campuses. They often find themselves reminiscing about their own college years, or simply about the days when they were eighteen. Although students are quick to acknowledge their desire to get out of high school, many of them seem overwhelmed by the choices now facing them. After showing initial enthusiasm about college materials, they may start to withdraw from the whole process. Conflict about deadlines and making plans for college visits and filling out applications seems to be de rigueur between seniors in high school and their parents. Most tend to look back on the year with a sense of relief after it is over.

Tension about whose decision this really is lies behind much of the conflict. Many parents believe that they know what's best for their children, and that it is their responsibility to select the schools to which their child will apply. One mother described emphatically how she had picked schools for each of her five children, because she thought she knew her children better than anyone else. Other parents bend over backwards not to interfere, and stay totally uninvolved. Most parents try for a middle course, sometimes rushing erratically from one extreme to the other. At some time during the course of the year almost all families find themselves talking about college admissions more than any of them find palatable. A student at the University of Michigan reminisced:

> I was scared to death my junior year in high school. I didn't want to think about college. I felt my parents pushed me too much. I needed them to push me, but not right away. I went to look at colleges the summer after junior year, but it was too much. At the dinner table it seemed to be the only topic of conversation.

And a freshman in high school complained:

> We spent this whole year talking about college, because my brother was applying. I got so sick of it I felt like screaming almost every night. I don't think my brother liked it any more than I did, but my parents never seemed to want to talk about anything else. No one seemed bothered by my problems. I guess they seemed unimportant by comparison. It really bugged me!

A New England woman explained how her studied attempt not to repeat her parents' mistakes backfired. Thirty years ago she had gone to Smith because her father wanted her to. At that time she vowed that she would never do the same thing to her children:

> When my oldest was trying to decide between Boston College and Springfield, I wanted him to choose BC, but I stayed out of

it. He chose Springfield, because he thought he would feel more at home there. Now he's finished with school, but he never lets me forget that he thinks I should have told him to go to BC. You just can't win.

Most college-bound students are innundated with college literature. National Merit Semi-Finalists may get as many as three or four hundred pieces of mail. Minority students with high SATs, musicians, and athletes often receive even more. The mother of a St. Louis high school senior wrote this description of her family's response to a typical marketing blitz:

The summer after Michael's junior year, the deluge began. Every day the mailbox was stuffed with viewbooks and brochures—all slick and glossy, with pictures of beautiful young students strolling under trees laden with yellow and orange leaves. It always seemed to be fall in the viewbooks. And in the few shots of winter, more beautiful students cavorted in snow under azure skies. Even in Minnesota and Maine it didn't really look cold.

Michael showed only minor interest in the growing pile of information in his room. He was amused by the brochure with a half-page picture of a girl in a bikini stretched out in a tanning booth. Neither he nor we ever figured out any remote connection between that blatant attention getter and the midwestern state university that sent it. Then there was the poster-sized picture of a moose in the middle of a field of wildflowers from a small New England school. He hung that one in his bathroom. We encouraged Michael to read the materials so he could set some preliminary criteria and begin to think in terms of types of schools that interested him. We thought we were being very reasonable, that we were providing gentle guidance, and that we would teach him something about decision making along the way. Well, he managed to ignore our increasingly direct suggestions about how to proceed, and he went off to a job at a summer camp, leaving the unread literature in a heap in the middle of his bedroom floor.

After Michael left for camp, my husband and I bought pendaflex folders, and made files on selected schools, complete with summary notes. We became obsessed with college guide books too, and read them over and over making lists and comparing notes. I don't know how helpful all our efforts were to Michael, but at least we felt as though we were taking some control over what was quickly becoming an overwhelming task.

Overwhelming is a word used repeatedly by parents and students when they describe the college admissions process. There is, first of all, the sheer quantity of the choices. And there is the intensity of the rhetoric. After a while one of the few things that most students and parents agree on is that all of the viewbooks sound as though they were written by the same person. "Have you ever found a school that doesn't claim to have an outstanding and accessible faculty, a diverse student body, and a commitment to excellence?" asked a bemused high school senior.

Choosing a college is the biggest decision the majority of seventeen- and eighteen-year-old applicants have ever had to make. And because most of them still tend to think in terms of absolutes, they are likely to feel very anxious about making the right choice. A lot of students respond to this anxiety by procrastinating every step of the way. They may wait until the last minute before they narrow down their list to a manageable number of schools. Their overriding fear is that the school they cross off is "the perfect one." They wait as long as possible before writing their essays, believing somehow that the right essay may be just the key that will make the difference between admission and rejection. It is not unusual for these students to carry their procrastination right down to the wire, exemplified by the enormous number of applications that arrive at admissions offices all over the country on deadline day via Federal Express.

Many students have a clear sense of what kind of college they want to attend. They make an informed choice, apply early decision and, if they are accepted, there is a familial sigh of relief: "I knew I wanted to go to Kenyon after I spent a weekend there last fall," said a freshman. "I sat in on three classes and slept in the dorm. I think I got a good feel for the place in three days. I was sure it was for me, and I still am."

Other students make their choice early, based on little knowledge about themselves or the college. They avoid information about other schools and refuse to consider alternative choices. If they visit the school, they look only for confirmation of the decision they have already made. The negative aspects of the school are avoided or unnoticed. They, too, apply early decision in an attempt to put the whole issue out of their minds. This method of coping probably causes less tension in the family than the more common one of procrastination. But both responses may be methods of coping with the anxiety inherent in the belief that there really is a perfect answer rather than a number of options for each student.

It is important for parents to realize that young people have diverse ways of dealing with their ambivalence about college applications. They also have different styles of making decisions. Some students want as much help as possible from their parents and actually would prefer it if their parents assumed all the responsibility for them. Others want no help whatsoever; for them it may seem too threatening to take any kind of advice from someone they still see as an authority figure, without feeling as though they have to follow what they have been told. Students need their parents to respect their individual styles, and to help them stretch as they assume increasing responsibility for their own decisions. This is a delicate balance that is rarely achieved without turmoil on both sides, as parents and their children negotiate this aspect of separation.

The college admissions process forces students to assess themselves, to face their limitations and define their values. As they go through the ordeal of writing essays and preparing for interviews, they come face to face with basic questions about their emerging identity. And for many, competition with classmates, even with dear friends, becomes a reality to be reckoned with.

A high school senior wrote the following as part of her application for admission to Dartmouth:

> When my older brother was applying to college, he became to-
> tally overwhelmed with the system of exams, applications and
> interviews. In fact, it came to the point where he wouldn't re-
> quest further information from any schools. His attitude
> amazed me. I mean, this was his future he was talking about,
> and he refused to take it seriously. I knew that when my turn
> came, there would be no problem. I would take it all coolly, set-

ting up deadlines and schedules, while behaving in a mature and sophisticated manner!

My perspective changed, however, once I was no longer the amused bystander, but the prospective candidate. When it came time for the PSAT, it was a scary feeling to sit down with my two freshly sharpened pencils and take the first of many exams that would supposedly affect the rest of my life. To think that filling in all those little circles could possibly help determine who I would become and what would become of me!

Senior year has definitely been a time of self-reflection and appraisal. When I went to my first interview, I was petrified. I could think of no reason why anyone would care to talk for a half-hour about me and my interests. I am basically a shy person, opposed to being phony or fake, so I was shocked to find myself talking to a stranger about such a variety of topics. I became flushed and animated. It was almost as if I were in a play, only I wasn't acting and there was no script. The whole time I had this terrible feeling that I was there to be judged, and heaven help me if I was not adequate. I think this is what has worried most of my classmates this year. We have had to look at ourselves and think, "Am I good enough? Am I an acceptable candidate?" That fear has changed some of us. People who have always been self-assured and poised refused to reveal their SAT scores, and blushed at the memory of their results. Everyone has become excessively competitive, and our school, though an excellent one, does not promote cut-throat competition. When preliminary class ranks came out, they were the topic of conversation for days. I criticized a friend who was complaining because she was number seven and not in the top five. However, I then found myself plotting murder to raise my class rank from number eleven to ten. I realized I was even gossiping over who deserved their class rank, and who didn't. This from a person who had always worked for her own satisfaction and pride, not to outdo anyone else!

The feeling of inadequacy and competition came to a head when I actually began to write my application. Academically, I have never felt inferior to anyone. Yet, when I looked at the questions and tried to answer them so they would reveal an appealing picture of me to the reader, they were not appealing, they were appalling! First I was afraid I was being conceited; then I worried I was not being revealing enough; then I was too sappy; then, affected. On paper, I could not truly show who I was.

As students struggle with who they are, a conflict may arise between their parents' hopes and dreams for them and their own emerging sense of themselves. Many parents notice that their children withdraw during the months when college decisions are being considered. Closed doors, blaring stereos, silent shrugs are familiar teenage strategies for shutting parents out. It is not unusual for communicative young people who formerly have been very close to their parents to retreat for a while. Conversations turn into parental interrogations or nagging sessions, equally unpleasant to parent and offspring alike.

A Philadelphia woman whose daughter recently completed her freshman year at Northwestern recalled:

> My daughter spent her senior year separating and rebelling. It was as though she had to make things really miserable here, so she could eventually leave. We fought a lot, and there were a lot of frozen silences. It escalated as the year went on. Nicole was always the kind of kid who spoke her mind, but this was a whole new ball game. She refused to go to family functions. She spent more and more time in her room with the door closed. She even withdrew somewhat from her high school friends, and talked on the phone a lot to friends from out of town whom she had met at a college summer school. Since I was in graduate school in social work at the time, I was very tuned in to the dynamics of what was happening. I made the mistake of telling her I accepted what she was doing, that I understood that she was separating from us and her friends. As I look back on it, that was not a helpful thing to say. It helped me to understand what was happening, but it didn't help her for me to try to explain it!
>
> The other thing I was aware of is how similar her behavior was to the symptoms of a substance abuser. You know—the typical clues about drugs to parents are a youngster who stays in his or her room for a long period of time, who is negative and secretive, who doesn't want to talk. I think this is also pretty typical behavior of a lot of high school seniors, and it's easy to misinterpret it. I think parents should maintain a healthy skepticism. You can't be naive about drugs. By the time you see what is going on, there probably is more than you think. But you can't jump to conclusions either. One thing that helped me to figure out what was going on with Nicole was that there were still times, usually at 12:30 A.M., when she was ready to talk. And when that happens you have to be ready to drop

everything and talk. Those precious conversations can help to distinguish the kid who is in trouble from the one who isn't.

This is all a tricky business. The kid's job is to grow up and separate from you and do things you don't approve of. And your job is to be sure that what they're doing isn't so serious that it will get them into trouble.

A rough time was right before the applications were due. At one point Nicole was angry that I wasn't helping her. Then her father offered to help her with the typing. That meant they had to cooperate with each other and there was lots of tension. But the absolute worst time was the waiting time. We all were on edge then, and Nicole just withdrew.

Many college students remember their senior year in high school as a time of tremendous ambivalence. They want to be told what to do—to be given clear-cut advice about the choices facing them—and they also desperately want to break away, to be independent. They are worried about letting down the people who believe in them. And, as mentioned earlier, through it all they are struggling with who they are and how they will manage to separate from home and friends. A sophomore at Johns Hopkins recalls the pain of her senior year in high school. Even now a return to her parents' house brings back many of the feelings associated with that last year at home:

The application process was a real self-analysis for me. Who is Lauren Gibbons? What are her interests? Why is she applying here and not there? Why is she getting in here and rejected there? And on and on. What are your strengths? What are your weaknesses? What word best describes you? It was an unpleasant process for me. Home is still tied up with that process. There are a lot of memories of senior year that are truly miserable. And when I go back they still surround me. I look on my bookshelf and find one more college book I forgot to throw out. And even though I'm happy here, when I go home it all comes back; there's that feeling of—I remember what that felt like. Every time I go home it gets a little better, but it's incredible to think how powerful those feelings are.

From October to March of my senior year we were all consumed with the college application process. There was lots of pressure. I had lots of self-pity. I remember thinking I don't do *this* well; I don't do *that* well. I disappoint my parents in *this* respect; my friends in *that* respect; myself in *another* respect. It was a time of very low self-esteem. I was very insecure about academics and SATs and all that.

The worst part was those few months when everyone in the world was asking: where are you going to college next year? I remember thinking over and over, what if I just said I'm not going to college? Then I would think, what would I do if I didn't go to college? What could I do? What would I be good at doing? Nothing. What do I want to do? Nothing, nothing, nothing! I felt really lost. I had no idea what I would study in college. I had no idea what I would really do in college. I began to worry, what would I do when I started missing Mom and Dad? What happens when my dog dies? What's going to happen to my friends from high school? Wait a minute, do I have any friends from high school? I started a total evaluation process of the people I'd been hanging out with for the past twelve years. Through the whole thing, I didn't talk to anybody about what I was going through. I just couldn't. I guess it must have been hard on my parents too.

Parental ambivalence about sending a child off to college, particularly a first-born, is common. The sense that family life will never be the same again, a sense of loss, even jealousy—all are likely to be mixed with the anticipated satisfaction of launching one's offspring. For many parents in the midst of all the hustle and bustle of daily life, this is a period of reflection— of poignant memories about times past. For many there is a coming to terms with one's own limitations, while exploring the ever-expanding horizons of the next generation. A father wrote the following description of his recent tour of colleges with his seventeen-year-old son:

As we worked our way through several campuses in New England, the visits started to fall into a routine. Always starting with registration at the subdued admissions office, we gathered up a multitude of materials, took the student-guided tour of the campus, and attempted to observe and catalogue our thoughts. Ever mindful of the role of overbearing parent, I tried valiantly to hold back on questions, deferring to Andrew, but each time finding it impossible not to keep probing, attempting to unlock the subtle differences among the schools.

What was Andrew thinking about the people and places we were seeing? Despite my urging him beforehand to actively probe his hosts, he was virtually silent on the student-led tours.

However, he reassured me, "Don't worry, Dad, I'm taking it all in." And I'm sure he was, just as he always had. Rehashing at the end of each day we seemed to be very much in sync in our views of what we had observed. While I sat happily conversing with this suddenly grown person in the same Cambridge restaurant and Maine lobster shack where I had carried him in my arms fifteen years earlier, my mind shuttled back and forth across time.

As the week wore on, it was clear that my excited anticipation of the trip was being realized. The sheer freedom of moving about a favorite part of the country, the energy of college campuses, and the increasingly precious time alone with my seventeen-year-old son, exhilarated me. How idyllic it all looked, too, even in the bareness of late winter, with the feel of old brick, patterns of walkways crisscrossing the campus, venerable old buildings with venerable names, and overburdened bulletin boards.

For a middle-aged adult, time spent on a college campus also brought some pangs of jealousy. In a period of life when career, family, and financial demands sometimes seem overwhelming, the prospect of spending four years in a peaceful environment, with almost total devotion to matters of intellect and one's own development, seems to be an incredible luxury.

The mother of a Williams student explained that she too felt jealous when she took her daughter to the campus for the first time. She found that she couldn't help making comparisons between her daughter's opportunities and her own:

My sense of envy surprised me. There is a certain irony to children budding into beautiful young women, when most of us are becoming more aware of aging. I've spent the last twelve years juggling career and family, and it's just beginning to get easier. When I took Carla to Williams for her interview, I kept thinking how wonderful it would be to be in that kind of environment with so much support and only oneself to take care of. I also started to anticipate the loss of Carla. I knew I was going to miss her, and I kept mulling over the question—where has the time gone?

In this era of single parenthood and blended families, separation and family dynamics have become increasingly complicated. For single parents the anticipated departure of a child may be particularly difficult, especially when that child is a treasured companion. Students from single-parent families often worry about leaving their mother or father alone, especially if the child is the last one to leave home. Sometimes the child has had to deal with separation at an earlier age when one of the parents left the marriage. And this may add another dimension to the college leave-taking.

The financial pressure of supporting a child through college is an issue for almost all families. Parents often find themselves sending a double message to their children. On the one hand they are saying that education is invaluable, and they'll pay a premium for the best. On the other they may imply that it is costing them a fortune, and the child had better take advantage of it. Taking advantage of it means different things to different families. For some the message is clear: get good grades and go premed. For others the implication is simply that it is okay to pay all that money for a so-called name school, but not for a lesser known private institution with a high tuition rate.

Robert Hedrick, director of admissions at the University of the South, acknowledges that parents today are concerned about cost. They see themselves as consumers. They are asking as they look at schools: Am I going to get my money's worth?

> If families are from a state that has a strong public system such as Virginia, Michigan, or California, they are going to look very carefully at private college price tags. Parents not only want to know about the quality of the university, they want to know how strong a specific program is. They ask questions about rankings and about the success of graduates.
>
> More students today have parents who have been to college themselves. They have a lot of hopes and dreams for their children. They are hoping the student will be happy, the roommate will be compatible, the courses will be stimulating, and the grades will be good. If at the end of the semester the student's grades come home and they are barely a two point, and the tuition bill arrives the next week, those parental hopes and dreams may turn into expectations—which will in turn feel like demands to the student. It is not unusual for money to be a source of conflict between parents and their children during the admissions process and throughout the college years.

A lot of parents fail to consider financial aid opportunities. They narrow their child's options unnecessarily by precluding all high-priced institutions from the outset. Though the financial aid literature is confusing, filled as it is with its own arcane language and acronyms, it is well worth taking the time to become informed about it. The best place to gather information is at the financial aid office of each college under consideration. There are a wide range of options, including combinations of grants, scholarships, loans, and work-study positions. Though there are no guarantees that aid will be forthcoming, many colleges offer extremely attractive financial packages that make attendance possible for highly qualified students who otherwise would be unable to afford it.

Discussions about finances and financial aid packages are often the first occasion that parents have shared such adult family matters with their children. Honest conversations about what the family can afford, and what the plans and expectations are, can prevent tension and resentment on both sides later. Parents need to be clear about their parameters. They should tell a child from the outset the extent of the financial aid package they will need in order for him or her to attend a particular school. The popularity of books such as *The Public Ivys* and *The Best Buys in College Education* is a telling indicator of the role that money plays in college selection. Finances may dictate the location of potential choices as well as whether the institution is public or private.

Financial considerations are only one factor in the decision about how far from home a student will go. Family tradition and unfamiliarity with other parts of the country, as well as the psychological impact of distance, all play a part in setting geographical parameters. A sophomore at Harvard who grew up in the Bronx, said laughingly, "My mother told me I could go as far as the West Coast to school—only to her the West Coast meant Philadelphia."

And a senior at Carleton stated that her parents, both college professors, were emphatic about the locale that they thought was appropriate for her:

My mother wanted me in the Midwest. She wouldn't let me apply to Stanford. She talked as though California was going to fall off the continent and slip into the ocean. Her objections had nothing to do with distance, but according to my mother, there are weirdos in California, and she didn't want me there in my formative years. I think she was afraid I'd wander off into a cult.

The headmistress of a private school in New Orleans explained that parents of her students feel very tied to the place where they live. For the most part they want their children to be within a day's drive of home:

> This has a lot to do with Southern tradition and a sense of place. It's also about identity and the comfort that comes from being a family everybody knows. Decisions about college are very much influenced by these family values. Sometimes the students' real needs get lost.

Acceptance and Rejection

After all the applications are finally in, there is usually a respite from the oppressively frequent discussions about college. But most students and their parents are still thinking about college admission even if they have stopped talking about it. As the notification dates approach, it is the rare family that isn't checking the mailbox at the first opportunity. A woman who thought she had put the whole admissions game into its proper perspective, and prided herself on not being overly invested in her son's success, sheepishly admitted that she was a bit more connected and anxious than she had realized:

> The kids and I were on vacation out of the country during the two weeks that Jim's college admissions letters were due to arrive. Jim seemed to have put the whole situation out of his mind, and I thought I had too. But the night before we flew home, I had a dream that the housesitter had thrown out all our mail, including Jim's college letters. I awakened in a panic.

When the acceptances and rejections start coming in, students and sometimes parents too, rush home to see if the letter is fat or thin. When the acceptances to first choice schools arrive, the dream seems to be in hand. All those years of preparation, the mountains of college literature, the essays and recommendations, culminate, or so it may seem at the time, in one appropriately fat letter that starts with the word, "Congratulations." Surely this is a time to celebrate with our children. But in their enthusiasm, parents unwittingly can convey the message that acceptance to Yale is the essence of their child's value. In their relief and excitement, they also may perpetuate the expectation of four years of bliss and happiness in New Haven. We are not doing our children any favor if we convey the message that acceptance into a particular college means they "have got it made"—or that a letter of admission is a ticket to success.

Some parents have become so emotionally involved in the admissions process that they take credit for the acceptance themselves. Their public comments about how much money the family donated in order to help an offspring get in, or references to the importance of Dad's alumni connections, can deflate even the most competent student's self-confidence.

Inevitably many students face rejection during the spring of their senior year. And for a lot of them, this is the first major rejection of their lives. The word slips throughout high school corridors instantaneously about who was accepted and rejected where. Unseen scoreboards are tabulated and friendships sometimes buckle under the strain. Parents may find themselves standing by, wishing they could comfort their inconsolable child. Sometimes, however, parents feel more devastated by the rejection than their children do. Both parent and child may suffer from a perceived loss of status and feel embarrassed to tell family and friends. Parents as well as students talk about feeling inadequate at this time. Admissions officers talk candidly about being deluged by phone calls from parents of rejected applicants, demanding an explanation or pleading for a reconsideration. One admissions director recalls his first year in admissions work at a highly selective school. As rookie of the staff, he was assigned the task of signing five thousand rejection letters. After they were mailed, his phone rang constantly for three weeks:

Congressmen called. Alumni called. Mothers, fathers, counselors called—crying, yelling, venting their anger on me. It
was a horrible experience, especially since so many of the students we turned down were highly capable.

The way a student and his or her parents handle rejection is
likely to have a major influence on the student's eventual
college experience. Parents can play an important role at this
time by sympathizing with their child, and then trying to be
encouraging about the remaining options. If the parent has
become overly invested in the first-choice college, this will not
be an easy task. Too often students report that their parents were
terribly disappointed about their rejection, and sent them off
begrudgingly to choice number two or three.

Unfortunately this kind of parental disapproval and short-
sightedness colors students' attitudes toward the school right
from the beginning. They often seem depressed and unmotivated from the time they arrive on campus. It may take a lot of
work on their part and assistance from deans and counselors to
help them separate their personal desires and aspirations from
those of their parents, or to relinquish their own lost dreams and
embrace current reality. Only then are they likely to make a
commitment to their college and their success within it. A
parent who helps a child to enlarge his or her perspective and
to understand that there is no such thing as the perfect college
is bestowing a valuable graduation gift.

Edward B. Fiske, former education editor of the *New York
Times* and author of the *Fiske Guide to Colleges*, urges parents
and prospective college students not to limit their horizons to
the few dozen, most competitive schools:

> The fact that you don't have a designer label on your diploma
> doesn't matter. There are hundreds of good schools. We have
> in this country a system of higher education that is the envy of
> the world. There aren't just ten places that are excellent. There
> are probably about three hundred. It's important to keep some
> perspective.

Once a student has been accepted by at least one college and
is actively considering options, the pain of rejection often fades
into the background. Some high school students have instituted

a ritual of rejection parties, requiring that guests bring at least one rejection letter to gain entrance to the celebration. Paradoxically, of course, the rare student who received no rejections will finally be rejected—from the party. The students build a bonfire and burn the rejection letters along with their collection of college viewbooks, a mock exorcism of the whole stressful year.

Making the Choice

For many students the stress continues throughout April, as they struggle with the decision about which of their acceptances to choose. This is a time of weighing definite offers against indefinite waiting list status. Is it worth waiting, or is it better to just get the whole thing over with? Questions about financial aid and comparative expenses add to the confusion. A Princeton dean suggests:

> At this point the best thing a parent can do is step back and help the child look at the pros and cons of each school. The key is to ask meaningful questions rather than give answers. And realize that after examining all the intellectual pros and cons, ultimately the decision has to be made with the heart.

The father of a student who was trying to decide between the University of Pennyslvania and Dartmouth asked his son to make the proverbial list of the pros and cons for each school. Then he told him to make his decision and keep it to himself for two weeks. His son made the list and struggled with it for a long time. And after he finally made his decision, he didn't tell a soul. He lived with his choice for two weeks and then came into his father's study and announced that he had picked Penn. His sense of assurance surprised even his father, who had suggested the process in the first place. The young man explained that although he still saw lots of pros and cons for both schools, when it came right down to it, "Penn just felt right."

Part of the decision is based on what a particular school's image means to the prospective student. What will it mean if I become a Smithie? Who will I be if I go to Oberlin? Will I be a different person if I go to a small rural college, or a big city university? Is it foolish to turn down a prestigious school for one that I think I'd feel more comfortable at? What kind of person do I want to become?

At a time when their personal identity is fluid and sterotypes about colleges abound, students often have a very difficult time making that final decision. The fear of closing off options can be paralyzing. The students may feel as though their whole future is at stake. It is not unusual for the decision to be made and remade several times before it is final, as this current college freshman described:

> When I first started thinking about college I wanted to go to Carleton or Macalester. Later it became Bryn Mawr or Brown. After I was accepted at both, it was an arduous decision. It was really an awful time. I had lots of wonderful reasons I wanted to go to Bryn Mawr, and I had lots of wonderful reasons I wanted to go to Brown, but the reasons were the opposite. Brown has a lot of freedom and opportunities. I kept thinking Brown is like the real world that has both men and women. But Brown doesn't offer particular encouragement to women. Even if I wouldn't be as encouraged there, I told myself that's what it's like in real life. So it's good to be in a real world environment. But the other part of me wanted to be at Bryn Mawr where I could develop, where I thought there would be more support for me as a woman.
>
> One day I decided—I'm going to Bryn Mawr. I told everyone I saw all day—my teachers, people who wrote my recommendations, my friends. I think I did that so I could hear it out loud. I wrote it all over my notebook. It made it more real.
>
> But the next day I changed my mind, and I had to tell everyone I'd changed. My parents wanted me to go to Brown. That's probably part of the reason I had decided against it at first. To rebel. My father kept saying a Brown degree means a lot. It's not as if Bryn Mawr is a second-rate college. I finally chose Brown, probably for a silly reason, partly because statistically I thought I'd have more of a chance to transfer to Bryn Mawr than the other way around if I didn't like it. Also, since I didn't know what I wanted to do, Brown has a lot of freedom and opportunities—freedom to design my own program, and I thought that would be good for me.
>
> For the first few months I was at Brown I couldn't even talk about Bryn Mawr. All I could think of was all the good reasons to go there and I hadn't, and I wasn't very happy at

Brown. But now I'm used to being at Brown, and I see that it's not perfect. Now I like it. Part of it is I'm settled in and have gotten used to it and see its good parts. Part of it is I've changed my expectations.

Rarely does the student make the college choice in a vacuum. The pressure to go to a prestigious school comes from parents, peers, and the secondary school itself. Students often buy the image of a college and the lure of the success it supposedly will bestow on them. Sometimes the most prestigious school or the toughest one to get in to isn't the best choice for a particular student.

Stephen Spahn, headmaster of the Dwight School in New York City, cites an example:

One of my students who has been accepted at several Ivy League schools really wants a career in theater. I think she'd be best off at NYU, but it's hard to turn down the more prestigious offers.

Spahn believes that parents have a responsibility to be involved in the college selection process, but not to dictate their child's choice. He sees the role of parents as path clearers, who know their children and can honestly assess their strengths and talents, as well as their weaknesses.

In choosing a college, parents should help their kids look at appropriate options, at paths that will use their assets. Then once the decision is made, they should give as much support and expression of confidence as they can muster.

And parents should put the college decision into proper perspective. Choosing a college is just one step in a process that begins when children are small. Parents start acting as path clearers for their kids when they encourage them to play soccer, or take violin lessons, or volunteer in a hospital. Each choice is another step along a particular path, each commitment a limiting of alternative choices, so to speak.

For some students the decision brings them face to face with the question of who they are separate from their parents. Family traditions and cultural values may seem to be on the line. Families who have always sent their children off to Harvard may find it hard to understand when their child rejects the school they had always assumed was the best and chooses Stanford instead.

A Washington University sophomore from an African-American professional family rejected her parents' preference for her to attend a black college. Her father, a New York attorney and an alumnus of Morehouse, felt strongly that the black college experience would be an important phase of the education he wanted for his daughter. She found it difficult to make a choice that was in direct conflict with her father's firmly held belief:

> I went to a private school where we started talking about college in eighth grade. By the time I was a senior I was sick of the topic. I applied to five schools. Only one of them was a black college, and the only reason I applied there was because my Dad wanted me to. I was accepted by three of the five, including Spellman. My Dad really pushed Spellman; it's the sister school to Morehouse. For a while I just couldn't talk to my Dad at all. It was so confusing. If I decided to go to Spellman, I didn't know if I'd be going for him or for me. My Dad and I are very close. We have that special father-daughter relationship; I'm his baby and all that. It was so hard for me to decide what to do. I finally decided to come here, and now I'm glad I did. I know my Dad was real disappointed though. He still holds out hope for my sister and Spellman. I respect him and want him to respect me.

Respect for their choice was what students said they wanted more than anything else in our interviews with them. They want to be supported by their parents for the choice they have made, and though they don't always tell their parents directly, they desperately want to know that their parents are behind them. Even students who choose the college that was also their parents' first choice want to know that their parents see the choice as the student's own, not as an extension of the family or its traditions.

The Pressure Is Off

Just at the time when students, parents, teachers, and counselors are sure that they cannot bear to hear another word about college, the race grinds to a halt. Students send in their reply cards to the colleges, and then don't want to think or talk about it anymore. Thoughts turn to high school graduation and to fun and relaxation. Many parents stand by and watch their seventeen- and eighteen-year-old offspring regress to childlike behavior.

One mother described with incredulity the scene she found in the den of her house a few days after her son's last high school class:

> I couldn't believe it when I walked in the door. There were my son and two of his friends lying on the floor playing with their old hot wheels cars! It was quite a sight. Three huge eighteen-year-old boys who are going off to Amherst and Grinnell and Macalester next fall, whizzing those cars around a yellow plastic track. They had Bob Dylan blaring from the stereo and a candle burning in the middle of the floor.

At last the pressure is off. Students brag about the crazy things they are doing and flaunt their irresponsibility. They watch TV more than they have for years, or go to the beach, or as they put it, "just veg out." There is a reprieve—some well-earned time before they turn their thoughts to the next phase. Many of them, even if they weren't particularly happy in high school, feel temporarily on top of the world.

Even as they are enjoying the freedom they haven't felt since the whole college marathon began, students and their parents are aware that their time together is going by fast. One young woman from New York said that from the time she decided to attend a midwestern college, she knew that she had made a decision that might permanently lead her away from her family, at least geographically. She knew that her mother realized it too.

> I was home alone with my mother for four years after my sisters were out of the house. After I graduated from high school, there were many times that my mother and I would be cooking dinner and my mother would say, "I can't believe you're not going to be here next year." And I'd say, "I can't believe it either." But we always said it lightheartedly, because we knew we were close and that I would come back for holidays and special times no matter what. We felt kind of

solid about the connection. But once I had decided to go a thousand miles away to school, I knew that meant I might never go back to New York to live. As a matter of fact, I probably won't.

Anticipation: Excitement and Anxiety

It is a long time from the fall of senior year in high school to the summer before the first year of college. Throughout that time, the anticipation mounts, a mixture of excitement and anxiety.

In interviews with prospective freshmen, we asked them to tell us what they were excited about and what their concerns were. Their answers to both questions were variations on the same theme. They told us they were excited about meeting new people from different backgrounds, but were concerned about getting to know different kinds of people, being lonely, and getting along with their roommates. They were excited about living in a more independent atmosphere and having freedom; at the same time, they were worried about handling responsiblity, making decisions for themselves, and managing their time. They were excited about having fun and wild times, and they were worried about handling parties, drugs, and alcohol. They were looking forward to intellectual challenges, and were anxious about doing well academically. And most of all they were excited *and* concerned about leaving home and family.

Just as students feel a combination of excitement and anxiety, so for the most part, do parents. At the crux of this duality is the pull toward the new—toward risk taking and fresh starts, as well as the tug toward familiarity and safety and family ties. And intertwined through all of this is the ambivalence about separation and letting go.

Parents and children express their enthusiasm about starting over. For many parents there is a reawakening of the feelings they had when their children were babies, feelings of the new possibilities that come with a clean slate. Perhaps John will finally get organized, or Carol will become more responsible or more social or more successful academically. There is always the hope that the so-called late-bloomer finally will blossom.

Students, too, may look forward to shedding uncomfortable labels. Those who were unhappy or unsuccessful in high school may expect to create a whole new "me." And those who were high school superstars may have the equally strong expectation that they will repeat their high school experience in the broader arena of college. Either expectation can be a trap.

When freshmen leave for college they take themselves along. They take their strengths, their weaknesses, and their capacity to grow and change. Even if college can't possibly live up to the idyllic scenes in the viewbooks, or the idealized images in their parents' memories, it can provide students with special experiences that will help them to make the most of their natural capacity to grow and change as they discover who they are becoming. And that is the vital expectation with which we and our children can approach the next four years.

Chapter 4
READY, SET, GO: THE DEPARTURE

Mid-summer—and the "livin' is easy"—or is it? Sometime during the balmy days of late July or early August—after the roommates have been assigned and the dorms designated—the countdown begins.

Ten . . . *A sudden catch in the throat as a parent realizes this may be the last summer that this particular twosome, buddies since kindergarten, still unself-consciously meander through neighborhood streets with such carefree abandon.*

Nine . . . *Do I need name tapes or a laundry marker? Maybe I don't need either.*

Eight . . . *A seemingly spontaneous—but carefully orchestrated—attempt to recapture frozen moments of family good times with a nostalgic trip to a favorite ice cream parlor, beach, bike path.*

Seven . . . *Will he stand still long enough to figure out what clothes he needs to take to college so that I, he, or we can get them?*

Six . . . *Standing over her while she cleans out her room: am I really so concerned about cleaning out seventeen years of debris or is this a good excuse to reminisce together, assuring ourselves that our memories will retain what is being carted off in boxes? How does one measure if a note written in class, a program to a play, a beloved pair of jeans is worthy of the keep and store pile, the Goodwill pile, or the trash pile? How do we reduce the past to plastic bags neatly tied with wire twists?*

Five . . . *Lists of things to get: extension cords, masking tape, hangers.*

Four . . . *A flash of anger—or is it fear—at finding crumpled dollar bills falling out of jeans pockets in the washing machine, the front door left open once again, reappearances in the early morning after sleepless nights devoid of telephone calls, full of worry—how can this kid make it on his own?*

Three . . . *Is it cheaper to ship via UPS or Greyhound?*

Two . . . *Nightly rituals of good-byes as gangs of friends move from one house to another, taping each other's music, exchanging addresses, philosophical viewpoints, and emotions ranging from casual disinterest to sheer terror.*

One . . . *Blast off—the day of departure, the launch.*

The Last Few Months

The prelude to the actual countdown starts with a familiar invasion of the mailbox—no longer overstuffed with shiny viewbooks as it had been last year, but now carrying a steady stream of letters about housing options, campus organizations, and course selections, all with the same increasingly familiar college logo—a relentless reminder of the fall to come.

Parents often discover these letters unopened days or weeks after delivery, scattered all over the dining room buffet, or discarded among the piles of dirty socks and magazines on the floor of their child's room. Noted writer Gail Sheehy describes an official looking form stuck under her daughter's journal:

> "What's this?" A small alarm goes off. "It looks like the forms for your meal contract at college."
>
> "Mmm, yeah." She starts humming.
>
> "You haven't sent in your contract yet?"
>
> Here it comes. She knows it.
>
> "Where is your head, Maura? Why can't you ever follow through?"
>
> "Thank you," not allowing a nick to show in her expression.
>
> "Now would you mind leaving me alone?" [1]

Words like ever and never and always are pro forma in these exchanges between parents and children—exchanges that know no geographic boundaries, but are familiar refrains repeated coast to coast. The underlying theme from the child's point of view: Leave me alone. Stop reminding me that I'm growing up and leaving. And from the parent's point of view: I'm not so sure you're ready to leave. I'm not so sure you can make it without me.

One mother from the Midwest describes her son's avoidance with an expression halfway between exasperation and amusement:

> The letter from Macalester sat on his dresser for weeks un-opened. My curiosity turned to concern and when I finally couldn't restrain myself another minute, I suggested that there might be something important in the letter with a deadline that needed to be met.

When her son grudgingly opened it, he found an announce-ment for a tempting array of freshmen seminars—special offer-ings of the kind that had attracted him to Macalester in the first place. The announcement went on to say that if he was inter-ested in participating, he was to choose one, and that each seminar was limited to twelve people and would be filled on a first come, first served basis. The young man barked at his mother, "Why didn't you tell me to open it?" She decided not to respond or attempt to make any logic out of this query—this from her tall, strapping, bright son who ordinarily bristles at intrusions into his life.

The summer between high school and college seems like a giant exhale—a release of tension, a respite from respon-sibility, perhaps perceived as a last gasp of childhood. To interrupt it with a series of new choices about meal plans, seminars, housing, and roommates seems an affront: *Somebody else attend to the nitty-gritty details for me. Let me be to wander with my friends, have a summer romance, do some mindless work that keeps my head free and my pockets full.*

A Harvard student recalls receiving a form to help with the selection of roommates—a form that seemed a "silly piece of bureaucracy"—a nuisance that he dashed off on the day it was due. When asked what kind of person he'd like to live with, he jotted down, "I don't care. I can live with anyone." He regretted it later when he found himself living with two eccentrics. There were indeed people he couldn't live with, and he spent much of his first semester sleeping on the floor of a friend's room.

A member of the residence hall staff at Hollins College suggests that students fill out roommate questionnaires as thoroughly as possible, but adds that they should not expect all their preferences to be fulfilled. She explained,

> When the system works well, a student who asks for a quiet sunny room to help nourish her many plants will end up with a corner single with an abundance of light on a quiet floor. But obviously, it doesn't always work that way.

Almost all schools want to know students' preferences about quiet halls, smoking, coed or single-sex living, and other basic conditions. Although residence hall staffs may not be able to provide ideal matches, students are more likely to find themselves in a compatible situation if they take the time to fill out the questionnaires thoughtfully and return them on time.

Parents may choose to offer advice about completing forms and meeting deadlines, but ultimately the responsibility lies with the student. Students who don't take the time to complete or send in forms learn to live with, and adapt to, the consequences. The young man from Harvard who found the roommate selection forms silly had a bit more discomfort his freshman year than he needed to have, but now he looks back with amusement and a new respect for and understanding of bureaucracy. The freshman who missed getting into the courses she wanted because she registered late often becomes the sophomore who plans ahead to make sure she doesn't make the same mistake twice.

Still, in their eagerness to see their child get off to a good start, parents may make a last attempt to take the reins. Even minor decisions can produce out-of-proportion hassles. A young woman from the Southwest describes her last summer at home:

All through high school, my parents gave me a tremendous amount of freedom. I never had curfews. I had a car much of the time. I was treated as a pretty mature person. So for them to suddenly act very protective, and a lot more parental, was a shock. My mother was very nervous; she had always been so rational, and now she was absurd. We were supposed to send in a picture to be in the freshman facebook. I didn't want to have my face in the facebook. I knew that it wasn't important, and she just had a fit. She thought it was crucial that I do everything correctly. I lectured them and reminded them that I was eighteen years old and could take care of myself and everything would work out and I wouldn't be rejected and I would have a social life despite the fact that my mother said that no one would ever call me if my picture wasn't in the facebook!

Although it is helpful if parents back off as their children assume the responsibility for the consequences of their own decisions, there are certain circumstances in which it is important for parents to be involved. If, for instance, a child has special problems or needs, parents should make sure that appropriate university professionals are informed. The health service should be told about chronic illnesses, the dean about learning disabilities, and the dean or residence hall director about family problems that may affect the student's adjustment—a recent death, an impending divorce, a severe illness in the family. Whenever a parent informs the college about special needs or problems, the child should know about it.

Alice Drum, dean of freshmen at Franklin and Marshall, receives numerous phone calls from parents about everything from course selection to health or learning disabilities. She explains:

I like to be informed, but, whenever possible, I prefer that the student make the call—or if this is particularly difficult, that the student and parent contact me together. This can be an important step in the student's assuming responsibility for dealing with his or her problems.

The residence hall and roommate assignments that arrive in the mid-summer mail begin to make concrete what up to this point has been a rather distant, vague, and idealized image of college living. Often students convince themselves that they have to get into a particular dorm in order to be happy, or that all will be lost if their roommate isn't a potential best friend. They may agonize over which tapes they will bring with them or whether to take a bicycle. They may pore over course catalogues, trying to pick the perfect schedule, or spend hours trying to decide what color blankets to buy. Instead of facing their general anxiety about leaving home, they may focus on something that seems totally out of proportion to perplexed parents. Tension in the household begins to build again.

Finding oneself assigned to the less popular East Campus at Duke or to a rooming house at the University of Wisconsin brings disappointment and even tears to some, as if being off-campus or out of the mainstream is a metaphor for being "out of it" for one's entire freshman year.

Because many prospective freshmen still see the world in terms of black and white, right and wrong, they truly believe that if they don't make the perfect course choices or get the perfect room assignment, the implications will be disastrous. Some parental reassurance may help students to see the subtleties and shades of gray. But logic and information and even the best intentions of parents, are not sufficient to change the beliefs of an eighteen-year-old whose view of the world is dualistic. It will take time and experience to promote a more mature appreciation of the less than perfect.

One young woman's comments reflect her cognitive development over the course of her freshman year at Haverford:

> I didn't dwell on it, but I was upset last summer when I was assigned to the "apartments." When I had visited and stayed in a dorm, the woman I stayed with said "anything but the apartments." I thought I was doomed. I had always imagined myself in the dorm when I thought of myself living there, and now I had to reorient myself. Actually there are some real positive trade-offs living in the apartments. I guess I discovered that anything is the best or the worst depending on your vantage point.

And the young woman at Duke who felt banished to the East Campus freshman year—"definitely not where the action is"—

chose to stay there for three of her four years, cherishing the quiet retreat at the end of a frenetic day of classes and activities.

> When I got my room assignment, I remember an up-perclassman I knew telling me that some people preferred East Campus, but I thought he was just trying to make me feel better. I even changed into an all women's dorm from a coed dorm second semester, because the rooms were a lot nicer and there weren't so many distractions. There is no way I would have listened to anyone who might have suggested that to me ahead of time. I was scared enough about just coming to college. I wanted a head start with a good dorm and a good roommate.

How does one know if the housing or roommate is "good?" There is no way to know ahead of time, of course; stereotypes are often all one has to hang one's hat on—so coed dorms are "good" and single sex dorms are "bad." If your roommate's name is Brooke, "she's probably a snob"; if he's from Nebraska, "he's probably a hick." Atlases are dusted off and brought out to check on roommates' addresses. Is Edina a rural town in Minnesota? No, it's a suburb of Minneapolis. Is Essex Junction, Vermont, even on the map?

Parents can be helpful at these times by simply recognizing their children's anxiety or disappointment, and by helping them put information in perspective, dispelling myths and sweeping generalities, as well as encouraging them to find out more information, if they can, from upperclassmen at their school.

Unfortunately, some parents are more intolerant and anxious than their children. Residence hall personnel rarely hear requests from students for roommate changes during the summer. It is the parents who are more likely to intervene because of a name or address that suggests a certain nationality, race, or social class, and parents' prejudices as well as their overprotective involvement take over.

One staff member at a midwestern university told of a mother calling him more than ten times during the summer wanting her son's room changed because his roommate was from Puerto Rico. It was clear from their conversations that she had all sorts of assumptions about this young man's background and social status—all of which turned out to be completely wrong. In most cases, residence hall staffs will not make changes unless it seems as though the situation will be truly problematic for all involved. Usually the student is not the one who perceives the situation as a problem, and often he or she is embarrassed by a parent's intrusion. Indeed, parental intervention of this sort may impede a student's growth. The university's diverse student body is a rich resource. To understand, tolerate, and negotiate with people whose values, habits, and cultures are substantially different is a large part of the out-of-the-classroom learning that can take place in college.

Many students seem to take housing and roommate assignments in their stride and suspend judgment until school is underway. Some do write or call their roommates, though, to begin to make contact. Finding that a roommate listens to heavy metal music, or likes to go to sleep at 1 A.M. may be a future freshman's first encounter with the inevitable compromises of dorm living. A woman from a middle class family in the Midwest recounted her shock when her future roommate from Virginia called and said she was bringing her horse to school with her. And a Chicana woman from New Mexico, on a full scholarship, recalled the awkwardness she felt when her roommate from the north shore of Chicago asked if she was bringing her stereo with her to Wellesley. The diversity of the college campus had invaded these students' limited horizons, reminding them in personal ways that life was going to be different from now on.

A young man from Pittsburgh, who was entering Colgate, was reassured after talking to his roommate:

> I called my roommate. We talked and found out some interests in common, who would bring what to school, and when we were going to arrive. As soon as I talked to him, I felt like I knew one person there. When I saw him at school, I just picked up from where we had left off. I asked him how his job at the pool that summer had gone. It really made a difference talking to him ahead of time.

Some students prefer to contact their future roommates by mail. Searching for words of introduction can be awkward, however. A vivacious young woman of many talents tried to think of ways to introduce herself to her future Berkeley roommate in a letter: "If I tell her I was a cheerleader, she'll think I'm just a boppy airhead. I can't describe myself in two paragraphs," she wailed. Music seems to provide a shorthand that helps youngsters to place themselves in a context. "He listens to the Stones and Pink Floyd; he can't be half bad," one young man from Seattle exclaimed after an introductory letter from his roommate-to-be at Evergreen State College. "She's into the Grateful Dead; she wasn't too thrilled when I mentioned Vivaldi," was the essence of a quick conversation with a Tulane student's assigned roommate. An entering freshman at Brown reported the good news—"She likes jazz, does sports, and goes to bed early"—and the bad, "It all sounded good until I mentioned the word 'feminist' in a sentence, and there was this silence—she just said, 'Oh.'"

Based on numerous interviews with college students, there seems to be little or no correlation between roommates' initial contacts and their ultimate compatibility. Too often, single letters or abbreviated phone calls encourage fantasies of becoming best friends and soulmates—only to discover later that a liking for yellow quilts and James Dean doesn't guarantee friendship or similar lifestyles.

For students entering large universities, the summer before freshman year often includes a visit to the campus for an early orientation program. Many large universities have tried to reduce the chaos and impersonal atmosphere of orientation and registration by scheduling summer orientations, staggering smaller group programs through the summer weekends. These visits often ease the transition process, but may also burst the bubble of idealized college life. The dorm rooms probably look small and bare, and the food isn't like home. Preregistration and the frustration of dealing with prerequisites and closed course sections introduce students to the realities of institutional bureaucracy.

This slice of college life may seem out of sync with the summer's steady pace—a frenzied few days of the new and unknown interrupting the security of familiar friends, family, and surroundings. Some students panic, usually just for a brief period of time, and wonder what they are getting into.

One midwesterner, despite the additional expenses of travel and time away from her summer job, flew to Burlington for the University of Vermont's summer orientation. The program included preregistration, and she was afraid she wouldn't get into the classes she wanted if she didn't attend. Although she had fallen in love with the school on an earlier trip by herself in the spring, she called home daily during the few days of summer orientation, teary and miserable. There were relatively few out-of-state students; most of the students who showed up drove with parents or friends from nearby cities and neighboring states. Many seemed to know each other from high school, and she felt lonely and worried that she might have made the wrong choice of schools. After several late night phone calls, her parents prepared themselves for the fact that she might withdraw and go instead to Indiana University, closer to home. As she stepped off the plane wearing a University of Vermont sweatshirt and beaming smile, they knew they had been premature in their assumptions.

The Last Few Weeks

By August, a flurry of activity breaks the relaxed cadence of long summer days. The students who are procrastinators continue to put off shopping or packing, but the tempo of their social lives may increase as time with friends begins to run out. Couples linger together, planning ways to stay connected during their next nine months in different locations. The seesaw of snapping tempers and unusually tender exchanges between youngsters and their parents are reminders of the ambivalence and the proximity of separation.

Wanting these last weeks at home to be quality time, parents try to restrain themselves from commenting as their children sleep away mornings or party away nights. Time becomes the most precious of commodities—moments together to be begged, borrowed, or stolen. Some of this is spent on the practical aspects of the move, the question of getting to school; who's going, when, and how; the shopping, packing, and sending clothes and equipment. Many colleges send suggestions, even lists, of what to bring, and hometown upperclassmen at the college as well as their parents can help prospective freshmen with these decisions. Much, if not all, of this can be handled by the student alone, but more often than not, parents are actively involved.

Sometime during this period the decision usually is made about how the student will actually get to school, whether alone or accompanied by a parent. In some families this isn't even discussed, especially when there are family traditions or norms:

> My older sisters flew to school by themselves. I'm not sure who decided to do it that way, but by the time it got to be my turn, I just assumed that I'd fly too.

In other families the child makes his or her wishes known directly, or economics and distance dictate a particular decision. But many families find themselves approaching this topic delicately. It seems laden with everyone's feelings about the impending physical separation and the simultaneous desire to establish independence.

Some students are very clear about their preference—wanting a family member to take them either for reasons of practicality, to stuff the car with the last minute accumulation of belongings—or for emotional support. Washington University's associate dean of freshmen, Delores Kennedy, explains:

> Freshmen may not spend much time with parents once they finally arrive on campus, but they take comfort in looking over their shoulders and seeing that Mom and Dad are there. If students express an interest in having their parents accompany them, it's probably a good idea to try to do it. It may boost the student's confidence just at the time he or she needs it most.
>
> Just the opposite is true for some students, who find making the trip on their own a great confidence booster. Those who want to go by themselves may feel more secure and better about themselves if they are allowed to do so.

But, as is true with so many of the decisions facing parents and students at this time, the impact one way or another isn't likely to be a major one. If parents don't accompany their child to school in the fall, they may find it even more satisfying to come later for Parents' Weekend when the turf truly belongs to their child. Those who do go, however, will have the chance to begin to put some names together with faces and places right from the beginning—laying a foundation for sharing experiences as the year wears on.

As they concentrate on organizing and checking off last-minute "to do" lists, parents and children often neglect attending to the central long-range issues that will involve their continuous interaction throughout the college years. Families might save themselves unnecessary friction and misunderstanding if they put aside some time before college begins to think and talk about four key areas of concern: communication, finances, academics, and values.

Most parents approach their childrens' college years with expectations and assumptions about these four areas, although they may not express them explicitly. As a matter of fact, they may not even be conscious that they have assumptions at all. But all too often, college students and their parents find themselves locked in frustrating battles about money, grades, a live-in boyfriend, or a dearth of phone calls home, because they were each operating on a different set of assumptions. Just talking about these issues ahead of time obviously doesn't create a united front of common assumptions, but substantive conversations and attentive listening ensure that each will have a better understanding of the others' expectations and views.

How does a family come to this understanding? Lectures by pontificating parents are definitely not the way, in spite of the fact that it can be tempting for even the most well-meaning parents to take that last chance to express a disdain for hard drugs, or expound on the financial sacrifices they are making and what they expect in return.

By the time a family has a child old enough to leave for college, their patterns of communication are well-established.

Some families actually sit down to talk weekly with discussions as focused as they are at an office meeting. Others sit at the dinner table in a leisurely fashion night after night as the conversation glides effortlessly from topic to topic. Still others manage to squeeze in bits and pieces of their ideas and thoughts on the run at unpredictable times, whenever the spirit moves them. Periods of intimacy and long discussions are interspersed with weeks of hellos and good-byes and grunts and groans from teenagers who are always in motion.

As families prepare for their child's departure, the most effective means of talking with each other will probably be the one that is most familiar. This isn't the time to adopt a new style of family communication no matter how well it works for someone else. If parents think through these issues, examine alternatives, and come up with a conscious set of assumptions and expectations, they can discuss them with their children in whatever way and to what extent feels most comfortable and natural. And in doing so, they will be setting the groundwork for the inevitable changes and challenges that they and their children will confront as time goes on.

Communication

How will we keep in touch?

It is helpful for families to come up with a tentative answer to this question before the miles separate them literally. It is best if parents make their own expectations clear, although parental expectations may vary from a proposed plan for the year to a much less structured request for a call sometime during the first week of school, with the assumption that they'll "take it from there."

Students may not actually tell their parents how important it is for them to hear from the family. They may not even realize it themselves, or admitting it may belie their independent stance and their attempts to separate. But students do count on parents to keep them informed about what is happening at home, in the family, in the neighborhood.

Some parents claim that they have nothing interesting to write about, especially those who also speak to their children regularly. But letters or e-mail notes communicate something more than the actual facts and events they describe. The mundane, the daily comings and goings of brothers and sisters, of neighbors and friends, bring a sense of permanence and familiarity to a tenuous time. It is no coincidence that we use a word that suggests a safe harbor, rootedness, a stability to describe the nightly television newscaster—anchor—steady and familiar. Parents, too, serve as anchors to disperse the news from home as reliably as Dan Rather or Tom Brokaw.

A freshman at the University of Tulsa spoke with affection of the regular mail she received from her mother:

> My mom would write about how the street looked in front of our house—or about our cats. She'd tell me that our neighbor painted his door red, or that my old school won its first football game all season. Football isn't really important to me, but home is, and she made it come alive for me in her letters.

Students may or may not write back regularly in the midst of their busy lives. But, whether or not they do, mail from home is almost always appreciated. Reassuring letters from family members can be read and reread, giving a boost to a wounded ego and reminding students that they are not forgotten. Their own identities feel shaky in their constantly changing external and internal worlds, and recognition and acceptance from home can restore a sense of continuity and self-worth. Some parents send clippings from the local paper; some just send the Sunday sports pages with a brief note attached. There are innumerable ways to stay in touch—to let your child know he or she is on your mind. Students rave about care packages and holiday cards and surprise gifts, no matter how small.

A Colorado College sophomore from Long Island spoke fondly of his mother's regular correspondence:

> I live so far from school that we don't talk on the phone too often, but my mother often sends me a quick note saying, "I'm at the office writing a report and was thinking of you." Or she'll send me a silly card. It's great just to be remembered and get something in my mailbox.

And a junior from Montana State reiterated, "Mail is important. Going to an empty mailbox is the worst. Parents should let their kids know they're out there."

Some parents are very casual about their expectations for written communication from their children. They don't expect to hear from them a lot, or they are comfortable with long periods of silence interspersed with spurts of cards and calls. Other parents have definite ideas about letter writing, and they make their expectations explicit and clear to their children. A Texas mother of three explained:

> The requests made of our children when they went away to school were few and simple; do your best and write real letters. We insisted on weekly correspondence. They followed through—most of the time. The early examples from each were pitiful, but month by month, we could see marked improvement. Their diplomas validate most of the knowledge and skills acquired in those four years, but fail to note that each had developed a personal, literate style of correspondence.

Some parents who request that their children write regularly, offer subtle incentives: "Every letter you write, I'll write back. An empty mailbox is no fun to look at."

Others are not so subtle:

> I told him his allowance was contingent on a minimum of two letters a month. In the beginning I could count on both letters arriving sometime after the twentieth, but after a while he developed the letter-writing habit, as it were. It was a pleasure to hear from him, and I could tell from the changing content that somewhere along the line he stopped thinking of the correspondence as obligatory.

A senior at Rice University reflected on her parents' request that she send home weekly letters during her freshman year:

> They told me they wanted me to write weekly so I'd have a record of my reactions to my first year of college. At first I thought that was bullshit, but said I'd go along with it. I'm not sure I'd recommend that other parents do the same thing; I resented their telling me what to do, but I guess it is kind of nice to have that shoebox full of letters that my mother has saved for me.

But some parents who start out demanding regular correspondence soon discover that what they receive is correspondence without communication. Their children's letters are
reminiscent of the postcards from summer camp that have to
be mailed before one is allowed entrance to the dining hall.
Perfunctory messages of the "How are you? I am fine." genre
are rarely satisfying to the writer or the recipient. And some
students who feel pressured to adhere to a schedule, may assert
their growing independence by refraining from writing anything beyond the most literal fulfillment of the obligation. All
a parent knows from such regular, but noninformative, letters
is that the child is alive and still at school.

Even mutually agreed upon communications plans are subject to change. One couple from upper Wisconsin made an
agreement that they and their children would write regularly,
but then adapted this request to their two children's different
individual preferences and needs:

> Before they left for school, we arranged that we would try to
> write to each other every week. Our son, Philip, likes to write.
> He communicates much more easily by letter than by phone,
> and we receive wonderful letters from him regularly. But as it
> turned out, Elizabeth, our daughter, really doesn't like to write.
> She's always been the kind of kid who would flop down in the
> kitchen and talk about everything—and soon after she went to
> college it became a habit for us to call her on Saturday morn-
> ings. We hadn't planned it that way; it just happened. She
> looked forward to those calls, and so did we. She tends to be a
> bit hyper and talking things out helps. She tells all. Philip's
> more reticent. With both, I think it is vital for us to be receptive
> to whatever they have to say. Sometimes we can help them
> work things out just by listening. The phone and letters are our
> way of counseling from afar.

Although these parents set out with the expectation that
letters would be the primary means of communication, it was
the communication itself that was their goal. As the weeks and
months evolved, they were flexible enough to shift gears to suit
their children's styles.

Many parents expect to keep in touch weekly by phone.
Some arrange to call their children once a week at a particular

time, often on weekends when the rates are reduced. For many families the regular weekly phone call works well, with little need for modification throughout the student's college career. A lot of students, however, prefer to do the calling themselves when they are sure to have privacy and to be awake, alert, and undistracted. For some students, regular phone calls from home seem intrusive and controlling. They would prefer to choose the time, as well as the topic of their conversations. Wanting family members to be there for them when *they* do the calling rather than the other way around is not a sign of selfishness, but another indication of a need to take charge of their lives. For example,

> I think it's important that I do the calling because then I don't resent them. If they call, and I'm grumpy, the whole conversation goes downhill from there.

> My mother doesn't seem to get the message. She calls me at eight in the morning and says, "I called because I knew I'd get you in." Of course I'm in. I'm asleep.

> There is a problem with parents calling too often. My friend's mother called daily. Everyone on the hall knew about it. It upset her—it was embarrassing.

Many students mentioned how much they appreciated their parents' open-ended invitation to call home—or even to visit, if they live nearby. A Tufts freshman recalled her father's parting words:

> He said, "You're only a plane ride away—a one-hour shuttle ride—if you ever want to come home for just the day." I never did, but knowing I could made a difference.

Anne Schroer, associate dean of students at Washington and Lee, suggests:

> Invite your child to call home when needed. Kids can't plan to limit their crises to Sunday evenings. Some parents tell their children, we can only talk for ten minutes—but you can't budget a child's problems. Often they need the first ten minutes to check out how everyone at home is—what's going on. They may be worried about their parents' relationship or other problems at home and need to deal with these before they

are ready to let you know about theirs. So try to include phone calls, especially in the first semester, into your college expense budget.

Parents should remember, however, that reaching for the phone at "down" times is a freshman phenomenon, and that parents often receive a skewed view of their son's or daughter's psychological well-being. The "ups" are reserved for friends and the "downs" for them. Moreover, most family budgets cannot absorb the strain of frequent, long-distance phone calls over an extended period of time, and even open-ended invitations to call may eventually evoke limits.

Whatever plan a family begins with is likely to undergo adjustments eventually, often after just the first few weeks of school. Students who share a hall phone with fifty other freshmen will have different needs from those who have private phones. And adjustments will continue over the long haul, as students and their families weather the predictable and not so predictable crises of this time in their lives.

Paradoxically, the theme of separation permeates this pragmatic discussion about communication and maintaining connections. The issues of control and independence, the need to touch base and yet establish autonomy, are at the heart of all the logistics.

Laurence Beede, associate dean of the faculty of Hampshire College, urges parents and students to think about the importance of communication and its role in the evolution of their relationship:

> College is a time for communication between parents and students. Parents who call the school at regular intervals to find out how their son or daughter is doing, without asking the student, are not likely to be really helpful during this trying and exciting time. On the other hand, students who refuse to tell their parents anything could possibly be inviting confrontation when it comes time for the parents to pay the bill. We try to encourage direct communication back and forth on every possible occasion. In fact, good communication should foster the process of letting go.

Finances

Money may not be the root of all evil, but it can become the rope that binds children to their parents in stifling knots with many strings attached. A clear discussion of expectations can help to prevent this and, in fact, sound financial planning can foster a student's growing independence. If parents can be straightforward with their children about financial realities, their children often will surprise them with their resourcefulness and willingness to assume responsibility.

Indeed, an increasing percentage of today's college students are taking financial responsibility for a portion of their education. It is not unusual for graduates of expensive private colleges to incur debts of $10,000 or more. So money is very much on the mind of today's college students and their parents. As a senior at a private university put it:

> I've got $4,000 in grants, $3,500 for being an RA, $3,000 from parents, $3,000 in loans, and the rest from summer jobs. I try not to think about it too much.

Filling out college financial aid forms may have brought out into the open a subject that has typically been taboo in many families—how much money do we have? What is the accurate picture of our financial worth? For many families, however, this is still an off limits subject, and some students leave for college with only a vague notion of their family's finances. Some simply know that they are comfortable and that their parents will support them financially and are not concerned about money. Others are confused by mixed messages:

> My parents never talk about money, but I can see them trying to cut corners all the time now. And I know it's 'cause of the big tuition bills.

> My parents say they are strung out by college expenses, but they just redecorated our house.

> My mother and father are divorced. My tuition is due and it's gone up substantially from last year. My mother says, "Ask your father." My father says he can't afford any more, but he just took his girlfriend on a cruise. Sometimes I feel guilty, and other times, I'm just plain mad.

It is important for parents to be straightforward with their children about what their limits are, what they will be contributing to, and what the student's responsibility will be. Before a student leaves for college there may still be some unanswered questions regarding money. Parents and students can often find helpful information about estimated living expenses in the official college catalogue or parents' handbook. It's also a good idea to talk to sophomores and juniors at the college to get specific questions answered. But only time will tell exactly how much will actually be needed for expenses, or whether the student will be able to handle academics and a part-time job. Some basic parameters and an open avenue for discussion while the student is still at home can set the tone for later negotiations.

Some parents feel comfortable with sending a prescribed monthly allowance for expenses. Some make it clear that they can contribute to tuition, room, and board, but that the student will be responsible for any added expenses. Other parents agree to pay for travel home or for books, but not incidentals. Said the mother of a Yale sophomore:

> We said, we'd pay for books. We didn't want him to pick his courses by the price of the books. But clothes and all other expenses came out of his summer savings.

The decision about who will pay for what is made on the basis of available resources, priorities, and values. Parents who are sensitive to the issue of developing autonomy will set up a system that allows their child room for financial choices and responsibility:

> My Dad asked me to keep track of my daily expenses for two months. From that we arrived at an amount for a monthly allowance. It was a good exercise for me because it made me realize what I spend money on. I decided to get a job second semester though, because I liked having a little extra in case I wanted to be extravagant or travel to see a friend.

> My parents used to send me money as I needed it my freshman year, but I really hated it. I always felt guilty when I asked for more, or like I had to justify where I had spent the money. Now

I get one lump sum at the beginning of the semester and that's it. I like it a lot better. I know what I have, and I can budget accordingly. If I want to blow it on a ski trip or a couple of six-packs, it's my business—and I'll scrimp for a while to make up for it.

My parents told me they would supplement my financial aid package and would take care of the remaining tuition and board. All the other expenses are up to me. I thought I had earned enough last summer, but I ran out by March. Luckily I picked up a part-time job to keep me solvent.

Most colleges and universities have banks on or adjacent to their campuses, making it convenient to have an account locally. Opening and maintaining a checking account helps a young person to feel more competent about handling his or her own affairs. For the student who has never done this before, it is one more step on the road to independence.

The parent of a William and Mary freshman describes her daughter's stumbling attempts to manage her money during freshman year:

It's been a learning experience. We're big on finding someone within the system to help you. Brenda found a "nice lady at the bank" who helps her. We told her we were not going to bail her out when she overdrew her account. Apparently she did from time to time, because once when she was home, an envelope came for her from the bank and before opening it she said, "Oh God, I've overdrawn." I asked her how she knew and she replied, "That's what the envelope for that looks like."

The same parent described how her oldest son, when he was a freshman at Williams, convinced the family that it would be a good idea for him to have a credit card:

It would never have occurred to us to give him a credit card. We're not a credit card family. He came home second semester and presented us with a rational plan for why he wanted one. He wanted to establish credit for himself; it made it easier for him to cash checks, and it would be useful in a crisis situation. This made a lot of sense to us. After that, we gave all of our children cards and told them that the first month they couldn't pay their bill would be the last month that they would have the credit card. Our middle child did miss a plane once and had only eighteen dollars with her. Nobody would cash a check, and with her card, she was able to spend the night at a hotel.

The major expense of college tuition may bring to the surface once again financial tugs of war between separated and divorced parents. Counseling services in colleges and universities regularly see students caught in the continuing crossfire of bitter ex-husbands and wives who seem to lose sight of the fact that their child is the loser in this battle. Obviously it is in the child's best interest if the financial arrangements are clearly spelled out and understood before he or she leaves for school even if it takes, as one divorced woman put it, "mini-summit meetings" to do it.

The child also loses when parents use money as an unspoken bargain, the "after-all-I've-done-for-you" syndrome. A pamphlet, written by Fred Reiz for parents of Wittenberg University students, advises:

> Some students feel that their parents use what they have done for them to bribe the students to be "good" or to do what the parents wish. Such coercion often courts exaggerated rebellion. Money can be used in that way . . . as a bribe or threat to produce the kind of behavior a parent wants. Students are very sensitive about being used as "ready made products." They want to feel some of their own control over their lives.

As students move through their college years and struggle to become increasingly independent, money and financial ties to parents inevitably cause concern. For many students, the struggles for separation and independence are complicated by their prolonged years of financial dependence. Parents can help loosen the financial cord by encouraging their children to assume responsibility for the management of their financial affairs, by being honest with them about family finances, and by being clear about their expectations right from the beginning of their children's college career.

Academic Expectations

"Just do the best you can." These are the standard parental words of advice to offspring when the conversation turns to the academic side of college. But, if "the best they can" has meant A's and B's until now, most parents simply expect that to continue. Many students complain of the double messages they receive from parents. "I don't care about your grades as long as you try" may have as its hidden message, "I know if you try, you can get an A." Students are acutely tuned in to their parents' expectations regarding academics and many feel enormous pressure to "pay them back for their financial sacrifice" with A's and B's.

A lot of students place pressure on themselves to get good grades. Actually, most of them want the same academic success for themselves that their parents want for them. They want to be excited about their courses, stimulated by their professors and they want to do well. They would love to get all A's and B's; there are even some who would be truly satisfied only with A's. Many have glided or plugged their way through high school without a C or a D, and as they begin their college careers they want, and perhaps expect, to keep up their stellar record.

Some of the superstars will find themselves in academic situations that are totally different from high school. In the most selective colleges that fill their freshmen classes with the upper 10 percent of high school students, 90 percent of the students will be in an unfamiliar position—no longer at the top of the academic heap. And half of them will be at the bottom half of their college class. Obvious as that may sound, it can come as a shock to students and their parents when they have become accustomed to the accolades that accompany acceptance to the most prestigious colleges and universities.

Parents of these very successful students may be particularly susceptible to heightened expectations about their children's academic performance. Some have even touted their children to family and friends as a "four-point" or a "three-point-eight," as though those numbers describe a total person. One who understands this numerical shorthand might do well to ask, what else can you tell me about him? Is she excited about what she is learning?

Parents of high academic achievers probably haven't spent much time worrying about their child's academic performance. They may have come to take it for granted and focused their concern on other aspects of development. Some even hope their youngsters will relax more in college, and take more time for friends and extracurricular activities. They may not realize that they have high expectations and assumptions about academic performance until their child hits an unexpected academic snag. One woman commented:

> We finally accept the idea that our children won't be all-American or Artur Rubinstein—but we still expect them to excel academically in all their courses. My son was a bacteriology major, took philosophy and got a D. We were shocked. We expected him to be good at all subjects. That may be as unrealistic as the mentality that says we should all weigh 110 pounds. If we can accept the fact that a kid who is 5'7" won't play college basketball, then we should be able to accept academic liability.

Parents whose children did not do well in high school may have thought a great deal about what they expect from them in college. Their expectations are often mixed with anxiety that the high school pattern will be repeated, and the eternal hope that the student will turn a new leaf at last. These are the parents who are more prone to giving late summer lectures to their children about study habits and discipline and buckling down. The more they lecture, the more their children turn a deaf ear. But the temptation "to tell her one more time" is difficult to resist, in spite of the rational knowledge that it's "out of our hands, and now it's up to her."

A Cincinnati woman whose son was about to leave for Oberlin said:

> Ted didn't really work in high school. He managed to do okay, but not great, with very little effort. I don't think he was ever turned on to a course. He just didn't get much out of school at all. He'll have to work harder at Oberlin, and I expect him to make a reasonable effort—to hit the books and stretch his mind. He doesn't have to get all A's and B's, but we're paying too much money for him to just jerk around. I'm not concerned just about grades; what I really want is for him to open up intel-

lectually. I want him to be interested in what he's doing. He's
so narrow now; he's not curious or adventurous intellectually.
I'm hoping Oberlin will be broadening for him. He's going to a
place that fosters caring about the world and other people. I'd
rather he become really excited about a European history
course and get a C, than take yet another math course that he
hates and get an A. I guess you could say that I won't be satisfied with his just making it. Grades that are merely adequate
are okay, if he's enthusiastic and demonstrates that all this
means something to him. But it is hard to get away from the
subject of grades. They are the inevitable barometer; they are
some reflection of what is going on.

For most parents, even if grades aren't paramount, there is
a grade threshold—some number below which a grade point
average becomes unacceptable. That number not only will vary
from parent to parent, but also from one child to another in the
same family, and for the same child at different periods of his
or her academic career. Likewise, the messages that parents
transmit may mean different things to different students. Telling some students not to worry about grades may be a license
not to go to class. To a young person who has always been a
plugger, the message, "Do the best you can," may simply
increase tremendous self-imposed pressure and the tendency
to be a workaholic. The same message to a more easy-going
sibling may not be clear enough; she will be likely to benefit
from more specific guidelines—perhaps even a mutually
agreed upon grade point average to aim for during the freshman
year.

There are some parents who not only expect a certain grade
point average from their children, they also assume that they'll
select a certain major—usually one leading to a high status
career. It is not uncommon for parents to introduce their children who are barely out of high school as: "Jane's our premed;
Jim's our prelaw." Some parents even threaten to withdraw
financial support unless their child follows a prescribed course
of study. Students who are embarking on their college years are
just beginning to explore their own interests and capacities.
Parental expectations and assumptions about what they should
study act as barriers to the student's development. The underly-

ing communication to the student is, "I know what's good for you better than you do."

Every college counseling staff in the country can tell war stories about students who have been pressured to study business or biology or engineering against their will. And though consciously trying to appease their parents, these students may be fighting for their own identity. Some finally come to a turning point during their later years of school, but only after having paid a painful price.

Eventually, if they are to separate and become independent, students must take responsibility for their own academic goals and the consequences of their performance. They have to decide whether they are willing to work hard enough to get the grades it takes to be accepted to medical school, to keep a scholarship, or to graduate with honors. They have to discover what they are capable of and what sacrifices they are willing to make. Many students feel more secure when they know what their parents expect from them at the outset. And perhaps parents feel more secure too, when they know they have made themselves clear. But as time goes on it will be up to the student to decide to what extent parental goals really fit with his or her own aspirations.

And the challenge to parents will be to remain supportive, and to be flexible and open to change.

Values

> I drank a lot those first few weeks. I found myself in situations that were really hard for me to handle, and I didn't handle them the way I would have sober. I finally woke up well into the first semester and realized I didn't have to be a "party girl" to have friends and a social life, but it was hard to get people to take me seriously.

> I smoked a lot of pot in high school . When I got here I decided to hang out with a different kind of crowd. They're into drinking, and sometimes it gets out of hand.

> One night I took a girl out and after the movie, I invited her back to my apartment. Before I knew what was happening, she

went into the bathroom and came back out without any clothes on. I panicked!

It is the rare high school graduate who hasn't had to grapple with personal decisions about alcohol, drugs, and sex: Should I or shouldn't I? How much? What kind? Where?

By the time students arrive on campus they are well on the way to formulating their own value system, usually based on many years of observing and listening to parents and peers. Their actual degree of experimentation varies widely, but almost all of them will find that college life brings them face to face with more choices than they have ever had before. More choices, more pressures—and now perhaps for the first time, no familiar parental boundaries to keep them in line.

Throughout their teenage years, young people have been used to a certain amount of structure and limit setting by their parents. "I have to be home by midnight." "My parents wouldn't let me walk out of the house wearing that." "I better not have another drink 'cause I have to check in with my mom when I get home." "We always go to eleven o'clock Mass as a family Sunday morning." Phrases like these have saved many teenagers from having to take a stand—making it easier to say no when under intense pressure from peers, refusing to try out a new behavior before feeling ready. Students may find parental rules arbitrary and aggravating, but often they depend on these very rules to keep their behavior within safe limits.

Sometimes college students don't realize that this parental backing is missing until they are in the midst of a problematic situation. No one in college will be checking to see when they come home, or even *if* they come home. Roommates and friends won't be checking for red eyes or alcohol breath. Students have to put themselves on the line; they are responsible for setting their own limits.

Brown University sends an annual letter to parents and guardians of freshmen, asking them to do their share in preparing students to live in a campus community:

> The freedom of our atmosphere has on occasion, unfortunately, led some to lose sight of their corresponding responsibilities to

themselves and to the community. We therefore ask your help in reminding your children that boundaries do exist at Brown and that serious penalties are imposed on those found guilty of overstepping them.

The letter expresses concern about the misuse of alcohol and other drugs, and makes a particular plea to parents to join the university as partners in dealing with this problem.

It is our hope that parents will take time to review issues of chemical use with their children, including their expectations for behavior at Brown. In a nation where rules and customs vary so greatly from region to region and where national norms are so few, students can easily be confused as they make choices of their own. Parental direction can be of great value to children and provide enormous service to those at Brown who wrestle with this vast national problem.

When Andrew Edmiston was director of the counseling service at Lehigh University, he wrote a sensitive and comprehensive monograph, "Life at Lehigh: A Conversation with Parents." He challenged parents to formulate and discuss their own values and to communicate directly with their children. On the topic of drugs he advised:

Every student and every parent is faced with the task of formulating his own personal position with regard to the use of various drugs.

There is never a guarantee that you and the student will see eye to eye on these matters, but mutual respect is a sound beginning. Furthermore, learning about drug types, drug usage, and possible effects helps to create a foundation upon which intelligent opinions can be built. Young adults respect those who are well informed and willing to discuss objectively the complex issues involved. Parents who recognize that the problems associated with drug use and abuse are complex can better avoid the pitfalls that occur from misunderstanding and misinformation.

There is an important difference between communication and confrontation. If you have concerns about these matters, share them. Do so in a manner that conveys your earnest desire to understand your student's world and the challenges he faces. Whatever else you may feel or do with regard to these matters, keep in mind that lectures, threats, and ultimatums may lead to doubt and distrust and sometimes result in everyone involved retreating into defiant and defensive positions.

Edmiston also tackled the issue of sexual conduct:

Your student may find, as many do, that his attitudes relating to sex will be challenged many times. He may be forced to do some hard thinking about his own attitudes, particularly so in a climate that encourages him to be his own person and to make up his own mind.

The foundations he brings to the University, upon which he builds or against which he protests, are those that have their origins within the family.

Parents are confronted with an infinite number of "teachable moments," and the challenge, of course, is to recognize some of them when they occur. The father of a Bucknell freshman described how he almost blew his chance to talk to his son in a meaningful way about marijuana use:

Two weeks before Tim left for school, I was driving home from work and reached into the glove compartment to get out a map. A packet of cigarette rolling paper fell out with the map. I could feel my blood start to boil. "Now he's smoking pot in the car!" was all I could think.

I barged into the house and was about to start in on a tirade, but something inside me stopped me and I calmed down and just presented him with the packet and said, "Come on in and talk. I'm worried about this."

At first Tim just looked at me sheepishly, and then he said angrily, "What do you want me to do? Tell you every time I smoke a joint?"

I said, "No, of course not. But you're leaving me evidence that you're smoking, and I'm concerned about how much, and what it will do to you when you're off on your own." He kind of relaxed and started talking—reassuring me, giving me space to ask more questions. I probed a bit, but mainly listened. He told me about a lot of stuff he'd been exposed to in high school and let me know he'd done lots of thinking about his own limits and how to deal with pressure from other kids. One thing led to another and before I knew it almost an hour had gone by and our conversation had run the gamut from cocaine and a messed up friend who was in jail for dealing, to spirituality in nature and organized religion. What was best was, he did most of the talking. And I was able to tell him something I've been wanting to say for a long time—that if he's ever in a jam, no matter what it is, I want him to feel as though he can come to me for help.

A Kansas mother of three gave each of her daughters at Smith, Trinity, and the University of Kansas the same advice at the beginning of their college years:

I will never relinquish my right to give advice, but at this point you are no longer obliged to take it. I have done what I can to give you the equipment to make your own decisions. Never let anyone else tell you what to do. Never make a decision and say, "she made me do it." If you choose drugs, sleeping around, whatever, it will be your choice. Don't close any doors behind you. Don't not do something because it's expedient.

Students fortunate enough to have older siblings who will counsel them often turn to them rather than parents for advice. A freshman at James Madison University recounted his pre--college conversation with his older brother: "He basically told me to wait until I was sure of what I was doing . . . to use my best judgment and not to do anything for someone else."

Another experienced upperclassman advised his younger sister, "Just make sure you always leave yourself a safety net. If you're going to drink a lot, don't go back to a guy's room with him. If you're going to go to his room, don't drink."

Counselors often see the "casualties" from the first month or two of college—students who have jumped into new life-styles too quickly without taking into account consequences or personal values. One counselor regularly advises freshmen not to make any major lifestyle changes during the first month of school: "It's better not to jump into dramatic experimenta-tion—whether the experimentation is with sex, alcohol, or a new religious commitment." Many students regret starting off by creating an image that doesn't reflect their own sense of themselves and find backtracking an awkward and stressful process.

Parents may think that being honest and direct about their own values and concerns seems fruitless and redundant at times, when confronted with, "Yeah, yeah, Dad" or eyes that roll back in disgust, or tolerant amusement when talking about such provocative topics. But, though loathe to admit it, students do care about what their parents think, and often these discussions at home can serve as a grounding to refer back to when the student is faced with difficult choices at school.

The Last Few Days

There does come a time finally when the suitcases are brought down from the attic or the trunk up from the basement. The very act of packing may be another reflection of the way a student handles leaving home.

Parents speak of their children's underpacking:

> The night before she left, she threw some things into a backpack and some duffels. I was horrified, but she kept reminding me that they sold tissue and toothpaste in Ann Arbor, so not to worry.

and overpacking:

> She seemed to be moving her entire room to Penn—her bulletin board, high school yearbooks, stuffed animals, wall hanging. We packed five or six large boxes to send UPS the week before, plus a trunk and the suitcases she took on the plane. I tried to explain that she would have trouble fitting all that into a small room with another person and her things, but it seemed so important to her—a way of bringing a piece of home with her, I guess. At the time, I thought I was being too indulgent, but it really seemed to help. She kind of "nested" when she got there and seemed to relax when she replicated a corner of her room at home in her new surroundings.

In these last hours of packing, the most ordinary actions can take on a special magnitude. Cleaning out a closet becomes a night-before-departure ritual, and the gesture of taping the last box is done with emphatic finality. All the while nostalgia permeates the scene.

In a letter to the editor of the *New York Times,* Deborah Frankel Reese, a New Jersey mother of two, writes wistfully of her own departure for Skidmore in 1959, as the images from that time mingle with the present reality of her daughter's leave-taking:

I believe that part of the mixed pain and joy I felt as we packed the college-bound boxes and bags were the memories of my departure for college more than twenty-five years ago. My own remembered clothes—Bermuda shorts, McMullen blouses, madras, and circle pins—kept getting tangled up in my daughter's very different clothes as we filled the suitcases.

Just as she, opening the doors to her new life, believes everything is possible, so did I. Her small cartons of books reminded me of the Emerson, Byron, and Camus I took with me, certain in the knowledge that I, too, would one day write a book. I smiled at the favorite stuffed animals my usually pragmatic, practical daughter gentled into her trunk, particularly the small, green kangaroo—given to me so long ago by the boy I was so certain I would one day marry.

Each leave-taking is unique and has the stamp of that child's own personality printed on its style and pace. A mother of two college-aged children recognized the characteristic patterns of their approaches to new adventures. Her sensitivity to their individuality helped her to support them in different and appropriate ways:

> When our daughter was young, she always rushed into things and then got scared. She would race to the top of the slide and then get scared at the top, and I would come and help her down. Our son, on the other hand, would stand next to me and watch for a long time until he'd figured it out and then he would attempt it without looking back. They left for college the same way. Steven went first to the University of Michigan. He researched it and spent time during the summer talking about it and planning. We talked over details endlessly. He was miserable for the first twenty-four hours, but never after. Stephanie didn't seem to want to talk or think about it ahead at all. She went to Michigan also, packed the night before and went off fearlessly, or so it seemed, but then she got scared and had a hard time. We did a lot of long-distance hand holding.

And so the journey begins. . . .

Chapter 5
ORIENTATION
AND DISORIENTATION

Imagine yourself standing at your front door with your bags packed, ready to leave on a long-awaited journey. This is a special trip, different from the family vacations or business travels you are accustomed to.

You are leaving behind everyone you know and moving to a new place where you have made a commitment to spend the next four years of your life.

When you arrive in this strange place, you look around and see a landscape of unfamiliar faces. A lot of these people talk differently from you; they have strange accents and use expressions you've never heard before. Some of them wear clothes that are different too. They all look smart, confident, and outgoing.

No one here knows anything about the status you had in your previous position—or about any of your past accomplishments.

You have left behind your family, friends, colleagues—all the people who are important in your life.

You're not too sure where anything is or who might be able to help you.

You have to share a small room with a perfect stranger. There are no set guidelines about bedtime, use of the phone, stereo, radio, or entertaining guests. You have to negotiate everything.

You have more work to do than ever before, but you're not too sure how you will be evaluated or what people will want from you. You may not get your first evaluations for many weeks.

You have a lot of unscheduled time and there are plenty of distractions: sports centers, concerts, movies, parties, clubs—and lots of attractive potential partners.

You have to handle financial and housekeeping matters that used to be done for you or, at least, you shared.

You're not too sure where your work and new relationships are heading and you don't know where or how you will ever fit into this new place. But everyone has told you that your whole future depends on your doing well during these four years—preferably better than those other bright, confident looking people who live here with you.

This is the freshman's journey. The student who arrives at college is confronted with a totally new world, as alien as a foreign land. And when seen from this perspective, we may wonder how anyone survives freshman year. Of course, most will survive—even thrive. Yet in many families, college has been a topic of family conversation for so long, especially during the senior year of high school, that parents may lose sight of the magnitude of the transition that freshmen encounter.

Orientation

Most colleges and universities plan carefully orchestrated orientation programs to help freshmen get their bearings. Though larger schools often get an early start during the summer, in many colleges orientation is a three- or four-day affair that kicks off the fall semester. The official orientation period, no matter when it takes place, is designed to take advantage of new students' eager attentiveness, imparting vast amounts of information and immersing them in social activities that encourage friendship and keep homesickness at bay. Seminars and speeches, parties, tours and excursions, a seemingly endless series of meetings and greetings fill the first days. And, through it all, upperclassmen, administrators, and faculty attempt to introduce freshmen to the resources, philosophy, rituals, and culture of their new home. In retrospect, students are often both grateful for and disparaging of the bombardment of back-to-back programming. But most of them emerge with tentative feelings of belonging to a new culture and new place, using campus acronyms and nicknames as though they had always known them, talking about "my friends" or "my advisor" with a possessiveness that bespeaks a longstanding acquaintance.

Parents who come to campus with their children are kept busy too. Many attend the brief orientation programs that are offered especially for them in an increasing number of schools, introducing them to the resources of the college, telling them what to expect, and encouraging the process of letting go. Most of the programming is planned so that parents and students are separated from each other for a significant portion of the day. Parents have an opportunity to ask questions without fear of embarrassing their children, and to gain a first-hand exposure to their child's new world.

Parent orientation is, to some extent, an exercise in reassurance. All parents want to know, of course, that they are leaving their children in good hands. Knowing how the advising system works, or what the Learning Center and Counseling Service offer, is not only reassuring, it is also information that may help parents to foster their child's independence. Later on, when a child calls home with a problem, a parent who knows what kind of assistance is available is more likely to suggest using the appropriate service on campus rather than trying to take over the problem and solve it. Parents who understand something about the rigor of the academic program will find it easier to give much needed support to a discouraged and tired freshman, rather than offer unsolicited advice about studying harder. College orientation directors and other administrators urge parents to take advantage of the sessions planned for them and learn how they can help their children find help for themselves.

Whether or not parents actually attend the orientation sessions on campus, they all have access to information about campus services and academic programs through bulletins and brochures, which can be tucked away in a readily accessible place. These might come in handy when least expected. Even if they are never used, most parents feel more secure just knowing where to turn if help is needed.

On the day fall orientation begins, the campus begins to bustle early in the morning with a steady stream of new arrivals. Some students arrive in airport vans with only a backpack and small duffel; others in their parents' cars, loaded with suitcases and trunks and racks of clothes. Though some have traveled across the country and others have commuted from across town, the air is thick with anxiety, tension, and excitement. Parents and their children can be heard snapping at each other, in spite of the fact that they all want this to be a perfect day. The new students walk uneasily, often with heads down, looking up as they pass each other and exchanging awkward glances. Many wear T-shirts with advertisements for the status they used to have—Silver Lake Tennis Team, Ypsilanti Basketball—or where they spent their summer—Yellowstone, Paris, Oak Bluffs. Others sport the names of their high schools or favorite rock groups, all in an attempt to hold on to and present to others who they are.

During those first hours on campus, it is easy to distinguish the freshmen from the upperclassmen who serve as resident advisors and orientation assistants. The RAs and OAs, as they are called at many schools, typically move with the grace and ease of those who are at home in their environment. They greet each other enthusiastically, share breathless tales of summer adventures and unself-conscious hugs. They all seem to look fit and tan and relaxed. It is not unusual for a freshman to look at them and wonder, "Will I ever be like that? Will this place ever feel like home?"

The very first moments of collegiate life are filled with the ubiquitous pastime of waiting in line. There are lines of cars in front of the residence halls, waiting for their turn to unload. There are lines to pick up orientation packets and keys, lines for luggage carts and elevators—all before the students even get into their rooms. Then there are lines at the bookstore and drugstore and bank and telephone service. And more lines to see advisors and financial aid officers and to register for classes. The larger the school, the more numerous and longer the lines. After all the preparation and anticipation and emotions of departure, college begins with a series of tedious waits.

Parents, too, feel the disorientation of arrival on someone else's turf, where customs and logistics are unfamiliar. Suddenly their child is just one of many, and the family unit joins the ranks of outsiders. Their son or daughter who had been eager for their presence may now walk self-consciously five or six feet ahead of them—already placing distance between them, reminding them that the time to part is near. One mother, when asked how the first day was going for her, answered bemusedly:

> As well as can be expected, considering I drove five hundred miles yesterday and now my son is telling me I can sit in his suite, but should stay out of his room—that it's okay if I talk to other parents, but not to students. He literally jogs ahead of me. He's keeping his distance. And he and his "friends"—he met them this morning—are going out for pizza tonight.

Many parents are surprised by the subtle and sometimes not so subtle cues from their son or daughter that their presence is a mixed blessing. As one faculty member said to an assembled group of parents at the opening orientation session of a small liberal arts college: "This person you brought with you who was clinging to you two hours ago, won't even know who you are three hours from now."

An exaggeration to be sure, but the pull toward separation and the desire to make the break are coupled with the wish for parental reassurance—or just a bit of help with the mundane tasks of moving in and getting settled. A student who emphatically tells his parents he wants to be alone and unpack by himself urges them a moment later to be back in time to meet him for lunch. Another, who had handled the packing and departure from home with utmost bravado, tells her mother she wants to spend the first night with her in her hotel. This desire to surge forward and then to check back with parents is a familiar echo of the separation behavior of the two-year-old, who careens off into new worlds, only to run back anxiously to make sure that mother is still there. The beginning college student is also plunging into new worlds, and the lure of adventure and separation from parents, as well as the need for security, may produce behavior during these opening days that is as inconsistent as it was those long years ago when he or she was a toddler.

Parents who bring their children to college with preconceived expectations of sharing the orientation experience in a particular way may miss the very rich experience that is actually available to them. Dreams of a last family dinner together at the best restaurant in town are often dashed by a scheduled orientation event or a spontaneous first meal with a new friend or floormate. Images of an idyllic shopping spree to buy plants and prints together may never materialize. Not only that, but the weather may not cooperate. Instead of the anticipated crisp, cool fall day, students and parents often find themselves moving in on the hottest day of Indian summer or in the midst of a downpour.

Expectations of gracious living are relinquished to the reality of lounges filled with worn furniture and long, dimly lit hallways. Even the glass and steel high-rises that dot many campuses usually reveal interiors that include modern amenities, but lack imagination. Parents are sometimes angered by the physical limitations of the residence halls, especially when at an expensive school. "But," explains Barbara Schmitter, vice president and dean of student affairs at Barnard College, "I'd like parents to understand that our focus is on quality education. Poshness is not one of the important offerings."

Parents may feel like awkward bystanders in a world that is quickly enveloping their child. Relishing the opportunity to provide tangible assistance one more time, they assume the roles of porters, go-fers, and personal shoppers. The mother and father of a University of Minnesota student laugh as they describe a frenetic thirty minutes at a Minneapolis discount store while their son was getting settled in his room:

> We madly ran from aisle to aisle filling our cart with essentials and nonessentials, everything from double-stick tape to plastic drinking cups; from a popcorn maker complete with a jar of popcorn to a big shiny red wastebasket. We even threw in a tie. We must have looked like those prize winners in a supermarket contest. "Fill your basket with all you can in thirty minutes!" The truth of the matter is we did it as much for us as we did for Ted. We knew he wanted to stay in the dorm and unpack by himself, and we had all this nervous energy and this was something concrete we could do. When we brought the stuff back to the dorm, it was clear that it was a hit. The popcorn maker was our best bet. We got a kick out of seeing Ted and his roommate leave for their first floor meeting, carrying the wastebasket filled with freshly made popcorn.

It isn't always easy to refrain from last minute hints about study habits and course selection and discipline and making friends. It may even be difficult to stand back and leave the bed unmade and the suitcases half full. A Bowdoin senior recounts:

> My mother hadn't set foot in my room since I was thirteen. When we arrived at college, she wouldn't leave until she had made my bed; it freaked me out. She got upset because I brought my favorite bedspread, which had holes in it. She was acting as if my college career was doomed because I had three holes in my bedspread.

It is not uncommon to hear students and parents fighting in the campus store about mundane decisions, such as what color sweatshirt to buy, or which type of desk lamp is best. Some parents even try to have dorm rooms switched, or show up at meetings for students and advisors, or make special requests to the RAs to look out for their children. All of these actions, no matter how well-intentioned, make it more difficult for the new freshmen to separate and assert their independence.

Though many schools invite parents to accompany their children to school, they also gently encourage them to leave campus after the parent programs are over. Phrases such as, "now that parents have departed," and "dinner with your classmates while your parents enjoy the restaurants in town" appear in most orientation schedules, pointed hints that it is time for parents to go. It is apparent to college faculty and administrators that even the most self-confident freshmen feel uneasy when their families linger on beyond the activities intended for them.

As the moment of parting draws near, many students seem anxious to say good-bye to their parents; others have last minute jitters and become tearful and panicky. The long imagined final good-bye may be, in fact, a self-conscious and hurried affair in the student-filled lobby. One father said wistfully of the last minutes at Kenyon with his son:

> Like most symbolic moments, we have a picture in mind of what it will be like, but it's not finished off like a Kodak commercial. I can't even remember the actual moment of parting, because he was surrounded by his RA and friends.

The orientation experience isn't picture perfect for students or their parents. But parents who approach this experience with open minds, who are flexible and willing to take their cues from their children rather than attempt to direct them, are likely to feel the deep satisfaction of having shared an important passage even as they are parting.

Disorientation: The First Few Days on Campus

"A whirlwind," "a blur," "a fog"—these are the words students use in retrospect to describe their earliest days on campus. Overwhelmed by new places and people and rituals, there is a sense of unreality and a world turned topsy-turvy. The first glimpse inside an ivy-covered, brick dorm is often a shock. And the dormitory room itself, bare and colorless, shows little promise of the home it will eventually become. A University of Oregon student recalls:

> When I got to my room, my roommates' stuff was there, but they weren't. I started putting sheets on the bed, and I broke down. It didn't look good. Anything that unfamiliar that I

know I'm committed to for the next ten months couldn't possibly have looked good—to sleep at night with total strangers—and wake up the next morning in this strange place.

And a Vassar student remembers:

I had a single and I was really glad about that. But when I saw it, I just couldn't imagine how I could ever think of it as my place. The first thing I did was set up my stereo, so at least the sounds would help me mellow out.

For a University of Vermont freshman, the first problem was finding her room. It certainly didn't seem funny at the time, but now she chuckles as she tells the story:

I asked my Dad to drop me off at the dorm, and made plans to meet him later. I knew I didn't want him to be there as I met my roommate. I grabbed two of my suitcases and took the elevator to my floor. When I got to the room, there were two girls already in there. It was then that I found out I was in the wrong dorm. I was too embarrassed to go back down in the elevator. I was afraid someone would see me and know what happened, so I took the stairs. Later that day I was supposed to go to a freshman barbecue, and I couldn't find it. Everything seemed to be going wrong. I was really in a daze. It was sort of like floating around in a sea of people. I felt very vulnerable.

Indeed, many college students talk about how vulnerable they felt during their first days on campus; they acknowledge with hindsight that the road to becoming a suave sophomore is paved with a series of minor embarrassments. They remember desperately wanting to make a good first impression, while trying to decipher the codes of their fellow students' behavior. As they meet their roommates and floormates with whom they will spend the next year, they are confronted with people whose lives thus far inevitably have been different from their own. Dean Alice Drum of Franklin and Marshall observes:

When students come to college, they bring a whole series of cultures with them: their individual family, their high school, their town, their part of the country. An only child may find herself rooming with someone from a family of ten. Even if the two students are from similar racial, religious, and class cultures, their personal family cultures are foreign to each other in

many ways. One has most likely never shared a room with
anyone; the other has never had a room alone. One student may
be appalled by the other's casual borrowing of clothes and
other possessions; the other may think that the roommate is
selfish.

And in this era of diversity on college campuses, a lot of
students will also find themselves living with classmates who
do come from different religious, racial, and class backgrounds.
They may use different slang, or even speak a foreign language.
Soon after their arrival, students are confronted with a melange
of styles, values, and attitudes—a coming together of many
worlds:

> My roommate went to boarding school. That wasn't part of my
> world. She had her friends from St. Paul's.

> My roommate was from Puerto Rico and spoke practically no
> English whatsoever. When my parents left, I thought—oh, no—
> I'm being left here and I don't know anyone and my roommate
> doesn't even speak English. I was jealous of the girl down the
> hall who had a Puerto Rican roommate who did speak English.

> I wasn't prepared for the racism I encountered here. It's some-
> times subtle and sometimes not so subtle—like if I play my
> music at the same decibel level as a white student, I'm the one
> the RA tells to lower the volume.

> I was very conscious of the eighteenth generation Harvard
> people because my father was so into the fact that his daughter,
> the daughter of an immigrant, was going to Harvard, the quin-
> tessentially American university.

> I'd never met anyone who was Jewish or black before. Half my
> floor was from Long Island and didn't even know where Min-
> nesota was, no less my small town. Everyone started calling
> me "blondie," and I thought, wait a minute, my hair is almost
> brown. It was overwhelming.

> I came here—to this Ivy League bastion—with a chip on my
> shoulder about prep schools, because I went to a big public,
> urban high school where half the class dropped out by senior
> year and most of my friends don't have much and a lot of them
> went to community colleges. I was surprised by how much
> people mix here.

Although many students find the discovery of this diversity exciting, parents sometimes intrude in an attempt to assure that their child won't stray far from the fold. A young woman from Cleveland recalls a series of phone calls from her parents the first week of school:

> My parents had talked to other parents when they dropped me off here. There happened to be a few other people whose last names ended in "ski" in the dorm, and Mom and Dad asked them if they were Polish Catholics. They wanted me to meet all the people on the floor who were Catholic . It happened that my roommate was the youngest of seven from a big Catholic family, and they thought that was really neat. They kept calling and asking about these people. They were really concerned that now that I had left, I was going to leave my religion too, and they wanted to make sure that I hit the Newman Center as much as possible.

Overanxious parents, even those whose own values reflect an appreciation of the richness of different cultures, may find themselves seeking out potential friends for their children. A freshman from suburban Atlanta exclaims mockingly:

> I can't believe my mother. She keeps asking me if I've gotten to know that nice Jewish girl from Bethesda who lives across the hall. My parents have never even noticed if my friends were Jewish before!

In response to the plethora of new people, some students themselves initially cling to anyone who is remotely familiar—a long-lost buddy from fifth grade, a fellow Bostonian, a former cabin mate from summer camp. Foreign students and minorities find it particularly comforting to make connections with others from their own backgrounds; indeed, they can be a lifeline to one another, and many schools plan special programs to help them meet. Some students respond with enthusiasm to the opportunity to meet so many new people and join the party crowd immediately. But even the most outgoing feel disoriented as well as excited by the fast pace and their new surroundings.

The hallways and walkways reverberate with fleeting conversations as strangers make their introductions—"What's your name? Where are you from? What's your major?" The questions and answers are an endless echo.

In spite of efforts to concentrate, it is impossible to keep names and faces straight. Two students may engage in an impromptu half-hour conversation at the soft drink machine and walk away without knowing who the other is. Time seems distorted, the way it does to travelers in a distant country who are bombarded with countless new experiences in the course of a day. Nothing is connected to the routines and rhythms of life at home. It is exhilarating and exhausting.

There are a lot of choices to be made, and students are often concerned about making the right ones. Is it important to go to the orientation session on note taking or should I skip it and play softball in the quad? Should I wear a Polo or tie dye? Would it be better to go to the freshman ice cream social or out for a pizza with the kids down the hall? Should I go to a French film with my roommate or party at the frats? What courses should I sign up for? What activities should I get involved in? How much should I drink at the party? Should I or shouldn't I try out for the choir? Do I want to be called Peggy or Margaret or use my middle name instead?

Parents may receive frantic phone calls from confused and overstimulated sons or daughters who just days before brushed off attempts at last minute advice, now wanting immediate right answers. The temptation of the father who is a pragmatic business executive to respond from his own perspective to the questions, "Do you think I should take cultural anthropology or economics?" is compelling. If he can take a deep breath and then ask some probing questions, he will be teaching his child something about decision making and will help him move toward independence. Questions such as: "What do you see as the advantages and disadvantages of each?" "How do the faculty compare?" "How does each course complement the rest of your schedule?" are more effective than a directive answer. The mother, who in her own college days was fiercely anti-Greek, and receives a bubbling phone call from her daughter, announcing, "I've gotten a bid from Pi Phi. Do you think I should join?" is challenged to pause and open a discussion that will help her daughter discover her own best answer.

This North Carolina mother reflects a year later on her handling of the sorority situation:

> I made the mistake of putting down sorority life when our daughter called. She did join anyway, but I never responded positively when she talked about it. It went against so many of my own values. But as time went on, I realized that it provided her with a structure for her social life that she needed—and also gave her better housing opportunities than she would have had on such a big campus. The bottom line was she had investigated all of this and had more information than we did to know what was best for her. I just regret that I wasn't more supportive at the time, and I've learned to trust her judgment more.

It is easy to succumb to the lure of simple black-and-white answers that these dilemmas seem to evoke. But these moments are a perfect opportunity for parents to promote and encourage independent decision making with an expression of support for whatever is decided.

At stake in the aggregate of these decisions is the freshman's sense of who he or she is going to be in this new place where the labels of high school and family and community no longer stick. What affiliations will he make? What groups will he become part of? What image of herself does she want to present? What commitments will she make? What is important? In the company of strangers, a clean slate opens up the possibility of developing a clearer identity—a more solid sense of self that is not merely a reflection of, or reaction to, parents and family expectations. It is exciting to think about the option of change, as well as frightening to think about the possibility of losing oneself. It is almost always disorienting, as exemplified by the comments of this Mills College sophomore:

> When I was first at school I felt like I was floating. I kept having to remind myself who I was—what my name was, where I was from. I felt like I always had to explain, this is my name, what I do, who I am. I needed to assert this all the time. With all these strangers it was so discouraging; I had to start all over again. Everything I had in Memphis didn't matter. It took me several weeks to realize that who I was hadn't really

changed. If I just went on living normally, people would discover who I am. I didn't have to keep putting it out like it was my resume.

A University of Rochester student from Omaha recalls:

In high school I was quiet and mild mannered. People saw me as an athlete and a scholar. My good friends saw the outgoing side of me, the clown, but that was reserved for them. It was fun coming to Rochester. A whole new beginning. Nobody knew Liza from Omaha and so I could start out anyway I wanted. I could be the clown or stay in my shell. I thought if I want to make college something I'll remember, I want to meet as many people as possible and especially in the first week. It was a fresh start. I could have my own identity here. No stereotypes were attached and everyone was in the same boat. We were all academic type people and there had to be someone to break the ice and provide comic relief, which I did.

And a freshman from Haverford explains:

When I got to school, I decided to use my real name, Amelia. It's a name most people don't have, and it's more sophisticated than Amy. Amy had served me well when I wanted to blend into the woodwork. I thought I would be happy if I could bring Amy, but call her Amelia.

The issue of identity is predominant as freshmen find ways to present themselves to each other. Having left family and longstanding friends behind, they are anxious to make connections that will begin to fill the void. They communicate who they are, not only by what they call themselves, how they dress, and what they do, but also by the music they play and the way they decorate their rooms. Most students plug in their radios or stereos before they even unpack. The music they select blares into the hall, a communiqué to passersby. It is an introduction, a way to "break the ice," an excuse to wander in—a common language, drawing together like-minded admirers. It also fills this alien space with familiar sounds that entertained and soothed them back home.

Throughout their rooms, students scatter bits and pieces of home, a reminder to themselves and a message to others. Pictures of family and friends and pets, beloved stuffed animals, posters, and yearbooks take their places of honor. Even those who were miserable in high school or whose home life is precarious, tend to bring some tangible part of their past for display.

Roommates stack up their beds double-decker style, or take them apart and put mattresses on the floor. Students build lofts and hang kites from the ceiling. Some strive for a white wicker and green plant look; others for sixties retro with Indian spreads and incense. One way or another they create an ambience and put their personal stamp on rooms formerly devoid of character.

Roommates who do this together face their first challenge: two strangers making the kinds of decisions usually reserved for intimate friends or couples. As they make plans about space and supplies and decor, they may have their first disagreements. These initial difficulties are a chance for them to begin to learn about accommodating each other's needs, about standing up for themselves and engaging in the art of compromise. Through dealing with each other they begin to develop skills that they will use in many other situations. And as the transformation of the room takes place, they also begin to build a bond between them; they feel more competent and independent. Parents who intervene and take charge of setting up the room before they leave, unwittingly deprive their children of an important opportunity, more important by far than the perfect rug and matching bedspreads.

Whether the formal orientation period lasts a day or a week, most upperclassmen look back on that time and smile at how naive, scared, and hyper they were. Emotions tend to be at a peak and change from moment to moment. In an address to the freshman class at Washington University, a senior reminisced about how terrified he had been three years earlier when he sat where they were now. During the question-and-answer period after the speech, a freshman raised his hand and said: "I don't think the word 'terrified' accurately describes how most of us feel right now. It's more a deathlike paralysis!" His fellow students roared with approval and burst into applause, momentarily united by a common plight. The next night the whole class was united in common joy, joking with each other and dancing to the strains of deafening rock music aboard a Mississippi River excursion boat. They bore little resemblance to the group that had filed into the auditorium to listen to speeches by the deans and the senior just the day before.

In more private moments, there are countless triumphs and defeats as students navigate the first few days of college life. They feel pulled in different directions. They suffer bouts of loneliness and homesickness, doubting that all these new people will ever measure up to their dearest friends at home. Everyone else looks happy and secure; it will take time to develop friendships and to find out that others share their doubts and feelings. Freshmen may enjoy the camaraderie and sociability of constant activities and impromptu get-togethers, but worry how and where they will ever have privacy and time alone in such close quarters. Many liken it to summer camp. Others remark incredulously that their fellow classmates "act like high school kids."

Students find themselves suddenly responsible for "grown-up tasks," arranging for a telephone, opening a bank account, interviewing for work-study jobs. As one young woman put it, "All of a sudden I feel like I have to be independent. I feel like my parents. I feel old; the child is gone in a second."

Even the hallowed collegiate rituals are confusing to a freshman who as yet has no context in which to place them. A freshman walks out of the convocation ceremony, where the provost has spoken, turns to his roommate and asks, "What's a provost?" His roommate shrugs his shoulders. Another looks with disbelief as a processional of faculty, dressed in academic regalia, streams into the somber chapel; she whispers to the student next to her: "Do you think these people are our teachers?" Later another student quips, "I wonder what we should call them: Professor? Doctor? Your Majesty? Hey, you?" And a student at Brown recalls:

> We have these gates at Brown. They're only opened twice,
> once at convocation and once at graduation. At convocation,
> the first day of classes, we all file through these gates in rows. I
> did it barefoot; I couldn't resist. There we are, all the freshmen
> with no idea what is going on. Some administrator I don't

know is telling me what to do. It seemed impersonal and strange. There were all these people giving talks we had to listen to and we're the ones who don't know them. It was all done as if they were doing it for our own good, but it had no meaning to us.

Some students become so absorbed in the euphoria and intensity of their new lives that promises to call or write home are temporarily forgotten. They lose track of time, and when they do think about calling it's 2 A. M. or there's a line for the hall phone. As one college dean told a group of parents, "If your children don't call home for a week or so, it probably means that they are busy, healthy, and haven't run out of money yet." Some students, though, call a lot in the beginning—perhaps even daily. They may want to talk about everything that is happening, or they simply may want to hear a parent's voice, yet offer little information or insight in return. Occasionally they tell just enough to set parents on edge. A Trinity student called home breathlessly a few hours after her arrival in San Antonio to report, "I'm in love with the guy who gave me a ride from the airport!"

Disorientation: Parents' First Few Weeks at Home

Of course, the world at home hasn't remained completely stable. A child's departure always has an impact on the parents who are left behind. Some feel the jolt at the moment of parting. Others find themselves reacting after the fact, their own feelings taking them by surprise.

During the weeks before his son's departure, the father of a Lawrence University freshman had been trying to console his wife, who was having a difficult time. He repeatedly told her that she should focus on the positive aspect of the upcoming event, that they had been preparing their son for this day for eighteen years and now it was time for him to leave. He urged her to think of this as a time for celebration, for after all, they had a terrific son who was going off to a fine school. It was all very logical. But after they dropped their son off at Lawrence and were heading back home on the interstate, his wife looked over at him and noticed his tear-streaked face. He describes that unexpected moment:

> I guess it didn't really hit me 'til then. I did feel really good about Kurt and about the experience I think he's going to have at Lawrence. But there was no way around it. We had just been through a passage, and I started thinking about the stage of life I'm in—that I just turned fifty and my mother is an old woman who can no longer share in this joy and that an important part of my life is coming to an end. My wife and I spent the next three hours driving through the cornfields, reminiscing about Kurt—both of us alternately laughing and crying.

A mother of three found that each child's leaving was different. She remembers most vividly the departure of her third:

> The last was the most difficult. In some ways it surprised me. I have a ritual—after they leave, I change the sheets and clean up their room. Jossie, the youngest, left a long, sentimental note and I found it under her pillow. I wept.

The factors affecting parents' reactions are innumerable, from their marital status, to size of the family, to birth order of the child or to how pleasant he or she was to have around. Most parents feel mixed emotions after they have sent a child off to college. It is a bittersweet time of excitement and nostalgia, of weighing and evaluating gains and losses. Waves of feeling tend to emerge and recede at unpredictable times, when walking past a daughter's uncharacteristically neat bedroom or glancing at her baby picture on the wall—after a son's telephone calls or long-awaited letters describing his new friends. One father whose son and last child left for the University of Denver told of placing a pair of his son's old track shoes in the front hall for weeks after he left to ease the hollowness he felt whenever he came home from work.

In a newsletter to parents of high school seniors, Barbara Kohm, a school principal in Clayton, Missouri, writes her impressions after her last child left for college:

> I love the freedom my husband and I enjoy, and I love the quiet orderliness of a clean house. I love having my car to myself,

and I love having the radio dial permanently set on KWMU, the classical music station.

At the same time I miss the exciting confusion that the children and their friends provided. I miss the dinner table discussions about parties, poetry, politics, and English assignments and the silly songs we sang as we did the dishes. I even miss helping them solve problems although my memory may be a little fuzzy here. I'm ready to go out to dinner more and to cook less, but I'm not sure I'm ready to have my primary parenting years behind me.

What hurts the most is that for twenty-five years I've thought of motherhood as my main job. Now that job is reduced to a weekly phone call and an occasional piece of advice—although even that isn't needed very often. I have a hunch that this bittersweet rush of mixed emotions will never entirely go away, that it will linger for the rest of my life, not as an irritant but as a reminder of the real depth and meaning of life.

Many women, including those who have longstanding, demanding careers, share this feeling that being a mother has been their primary role, and the bonds that they have formed with their children often make the separation process more difficult for them than they had anticipated. When her own daughter left for college, Pulitzer prize-winning columnist Ellen Goodman wrote:

A long time ago, I thought that mothers who also had work that engaged their time and energy might avoid the cliché of an empty-nest syndrome. A child's departure once meant a mother's forced retirement from her only job. Many of us assumed that work would help protect us from that void. Now I doubt it.

Those of us who have worked two shifts, lived two roles, have no less investment in our identity as parents, no less connection to our children. No less love. No less sense of loss.

Tomorrow, for the first time in 18 years, the part of my brain that is always calculating time—school time, work time, dinner time—can let go of its stopwatch . The part of me that is as attuned to a child's schedule and needs as it is to a baby's cry in the night will no longer be operative. I don't know how easy it will be to unplug. [1]

For single parents, a child's leaving may be particularly poignant. A divorced woman who holds a high-level position in a major corporation describes the change in her home life:

> Eliot and his sister have been the focus of my family life for more than ten years. Eliot's father took him to college, so I missed out on all of that. I tried to get my former husband to describe everything to me, but that didn't work. His values and perceptions are so different from mine (that's what split us up in the first place) that when I'd say things like, "How's the dorm room?" he'd say, "It's messy!" That's not what I wanted to know. Anyhow, the weekend after Eliot left, I cleaned out the garage. I kept imagining Eliot's voice. I kept expecting to turn around and hear him say, "Hey, Mom, it's looking good," in that characteristic way of his.

Just as the freshmen are orienting themselves to the college world they have entered, their families back home are changing old patterns and finding ways to adjust to the new configuration their own world has suddenly taken. Siblings' relationships change; the threesome that was always a study in shifting alliances becomes a united duo. A father suddenly finds himself the only male in a family of women; he'd never thought about his daughters' common bond with his wife before. A divorced mother finds herself living alone for the first time in her life; she alternately revels in her freedom and weeps at the solitude. A couple look at each other across the dinner table night after night, wondering what is left of their marriage, or cherishing the opportunity to talk at last without interruption. The only child still at home challenges her parents not to be boring—to pay more attention to her now that a favorite brother is no longer there to joke and commiserate with her.

While parents are struggling with a sense of loss, a younger sibling may rejoice at the possibility of her new position in the family. A Los Angeles woman smiles as she recalls what happened the day after her first daughter left for the University of California at Santa Barbara:

> The next morning I got up very early and was engrossed in typing a long letter to Molly, trying to tell her all the things I'd forgotten to say, without letting on how much I missed her. I

felt very emotional, crying as I was writing. Suddenly the
bedroom door opened and in bounced Beth, my youngest,
dressed totally in Molly's clothes!

In many households, as soon as the departing child walks
out the door, the rest of the family scrambles for the space that's
suddenly available. Brothers and sisters who have shared
rooms grab the chance to have one of their own. Empty nests
are replaced with newly redecorated studies or exercise rooms
filled with the latest equipment. Parents may later be surprised
when their children are hurt or angry at finding their room
redone or taken over; their reaction seems out of sync with their
self-proclaimed independence. But when everything else is
changing in their lives, their room and all their childhood
memorabilia represent grounding and continuity. Clearly, cor-
doning off an underutilized room in an overcrowded apartment
or house is impractical. But it is the wise parent who discusses
these changes with sensitivity *before* they are carried out.

The period of launching children typically coincides with
the normal developmental issues of middle age. Parents of
college-age children are often concerned about elderly parents;
they may be caught in the middle, assuming financial responsibility for parents at the same time that they are taking on the
burden of college tuition. There is anxiety about finances, both
present and future. Women are approaching or going through
menopause. No longer taking their health for granted, men and
women become more concerned about staying fit and taking
care of themselves. Stimulated in part by the excitement and
possibility of their child's new adventure, they may be reevaluating their own careers, thinking about switching gears,
about increasing or decreasing work or community commitments. Or they may be coming face to face with their own
limitations and letting go of long-held dreams. The changes
implicit in a child's leaving for college may heighten parents'
awareness of other changes in their lives, and although still in
home territory, they often feel a sense of disorientation themselves.

And so at a time when children may be checking back for
the reassurance of the routine and familiar, family members

may be feeling shaky and off balance as they shift to accommodate the loss of one member. On the home front, senses are heightened and emotions more raw, swinging between elation and deep sadness as the reality of the loss becomes evident in the routines of an ordinary day—unconsciously setting the table for four when only three sit down for dinner, hearing the silence of an evening without the abrasive interruptions of the phone ringing, suddenly aware of the freed-up Saturdays that had been spent watching high school football games.

Young men and women ask for little more at this time than a steady and rooted home base to return to just as they had many years ago when they hurried back from their adventures across the playground to find mother sitting on the park bench where they left her. How to provide this sanctuary and still stay out of the way is often an artful balancing act. It requires sensitivity to the often confusing dynamics of separation and to the long journey the freshman has begun.

Chapter 6

THE FRESHMAN YEAR: ACADEMIC LIFE AND THE COLLEGE SCENE

The academic year on college and university campuses has its own predictable rhythm, but that rhythm—the markers and intervals—may be quite different from those that parents and children have grown used to at home. As parents pull sweaters out of mothballs, feeling renewed and invigorated by the clarity of the cool autumn weather, their freshman sons and daughters may be approaching midterms, feeling especially jittery and vulnerable as they prepare for the first tangible measure of their college work. Campus traditions and rituals become part of the fabric of students' lives: fraternity and sorority rush, fall break, homecoming, winter carnival, registration for the next term, housing selection, reading period, and finals.

The particular markers and their exact timing vary from school to school, and the reactions to these events vary from student to student. But within all this variation there is a common flow, common rituals and patterns that pervade college campuses at particular times of the year. And since the campus environment is different from home, with different priorities and different cycles, it is no wonder that parents and children sometimes feel out of sync when they talk to each other across the miles of their separate worlds.

To Every Season: The Rhythm of the Freshman Year

During the first few weeks of school, the frenetic pace set during orientation continues. Classes begin, teachers are sized up, and students approach the freshly printed syllabus for each course with good intentions and high expectations for success.

They may shop for courses, sitting in on numerous classes before they actually finalize their schedules. Trying to integrate their own impressions with the collected wisdom of their advisor and the upperclassmen they talk to, freshmen often drop and add courses until a cut-off date forces them to make their first academic commitments. They tend to want certainty, perhaps believing that if they search long enough, they will find the right courses that will comprise the perfect schedule. "It was so confusing that first semester," recalls a current junior:

> When I came to school, my advisor told me to look at the catalogue and just pick my courses. She told me I could drop and add later. I was already having enough trouble just having all these choices in that huge catalogue. I just wanted somebody to tell me what to do. Telling me that I could change my mind made it even worse. I was holding on to an old high school idea that you can't change your mind, that if you start something you have to finish it. And if I changed, I'd be responsible for that change, and what if I didn't make the right choice?

Beyond the classroom, freshmen are faced with an explosion of activity: parties and sporting events, concerts and plays, and a tempting array of extracurricular organizations all trying to lure freshmen recruits—not to mention a seemingly endless series of impromptu get-togethers as students wander from room to room in the residence halls, listening to music together and talking and wondering how they will ever get any work done.

Everything is new—exciting or frightening, overwhelming or stimulating. Some students thrive on the onslaught of activity and choices, hyper but happy with the overstimulation. Others seem bewildered and overwhelmed and retreat into bouts of homesickness and self-doubt. Students' reactions to school tend to be intense during these early weeks; they either love it or hate it or alternate between the two extremes, sometimes in the same day, sometimes even during the same phone call home. Almost unanimously, they complain about the institutional food, announcing that they can't find anything edible except salad and pizza.

Three or four weeks into the semester freshmen tend to settle down a bit, to come to the realization that this is not just, as one student put it, "summer camp with homework," and that they have made a long-term commitment. It is often a sobering time:

> I suddenly realized that I was staying—that this wasn't like camp or a vacation from home, that this was real life, and I got a funny sort of feeling. I had been swept along by the excitement of it, and I hadn't really let it sink in that this was now my home.

This realization may evoke homesickness from students who were euphoric during the first few weeks. Many reach out to high school friends at other schools, and they wonder whether they will ever find comparable friends at college. Letters, phone calls, and even visits from campus to campus are common attempts to establish continuity in an ever-changing period of transition. Meanwhile, students who were overwhelmed and homesick at first may find comfort in the familiarity they are beginning to feel with people and places and the day-to-day rhythms of life in college. They have taken the first of many steps in the year-long freshman task of finding a niche.

As classwork progresses, idealized expectations of intense intellectual discussions in the local coffee house give way to solitary sessions in the library or bouts of boredom in the classroom. Freshmen discover that long stretches of daytime with no classes and no assignments due the next day make it easy to succumb to the temptation to sleep late and watch "All My Children" on the lounge TV. For some, serious studying is limited to a nocturnal activity, the only time when, along with the brightness of daylight, the distractions temporarily disappear. Others find themselves filling every available hour studying, often inefficiently plowing through what appears to be an endless amount of reading, unable to decide when one is allowed to take time out to play.

During this second month of school, social life also may start to be tempered a bit as the pace slows down. First impressions begin to fade, and students who were wary at first learn that they can live together in spite of different backgrounds, values, or taste in music and wall posters. Students who formed instant friendships during the first few weeks of school, however, may find that the novelty and comfort of those relationships are starting to wear thin. The roommate who had been a constant companion during mealtimes and sojourns to the library may now seem more like a leech who never seems to be out of the room and whose obsessional neatness is nerve-racking. No longer treating each other with the tolerance accorded strangers, roommates often have their first major disagreements at this time of the year, and complaints to residential life staff about roommate problems inevitably increase. Students gravitate toward loosely-formed groups in their search for companionship and a sense of community. Most are still wondering just where they will fit in.

As the semester approaches its halfway point, first major papers are due and midterms are scheduled, and an air of tension envelops most campuses. Students move across diagonal pathways to and from libraries, labs, studios, and computer centers, heads down, faces serious—even somber, carrying the weight of several academic texts in the ubiquitous backpack, which this generation slings over one shoulder giving the body an oddly asymmetrical list. Many freshmen pull their first all-nighter during this time, a rite of passage—a time of desperately seeking to reclaim the many hours that seem to have disappeared during the previous weeks. They spend an inordinate amount of time studying and worrying about studying. Not surprisingly, the campus health service treats a constant stream of exhausted students complaining of sore throats, colds, and the flu. And the counseling service readies itself for the onslaught of students who are trying to cope with the psychological stresses that predictably emerge during this pressured time.

The aftermath of the first set of midterms often evokes a period of intense self-doubt. Students who sailed along effortlessly in high school may be shocked to realize that the success they had come to take for granted is no longer necessarily going to be theirs. The first failing grade, or even a C in a course, can be an affront to the confidence of many students, especially when their identity has been so tied to their academic prowess. They may even start worrying that the admissions office made a mistake when they were accepted and begin to think, "this is the wrong school for me." And the premed who encounters a disappointing grade in biology or chemistry may panic and question his or her whole future.

Some students breathe a sigh of relief when they see the results of midterms. Intimidated by war stories of parents and high school teachers, suggesting that they will no longer be able to get A's and B's when they reach college, those who do continue to do well feel the satisfaction of getting past the first academic hurdle of their college career. Whether or not their initial academic ventures have been successful, once they have moved beyond the mid-semester point, most students begin to see the differences between the demands of high school work and the more sophisticated academic challenges of college. And, at this point, some of them begin to make the adjustments necessary for their academic success.

By late October students start to talk eagerly about their Thanksgiving holiday plans. Some feel homesick for the first time. In numerous parts of the country November brings signs of gloomy, wintry weather, adding to the anticipation of the upcoming holiday and a break from campus life. For children of divorced families, the question of where to go for Thanksgiving often resurrects painful family conflicts and questions of allegiances. Some students who don't go home for the vacation struggle with an outbreak of homesickness, missing the familiar traditions of this family-oriented holiday. Others delight in the opportunity to be independent and try something different, whether it is a visit to a roommate's home, a trip to a nearby city, or cooking turkey with friends for the very first time.

Although many students can't wait to get home, once they arrive and check to see that the refrigerator is stocked and the old place looks pretty much the same, they are out the door for an extended round of visits to high school friends. Trying to explain their new worlds to each other, students begin to realize how much has happened to them in the few months since they left home. In the midst of the excitement of reunions and rounds of parties, it is often a confusing and disorienting time.

In spite of the brevity of their time at home, some students take this opportunity to let their parents know that college is changing them. As they try on different identities, students may surprise their parents with new hairstyles, modes of dress, accents, or food preferences. One bemused mother recounts:

> Three months ago all Tim would eat was spaghetti, hamburgers, and fries. When he came home for Thanksgiving I fixed all his favorite foods only to find out that all he wanted was tofu and brown rice.

Most students return to campus from Thanksgiving break to face several weeks of intense work, culminating in their first set of final exams. "It's hit the wall time," explained one student. "It can feel pretty grim in spite of all the campus preholiday traditions and hoopla. We all show up at these Christmas get-togethers tired as hell. But of course we manage to squeeze in our share of partying too."

As the days before winter break come closer, students struggle through long hours of studying and writing final papers and trying to hold themselves together until the long awaited holiday. Freshmen have a foot in both worlds, immersed in their studies and new college friends, while fantasizing about going home and being taken care of and reconnecting with old friends from high school.

Most students want nothing more than some time out when they arrive home for winter break. Parents are often dismayed by their first glimpse of their exam-weary son or daughter, red-rimmed eyes with dark circles, pale skin, and ten pounds heavier—or lighter—than usual. The typically energetic freshman is likely to want to sleep or "veg out" in front of the TV for a few days and consume as much food as possible. Parents, meanwhile, energized by the hustle and bustle of the holiday season, may want their son or daughter to get moving, to participate actively in long-established family traditions. They may even feel angry at this apparent inertia and cynically question why they are spending so much money on education if these are the results. For a while, at this particular juncture, the rhythms of the calendar and academic years seem markedly mismatched.

Winter break is a much needed refueling time for students. It is also a time that evokes for parents and their temporarily returned offspring new struggles over separation and letting go. Students often make emphatic attempts to assert their independence and establish their emerging identity. Coming home night after night at 4 A.M., sporting multiple earrings and multicolored hair are some of the more visible manifestations. There are, of course, deeper and more subtle pushes and pulls, as students test values and limits and new ideas in the context of old, familiar ground. Students struggle too with questions of intimacy, wondering if their new college friendships are truly meaningful, and at the same time questioning if they will be able to, or want to, maintain their old friendships at home.

When the winter break is over and students return to school, the residence halls are filled with the excitement of coming together again. Animated meetings and greetings, warm reunions among friends and roommates, and eager attempts to catch up with each others' worlds, are a telling contrast to the hesitant, self-conscious arrival on campus of this same group of freshmen the previous fall. For many students this is the moment of recognition that they actually belong to a community, that this place has become a focal point in their lives. For some, it feels like coming home. They have finally begun to believe that the place is theirs.

As they settle into the rhythm of the second semester, many students thrive on the comfort of knowing the ropes, of knowing where things are and who does what. They often are beginning to see their college friends as their close friends; many are giving up the illusion of the perfect high school group. They approach their coursework with a new-found confidence. Although still wavering in their attempts to manage time, they have learned something about pacing themselves and setting priorities. The sense of urgency and anxiety they felt first semester is replaced with the satisfaction of having more control over their lives, and as one student put it, "knowing what I have to do and what I can get away with."

Some students, however, feel let down and homesick when second semester begins. They may find it hard to readjust after being at home, comfortable and secure with few responsibilities. The long list of academic demands looms ahead of them and, still feeling burned out from first semester, they wonder if they can survive the same cycle of papers and tests all over again. Those who did not do well first semester often feel a combination of self-doubt and determination to do better. Many students rethink their initial plans. Premeds often question their choice as they plunge into the second round of courses in a rigorous curriculum. Freshman deans hear from a lot of students during this period who are thinking about transferring. Feeling lonely or perhaps uncommitted to anything at the school, they worry that they have made the wrong college choice. Some send away for catalogues and applications to other schools. Others make their first commitment to an activity outside the classroom, taking another step toward creating a niche for themselves.

In many parts of the country the first two or three months of the semester coincide with dreary winter weather. Not surprisingly, students' moods often plunge with the temperature. Midterms, which usually come at a particularly bleak time of the year, only exacerbate the situation. Most schools in cold climates plan special events and festivals to counter the frigid weather. And many students head south for a respite and the time-honored tradition of fun in the sun during spring break. Others use this vacation time to explore summer job opportunities and set up interviews in their home towns.

When spring finally arrives on campus, the social pace picks up in earnest. Students revel in their access to the outdoors, and impromptu frisbee games, concerts, and parties pop up all over campus. This can be a wonderful time for students who are comfortable in their friendships or who have found romance. But for some, spring can trigger feelings of intense loneliness.

As couples pair off, those who are unattached see a tableau of their classmates, walking hand in hand among inviting greenery. It looks as though everyone is in love and carefree, making it all the more difficult for the many students who are neither.

Most freshmen agree that the second semester goes by more quickly than the first, and before they know it the end is in sight. They have a pile of papers to write, exams to study for, and a host of decisions to make: Who am I going to live with next year? Where will we live? Do I store my things here or ship them home? How am I going to get home? And then there are the concerns about how to finance next year's college expenses and what to do during the summer. Students flock to the financial aid office in search of the latest information on available money and to the placement office in search of summer jobs.

For most, the academic year ends with rushed good-byes and promises to friends to keep in touch over the summer. As soon as they have finished their last exam, tired and bedraggled students throw their belongings into suitcases and storage boxes. They depart a few at a time over the course of several days, in a very different fashion from their simultaneous and emotion-filled arrival the previous August or September. The last to go find themselves wandering through quiet hallways and lifeless rooms, perhaps realizing more than most how much their feelings about college are intertwined with their fellow students.

For many the decision to go home for the summer raises familiar issues about separation, as well as independence, identity, and intimacy. Is it possible to go home and maintain a newfound, but still shaky, sense of independence? Is it feasible to hold on to a separate, emerging identity and not fall back into the role of family peacemaker or jester or superstar? What will it be like to separate and leave behind intimate college friends, or a lover who is a constant companion?

Some students decide that they don't want to spend the summer at home. They may get jobs near the campus, surrounded by friends who have made a similar choice, all hoping to enjoy the college environment without the pressure of academic demands. Or they may choose to work abroad or at a resort far from home. Parents who had been looking forward to their child's return are often disturbed by such decisions, and it may be hard for them to accept that their child wants and needs this opportunity. Once again parents are challenged to let go.

By the time summer vacation rolls around college freshmen have been away at school for approximately nine months. Their sense of time is likely to be very different from that of their parents. As one freshman put it, "Every day goes by so fast, but it feels like I've been here forever." They have met a whole new set of people; they have struggled with new ideas and knowledge and values. There have been countless firsts in all arenas of their lives. "My world has exploded," said a nineteen-year-old from Minneapolis. "There are so many new elements—I find it hard to figure out where my parents fit back into that."

In the context of parents' lifetimes, nine months have been but a moment, and, in comparison to their college student offspring, their universe has remained relatively stable. Fitting back in is a given; parents expect their child to have matured, to be more reasonable, to have become more independent. Their idea of independence, of course, is that their child be more responsible, more considerate, and tell Mom and Dad where he or she is going each night and for how long; their child's idea of independence is that he or she be trusted, and left alone and not accountable. The freshman year has ended, and the family has come together again, if only for a while. So much has changed; so much has stayed the same.

To follow the sequence of the freshman year from fall to summer in a linear fashion captures the peaks and valleys of the year, but misses the complexity of any given time. Simultaneously trying to adapt to academic demands, new social relationships, and the freedom and responsibility of the campus scene, college freshmen are deluged throughout the year with challenging experiences in all domains of their lives. The combined effect is more than the sum of the parts. Students don't have the luxury of compartmentalizing the challenges they face, or handling them sequentially. It is not possible to wait until homesickness is conquered, the roommate problem is resolved, and the noise and excessive drinking in the hall settle down before tackling the first big chemistry exam. Students have to try to handle everything all at once, and through the course of the year most of them do.

Yet, for parents to understand more about what the freshman is going through, it helps to examine separately each of the central elements of the freshman experience: academic life, friendship and social life, and today's campus scene.

Academic Life: The Freshman Perspective

Paradoxically, the area of a college freshman's life that parents are the most interested in is the one students may speak of least. To transmit in a letter or a short phone call the excitement of new learning or the heady feeling after a provocative seminar with a talented professor is difficult at best. Moreover, for many students, the academic side of life has been too closely associated with grades and expectations. A parent's question "How is your English class?" may be heard as "How are you doing in your English class?" or "Are you keeping up with the work in your English class?" As a result, a student may cut off the conversation with an abrupt "fine" and move on to less threatening subjects.

Some students are turned on by their courses and long to share their excitement with their parents. Parents who give them the opportunity speak of discovering in their children a new and previously untapped curiosity about art or politics, philosophy or physics. Some students call home and spill forth their delight in a particularly brilliant lecture by a favorite professor, or their first glimpses of the connections between renaissance art and literature.

When a parent responds seriously or in jest by saying "What can you do with art history to put bread on the table?" or a student even senses that a parent's thoughts may be moving in that direction, the conversation turns flat and the wind is knocked out of the student's sails. But parents who set a tone of openness and interest, who reflect the enthusiasm they hear and ask for more details, may be rewarded by hearing about the best that college has to offer.

Questions such as, "What's your favorite class? Tell me about it". What are you reading? What's the professor like?" convey the message, "I'm genuinely interested. I want to know what your new world is like, what you are learning, how you are maturing, and I appreciate you discovering your own interests, opinions, and strengths. I value your intellectual development and growing independence."

Parents can participate in a student's experience in other ways that show they care. One student who discovered women writers during her freshman year recalled:

> I read *The Awakening* and just loved it, and when I told my Mom she went and got it and read it too, and we had this great discussion about it at Thanksgiving break.

Many students assert their independence, however, by holding on to their new discoveries, protecting their new turf and emerging self from any infringement by family—perhaps fearing the pull back to an earlier, more passive academic self. Spending an evening discussing the pros and cons of divestiture of South African interests or the intrigue and complexity of a computer program can be exhilarating extensions of classroom learning—cherished private moments with fellow students. To question, to challenge, to explore established values are crucial steps in the educational process, but these new ideas are still unformed and to share them with parents may open them up to criticism or scorn. The freshman daughter of two New York attorneys explains:

> I was brought up with the idea that you have to be able to back up your opinion with logical arguments, even about small things. So now, when I'm changing my opinions about things I think are important, like politics and art, I'm not ready to talk to my parents about it yet. It's not that they'll jump down my throat or anything. I just want to be clearer about what I think so I can talk to them on a more equal level.

Students frequently appreciate it when their parents express interest in their academic life, and it is not unusual to hear students complain about parents who fail to do so. But no matter how well-meaning and interested parents are, some will discover that their children do not want to talk about their courses. They want their parents to respect their need to keep this and other parts of their lives to themselves.

Not all students will find all, or perhaps any, of their freshman classes intellectually stimulating. A scenario familiar to many parents is one that starts with a student's phone call home complaining about one or more courses. Parents may have an instinctive reaction; they may be angry—at the child or the school; they may be disappointed; they may worry that he or she is at the wrong school or taking the wrong courses. They may resent complaints when they are making sacrifices and spending so much money. The reality is that parents know little about what is actually going on and can't fix it no matter how much they wish they could. What parents can do is listen empathically and encourage their son or daughter to make the best of a less-than-perfect situation.

Whether or not they talk to their parents about the academic side of their freshman experience, in one way or another freshmen all struggle with some of the gaps between expectation and reality. Initially they may walk into intimidating surroundings, ranging from cavernous lecture halls, where they are sentenced to anonymity, to small seminar rooms where there is no place to hide. The professor, whom the viewbook suggested would be a friendly sort who would get to know you on a first-name basis, may be instead a distant figure standing behind a lectern and speaking into a microphone.

A Cornell student wrote in a parent newsletter about a freshman class she had attended, "where the overflow of students went downstairs to watch the lecture being broadcast simultaneously on a special circuited television—"Psychology 101"—more than sixteen hundred students." And a freshman at Emory said, "Big classes were a real shock. You're nobody, not even a face, to the professor. In high school people knew who I was."

Large lecture classes usually are interspersed with small discussion sections led by TAs (teaching assistants), most of whom teach to support their graduate work, which is their first priority. A Berkeley senior recalled the first class she attended her freshman year, "I knew I was in trouble when I went to calculus and the teacher didn't speak English." Foreign graduate student TAs, whose command of English is limited, may be the only available resource people in a large popular introductory freshman course.

This situation is not unique to Berkeley. A survey conducted for the Mathematical Association of America revealed that 45 percent of the total number of classes at leading math departments are taught by TAs or part-timers, and one-third of math TAs are foreign born. More than half of the foreign born TAs at a well-respected midwestern engineering school failed a spoken English exam. Though many schools are now taking steps to ensure that their TAs have adequate language skills, the fact remains that a disgruntled student who complains about not being able to understand the teacher may be dealing with a common and realistic problem. Although a parent's instinct may be to get angry along with the student, it is more useful to acknowledge his or her anger and then turn to brainstorming some ways to cope with the problem. Students may decide to seek out help from upperclassmen or fellow students or to get a tutor from the campus learning center. The student will have to be resourceful to find the best possible way to make the most of the situation, and it is helpful if parents encourage and support that resourcefulness, rather than try to take over the problem.

Not all freshman classes are so impersonal. Even large schools such as Cornell and UCLA offer freshman seminars with as few as fifteen students. Although designed to introduce freshmen to the process of intellectual inquiry in an intimate and nonthreatening way, this format can be frightening in its own right. Though many students find these small classes intellectually challenging and personally warm and inviting, the expectation to participate in class is intimidating to some. The atmosphere of open inquiry and multiple points of view can be confusing for the less intellectually developed student who is searching for the right answer, and may conclude that, "it's better not to say anything unless it's something brilliant."

Occasionally freshman seminars are taught by the stars of the faculty. Even senior administrators like the president of Tufts or the provost at the University of Pennsylvania have been known to teach freshman seminar sections. At Princeton, full professors have begun to teach select small freshman seminars, attracted by the enthusiasm and openness of first-year students. At some schools such as Grinnell, every student participates in a freshman tutorial, designed to develop research and writing skills. Freshman seminars often are noted for their innovative topics or interdisciplinary approaches to more traditional fare: "Freedom and Authority," "Cross Cultural Views of Adolescence," "Contemporary Civil Rights Movements," to name just a few. Many schools have adopted a course model known as University 101 developed at the University of South Carolina. These classes are designed to introduce freshmen to skills and resources that ease the transition from high school to college. It's not unusual for these seminars to become an important part of the student's life, evolving into a support group, an anchor of sorts for the freshman who feels adrift in an otherwise turbulent academic and social sea.

Opportunities for freshmen to take courses unavailable in high school are enticing—anthropology, philosophy, psychology, art history, management, marketing, communications—a smorgasbord of new academic treats. But for some, the course title that suggested an unknown exotic realm, in actuality turns out to be a bore. "*This* is philosophy?" one student moaned after three weeks of reading Plato. Somehow philosophy had brought to mind groups of eager and intense students questioning the meaning of life—*their* life, not Plato's. And introductory psychology classes are filled with young men and women who had anticipated dealing with the complexities of their own developing, fascinating psyches, only to find themselves studying color wheels to learn about perception or mazes and rats to learn about conditioning. "What about people?" they lament. Typically, the introductory courses are just that—introductions to the basics of a discipline, exposing students to the inevitable frustrations that accompany first encounters with challenging materials.

"All classes look great in the catalogue, but what goes on in the classroom is another story," sighed a cynical freshman two weeks before finals. His harsh comment can be attributed, in part, to his negative frame of mind at the time, but there is more than a hint of truth in his remark. All students learn that even the most wonderful courses have moments of tedium, that you have to memorize symbols and data, and struggle with new methodology before you can use them creatively.

Most freshmen are surprised and confused by the level of sophistication that their professors expect from them. Moving beyond the more literal mode of high school, they are expected in college to be able to present and support complex arguments. Students who arrive at college, secure in their abilities to read and write well, find that now they are being asked to read more actively than they had in the past and to write, not just reports, but analyses. They struggle with learning how to think and write critically ; how to synthesize material ; how to make connections between facts and theories, and between different concepts in different courses. Many of them find it very difficult to make the connections; others are excited by these new demands. A Cal Tech sophomore recalls:

> The problems in math and physics were on a different level, a higher level than what I was used to. The problems were much more intricate. You had to know the principles; you couldn't just go to a formula. It was frustrating, but stimulating to see if you could achieve a new level.

Students discover that scholars disagree with each other, and that they must begin to rely on their own opinions, supporting them with coherent logical arguments. A brochure written for parents of Cornell University students, describes an important transition freshmen have to make:

> Students who knew how to produce the "right" answers in high school are often confused and frustrated to find that the techniques which helped them succeed in the past are no longer ade-

quate. After the first round of prelims, they will wonder what the professor is "looking for." But somehow or other, they will have started learning how to learn.

Linda Salamon, dean of Columbian College and Graduate School of Arts and Sciences at George Washington University, explains that this transition is at the heart of the educational enterprise:

> The overall goal of the undergraduate education is to shake students out of complacency in the set of ideas and values with which they have grown and teach them a relativistic view of the world—to teach them that there are a lot of different perspectives on any given subject, that the power of the intellect is to imagine a point of view, to create a perspective on an idea, and that the job of a young educated person is to have opinions of his or her own.

She continues with a description of a scenario she typically encounters with freshmen:

> Three students came in to see me because they were unhappy with the grades they had received. They had been asked to keep a journal, giving their reactions to major texts in American literature that they had read—Thoreau, Melville, Emerson, Hawthorne. The professor had said, "It doesn't matter what your opinion is." He just wanted a reaction, a reasoned response. He had written on their journals such comments as: "Good idea, can you give specific examples? What about the text gives you this opinion? Don't just say you don't like transcendentalism. You have to engage the idea of transcendentalism, and if you don't like it, that's fine, but you must do so on the basis of a reasoned argument."
> We are trying to help the young see what argument is, what evidence is, how to support an opinion. This is our principal goal, whether it's taught in history or philosophy. We're teaching different subjects, but this is the constant subtext: a level of analysis and an understanding of where intellectual authority comes from—how to have confidence in your own views.

Professors who teach freshmen are often deluged with questions about procedures and expectations. "All students want direction," said one professor of political science. "Freshmen just want a lot more direction than the others. They want to be safe, to be sure they are doing things right. And they really expect that there is a right way and a wrong way to do everything."

Students may work industriously, putting in long hours, spinning their wheels—often on the wrong track. They compare notes with their peers and reinforce each other's ignorance, raising each other's anxiety level as well. They study for tests, trying to memorize an overwhelming amount of facts and figures, often concentrating on the details without a grounding or conceptual understanding of the theory. This can be a disaster, particularly in the physical sciences. Students are often engaged in what one bemused provost calls "intellectual bulimia—stuffing themselves with volumes of factual material and then regurgitating it back for the professor, maintaining for themselves little of nutritional value."

Many freshmen complain about ambiguity, and about professors who do not follow the syllabus. No longer required to do daily assignments as they were in high school, students are both relieved and unnerved by the freedom. A professor of French at a midwestern university describes the typical behavior of her freshman students:

> My freshmen are faced with long-term assignments and projects, many for the first time. When they are assigned a book, they ask, "How many pages a night do you think I should read?" For instance, when I assigned *Madame Bovary* to my third-level French class, I told them we would be discussing the book one period a week over an eight-week period. The freshmen in the class asked me which pages they should read for each class. They wanted me to be directive and tell them exactly what they were responsible for. I, on the other hand, want them to dig in and make discoveries for themselves at their own pace.

Without the routine of daily assignments and regular feedback about their performance, many freshmen feel adrift academically, especially during their first semester. When parents ask students midway through the semester how they are doing in their courses, they are apt to answer, "I don't know." Students may be trying to evade the question, but more often than not, they really don't know. Or what they know is limited to their scores on a few tests or papers, and is based more on their own hunches than on someone else's feedback. College may seem deceptively easy the first few months. Rarely is anyone checking on how thoroughly they are doing their work, or how much progress they are making on long-term projects. Some students welcome this new-found freedom to set their own rhythm and pace, while others find it difficult to function without external motivations and rewards.

Freshmen may put in many hours studying inefficiently. When they work inefficiently, they ask themselves, "Am I just plain dumb or inefficient? If inefficient, should I take the time to get organized, or is that a waste of time? If I take the time to get organized, how do I do that?"

Students find that they have to read some assignments two or three times just to understand them. But if they were to read everything two or three times, they'd never get through the semester. There are other assignments that they have to skim. A lot of freshmen don't trust themselves. They have to learn when to read things over, when to skim, and when to skip, and this takes time.

A junior majoring in English recalls:

> In high school, if a book was assigned and you were told to read it, you had to read the whole thing. And almost always, you just read it once. In calculus, you just did the problems you were told to do. When I came here I realized sometime during freshman year that it was up to me to decide how many problems to do, to decide if I had done enough problems to grasp the material that was being covered. Sometimes it might be enough to do three. Sometimes I'd have to do ten. It was hard to adjust to having that responsibility—to letting go of that old high school idea of just doing what the teacher told you to do.

Learning how to manage time is the biggest academic hurdle of all. Procrastination runs rampant among freshmen. Faced with the challenge of new disciplines and the heightened expectations of college faculty, many students fall into the trap of perfectionism. Hesitating to hand in papers or assignments until they are "good enough," they fall further and further behind—sometimes leading to a failing grade or an incomplete. Students also procrastinate as a way of resisting courses they don't like or rebelling against authority of any kind, and end up sabotaging themselves. Some find the brinkmanship of last-minute cram sessions and all-nighters exhilarating, but a steady dose of these eventually takes its academic and personal toll. Some find it difficult to be motivated when they are unsure of their academic goals. And some students procrastinate simply because there are so many distractions, and they have not learned to resist the full range of seductive inducements to play now and work later.

In addition, their lack of experience with college-level courses makes it difficult to schedule study time. So much of what they are being asked to do is a "first." A junior looking back on her freshman year comments:

> Things always took longer than I planned. I was always frustrated. I had no idea how long it would take me to do a particular task. If you've never written a twenty-page paper before, how can you know how long it will take you? Plus, a lot of kids grow up having their own space to study, to play music, or to be quiet. In college it's hard to find a place to do any of those things. You have to write the kind of papers you've never had to write before, under conditions you've never had to deal with before.

And a sophomore at Princeton reflects:

> My freshman year computer science course taught me the relative value of time and grades. They teach you to program here by sheer volume. I learned there was a limit to the amount of time I was willing to put into it. My time was worth more than a grade.

For those whose identities have been closely tied to their academic success, the reality of competing with others as bright or brighter than themselves is a stunning shock. For those students who see the world in polarities, even an A- or a B+ is seen as a failure, a blot on their past 4.0 record and their future GPA.

Many students feel a responsibility to parents and to whole communities who have encouraged them—and the humiliation and sense of failure at not living up to these expectations can lead to a general lack of self-regard. A freshman at Yale lamented, "No one here feels special anymore. Kids need to know that they're still special to their parents, even if they're getting C's."

Whether or not they have excelled in the past, students worry about how they will be judged in this new setting. Will they lose the "specialness" they felt in high school, or will they once again move to the top of the pyramid? Will they finally get it together and do well after years of just getting by? Will they be found out as frauds and fail for the first time in their lives? Will they waste their parents' money by getting C's instead of proving their investment was worthwhile by getting A's? Will they ruin their GPA and be blown off the track to law or medical school?

The pressure to excel comes from families, graduate schools, financial aid offices, professors, and peers; and often the greatest pressure comes from students themselves whose fragile sense of self-worth is tightly bound to external confirmation. In the academic domain, this confirmation takes the form of grades. From the mother of a University of Chicago freshman:

> When she first went to college, Elise was very glib. She'd call and say she didn't know why people had so much trouble adjusting. Then one night in the middle of first semester, she called home crying hysterically, which was out of character for her. My first thought was—she's pregnant. But no that wasn't it. She had gotten a D on a test. The issue was her loss of identity as a high achiever.

Grades are an indicator of a student's academic success. And there is no denying that they will eventually influence students' chances for acceptance to graduate and professional schools and slots in corporate training programs. But parents who gauge their youngster's total college experience simply by looking at a list of letters miss the complexity of the educational enterprise. Professors, after all, have different goals in mind when grading. The same paper may receive an A from one professor and a C from another. There are, to use the student lingo, "bite" and "blow off" courses; studio, lab, and reading courses; courses that are graded on a curve and others that are pass/fail. Most students would agree that grades mean little out of context.

It is not unusual for students at even the most selective colleges to have a rocky freshman year. Deans and advisors often explain to parents that freshmen are likely to perform at a lower level than they did in high school. Each fall they make a common plea for patience and understanding and urge parents of entering freshmen not to put undue pressure on their children.

Unfortunately, some parents exacerbate their children's anxiety about performance, which is often high to begin with, by putting pressure on them to do well in everything. This attitude not only creates undue stress, it may inhibit students from taking academic risks; they may stick to courses in which they know they will get high grades, missing opportunities to take a course from a particularly brilliant teacher in an unfamiliar discipline or avoiding a quality class that is known to be difficult. Students benefit from their parents' encouragement to challenge themselves; those who know that Mom or Dad will be there if they temporarily fall on their face will have more courage to stretch their intellectual horizons.

Dean of the undergraduate college at Bryn Mawr Karen Tidmarsh states:

> Most frustrating of all is when parents have sets of expectations that are totally out of sync with the college's philosophy—when they say, "I expect you to have a GPA this year of such and such if I'm spending this much money."
> The GPA may have nothing to do with the ability of the student or reflect the learning that's taking place. These parents decide a standard and take the most artificial one available, and then hold it over a student's head. We make every effort to deemphasize grades—no dean's list or Phi Beta Kappa."

And associate professor Kiki Smith of Smith College notes:

I'd like to hear more parents inquire about what excites their daughter rather than what grades she is getting. They always seem to want to talk about grades. And the questions I'm asked on parents' weekend are almost always numerative: How many students on dean's list? How many in academic trouble? How many go on to graduate school?

Students are paranoid about their transcript. They assume that it is going to follow them wherever they go. They would be amazed . . . and are . . . how few people ever look at it after their student days are over.

Grades can be a barometer, however, when they are viewed in context. They can be a catalyst for discussion between students and parents. They may represent growth and progress, discipline and hard work, or innate talent. A sudden drop in grades may indicate emotional, social, or chemical dependency problems. Grades may soar and plunge as students fall in and out of love, as they become absorbed in campus activities or worry about problems at home. Grades that are consistently low may indicate that a student is taking too many courses or inappropriate ones. They may suggest that a student is feeling pressured to pursue a particular discipline or even that the student is at the wrong school.

When parents respond to a student's grades with accusations, expressions of anger or disappointment, or simple bromides such as "get down to work," the conversation is over before it has begun. The opportunity is lost to find out what these symbols really mean. Too much emphasis on grades, even high grades, can be disconcerting to students, but a parent's balanced sense of perspective is appreciated, as indicated by the following student comments:

Academically I'm a hard worker—always done three days early. I'm challenged more at Haverford, but I'm doing as well as I did in high school. I hate talking about grades. As soon as you say them out loud, they become someone else's property— parents' and grandparents' accomplishments. It's nice to keep it quiet and feel kind of smug.

My mother always gives me perspective on things. Every time I say I'm failing, which she knows I'm really not, she says "C is for celestial; D is for divine." She always tells me, "Your grandmother failed at this, and I got D's in that." It makes me feel a lot better.

I was so homesick first semester, I got really into my work. All I did was study, and I got straight A's. My parents were thrilled.

Second semester I started to feel more at home. I made friends and got involved and my grades dropped. My parents wondered what was wrong.

Parents of freshmen are often shocked to learn that since the passage of the Family Educational Rights and Privacy Act of 1974, more commonly known as the Buckley Amendment, they may not have access to their son's or daughter's grades. Colleges take a variety of approaches to the question of access and usually explain their policy in parent or student handbooks. At some schools students have the option of signing a waiver that allows their grades to be sent home to parents. Said one father:

We couldn't believe it. We're paying eighteen thousand a year for our son's education, and they have the gall to say they won't send his grades!

And from a Harvard freshman:

We have to sign a thing, saying I will let my parents see my grades. But if you don't sign it, your parents will get a letter saying something like—Dr. and Mrs. W: your son Nicholas doesn't want you to see his grades. So it's a Catch-22. My parents are so offended by that. They're paying all that money, and they think they damn well better see my grades.

If grades have been a battleground upon which students have felt bruised and thwarted by parents in the past, then the Buckley Amendment may be one more weapon they can use to assert some power in their struggle. For students who feel comfortable discussing grades with their parents, this barrier may never even become an issue since conversations about their progress are shared regularly. One young woman, whose parents are divorced, said:

My Dad has always pressured me to get straight A's. I'm afraid he'll pull me out of school. That's my biggest fear. I don't tell

him my grades; I lie through my teeth. I tell my Mom everything. She can deal with anything I tell her. I think most students deal with grades the way I do. If a parent puts on lots of
pressure about grades, they just don't tell them the truth.

Freshmen are bound to get discouraged at various points
during the year, questioning their ability and their whole sense
of themselves. They may complain of stress and exhaustion and
call home, hoping for sympathy and support. Parents should
realize that some stress is part of any college experience. If a
course is not difficult, if it is not stretching the student, it is
probably not a very effective one. The whole purpose of taking
a course is to be challenged. But when stress is paralyzing, it is
detrimental. Parents can help their children deal with discour-
agement and stress by listening, by asking them to describe
what they are doing, and by acknowledging that what they are
going through is tough.

Specifically, they also might ask them where they are studying and how they are dividing their time. Spending hour after
hour trying to study in a noisy residence hall with one eye on
the social scene outside the door is rarely effective. When
challenged to think of alternatives, students often come up with
imaginative options, such as finding secret study niches in an
Asian Studies library, campus art gallery, or departmental
lounge. And upperclassmen are usually happy to pass on some
tips, enjoying the chance to demonstrate to freshmen the wisdom of their years.

A lot of students work themselves into a froth and call home
before they have even tried to get help. A parent might assist
by encouraging the student to seek out help from the professor
or TA, to try to get a tutor, or to take advantage of the academic
learning center or other academic support services that exist on
most campuses today. Some students have too much pride to
ask for assistance, and parental encouragement may stimulate
them to take the steps they need to get help. Inadvertently, some
parents discourage this process. The dean of a small liberal arts
college sighed with exasperation when he recalled one incident:

> When I asked a student in trouble why he hadn't come in earlier, he said, "Before I came here I asked my father what deans were for, and he told me, deans are something you avoid whenever you can."
>
> I guess it was his father's way of being funny, as well as saying there are all these bureaucrats—keep away.

It is more difficult to get academic assistance on some campuses than others. Students may have to be persistent, but if they seek out help in enough places they will almost always find it.

Advising programs on many campuses fail to measure up to their descriptions in the admissions literature. In many instances advisors are faculty members, saddled with what they consider an unrewarding, bureaucratic task. Knowing little about departments outside their own, and caring even less, they take a laissez faire approach and sign students' schedule cards, no questions asked. Students may need to look for other resources on campus—peer advisors, upperclassmen, counselors, and deans, for the academic insight and advice they need.

Students who do have good advisors often turn to them first when they want academic assistance. One faculty advisor who takes her job very seriously explains her frustration when parents interfere with the advising relationship:

> When parents override a decision by a student and an advisor, it undermines the advisor and the student. For example, as a freshman advisor, I helped a student decide to drop a course in mid-semester. The fifth course added pressure that wasn't necessary. The student wasn't organized enough to handle everything. His parents told him it wasn't appropriate to be a quitter, and they refused to let him drop the course. It made the student furious and frustrated, and it tainted our relationship. Ever since then I've been nervous about advising him.
>
> Even in crisis situations, generally I prefer the student to let me know rather than have the parents call.
>
> If parents sense, however, that their child is having a difficult problem and know that he or she won't talk to anyone, then—and only then—the parent might want to intervene. There have been times that I found out things after the fact and wish a parent had called—not to be directive and tell me what

to do—but to say, "I'm concerned. My kid is in what looks like a bad situation."

Freshmen don't really expect or want their parents to solve their academic problems, but they do want them to care and to show that they are interested. A University of Vermont student's comments seem representative:

> I looked to my parents for support a lot freshman year. I needed to know that it was okay to tell them I was going through a hard time. I felt there was no way they could help me specifically. It didn't work when I asked for help with specific problems, because the specifics were all joined together in one giant process—sometimes it felt like one giant mess.
>
> What helped was to hear them show interest—show that they had faith in me. It was important to me that they be concerned that I wasn't doing well. I needed them to be calm, to listen, not to lecture. They were terrific and that really made a difference even though I had to work things out for myself on campus.

A pamphlet sent by the freshmen dean's office at Harvard to parents of entering students explains the crucial step that all freshmen must take if they are to thrive in the college environment:

> The word "freedom" is bandied about pretty frequently in a student's college years, and many freshmen misinterpret it at the start. . . . So long as a student is performing satisfactorily, no one here is going to hound him or her to do better. What we are trying to do, it seems to us, is to shift the responsibility for education from school to student. Final choice of courses is the responsibility of the individual student (with plenty of help available). Each student must decide how time will be spent. Acceptance of this transfer of responsibility is often difficult for a new student, but until it is understood and accepted, he or she will not experience the unique satisfactions of a fruitful and effective life in college.

Throughout all the struggles and triumphs of the freshman year, students are sorting out what part academics are going to play in their lives. Will they devote most of their time to their studies and shoot for the top of the class? Or will they try a more eclectic approach? How important is academic success?

What is academic success? They jockey for position with their peers and measure themselves against their own expectations.

Many who started the year with clear goals find themselves not nearly so certain in May. Others have discovered new intellectual passions and are beginning to look toward the future, wondering what they will make of it all. Armed with new ideas and abilities, they spend enormous amounts of time thinking about who they are and who they are becoming. Nothing looks quite as simple as it once did.

The College Scene

> I needed to find the ground of my own personality. I'd spent too much time just being a student in high school, doing the things that people told me. Then I came to college and there was no one paying attention to me ; I didn't have to answer to anybody. All of a sudden, I just felt afloat. School work didn't seem as important to me as becoming responsible in a different kind of way, finding out what kind of fabric I was made of, finding out what I could do—not just on paper. And that goes for relationships too. What kind of friend I was capable of being—how responsible I can be as a friend. There were a lot of things happening to me and most of it wasn't what my parents seemed to care about. It had little to do with my courses and it was being denied by the official reality of the institution.

Caught in the web of his parents' and the college's reality, this introspective Northwestern senior looks back at his freshmen year as a time when his primary learning took place outside of the classroom. He speaks of his frustration at not having his reality validated by the adult world around him. The college environment provided him with opportunities and choices beyond his expectations and beyond the experience of his parents' generation. But where was the official sanction for, or recognition of, the many days and nights spent dealing with the out-of-the-classroom decisions and dilemmas?

The college scene is often chaotic, exciting, and over-stimulating, from time to time depressing and deflating, leading to bouts of intense introspection or episodes of bacchanalian abandon. It is a rich tapestry of relationships, activities, and possibilities. And these are competing perpetually with the classroom experience for the student's attention and physical and emotional energy. The dearth of structure and rules results in an abundance of choices and, at first blush, seemingly endless—and joyous—freedoms. But freedom brings with it the burden of personal responsibility and all the attendant anxieties and possible consequences of difficult decisions.

Roommates, Friends, and Lovers

> I just can't concentrate. There are three of us rooming in a room meant for two and now Beth's got a boyfriend who spends the night almost every night. There's no privacy; I have to go to the bathroom to get undressed—to say nothing of the fact that they're having sex a few feet away from me. And my other roommate says I'm a prude because it bothers me. Am I a prude? Is there something wrong with me? Am I immature? When I sit down to study, all I can think about is how I'll handle it tonight when I go back to the room.

For most of us our home is our sanctuary, the one place where some privacy can be found, where the rules and customs are known, if not always adhered to. A loud stereo might evoke a request to lower the volume or an equally loud but familiar argument with a brother or parent. But in a college residence hall, the stereo player or the smoker or the roommate who borrows things unasked is barely an acquaintance, and students may be inhibited about asserting themselves with neighbors and recently acquired friends.

Parents are often shocked, dismayed, and angry to discover that the burden of change lies with their child, the one whose rights are being infringed upon. "We're paying for that room; there must be a policy about other people living there. Why don't they do something!"

The prevailing philosophy of student development on college campuses today encourages young men and women to solve their own problems with little authoritative intervention. To live with a total stranger on a floor with all new acquaintances provides numerous challenges and opportunities for learning assertion and problem-solving skills. Residential life

personnel usually act as coaches or facilitators of these interactions, only intervening after other avenues have been exhausted. As a result, students may spend a great deal of time
trying to handle day-to-day interpersonal problems with their
roommates and other residents of their floor.

Likened to an arranged marriage, college roommates, two
strangers matched by little more than their smoking habits,
come together in a very small space that becomes the bedroom,
study, living room, retreat, and playroom for each. When it
works well, which is more the exception than the rule, students
have a companion, company for dinner, someone to let off
steam with, an instant cure for the first month's loneliness, and
the potential for lifelong friendship.

Students find themselves living with roommates from
different cultures. "At times, they misunderstand each other
simply because their backgrounds are so different," says Janet
Loxley, a counselor at the University of California's Irvine
campus:

> Even in the initial getting-to-know-you conversations, they
> may unwittingly offend each other. For instance, black and
> white students may tend to talk openly about their families. But
> Asian students may think it's rude to inquire, "What does your
> father do? How do you get along with your sister?"

Sometimes differences in personal habits are more
problematic than differences in backgrounds. A young man
from a rural community in the South and a cosmopolitan New
Yorker may suit each other well if they both like to go to bed
early and keep their rooms neat. But a student who has always
had her own room may find it difficult to share space; and her
roommate, one of six children, may be intolerant of her complaining. They may make awkward attempts at discussions
about letting each other know if something bothers them. Some
schools even have structured exercises for roommates to do
together to help ward off tension. At least one, Hood College,
has published a booklet, *The Roommate Negotiation Workbook*
by Barbara Engram, to help roommates communicate with
each other, and some universities such as Ohio State have

established student mediation centers. Most students will struggle, however, with the disagreements that are inevitable when two people live together in such close quarters.

An attractive, impeccably dressed freshman at the University of Pennsylvania's Wharton School recounts her first impression of her roommate:

> My roommate seemed very strange, tiny, glasses, braces, no make-up. She wore only army fatigues, and I was totally intimidated by her—and found out later that she was of me. We were very accommodating and compromising—otherwise it would have been a big hassle to change rooms. Much to the surprise of both of us, we eventually became great friends.

But lifestyles can be so different that accommodation is difficult. This Carnegie-Mellon freshman describes his frustration:

> I need my sleep, and I'm a very light sleeper. He's a night person and a fine arts major, and he keeps the light on doing his projects late at night. He says he has no other place to go because all of his materials are in our room, but I just can't go to sleep with the noise and the light. It's finally gotten to the point that I'm barely speaking to him. You can cut the tension in our room with a knife.

Or consider this vivacious freshman from the University of Texas:

> Everytime I come into the room, she's here staring at the TV. I've tried to be friendly, but she's sullen and uncommunicative. And she obviously doesn't like my friends, so I feel guilty whenever I have someone in the room. At first I kind of felt sorry for her, because she seemed depressed, but now I'm just fed up. I want out.

And accommodation may raise fundamental questions of autonomy and compromise. How much of myself am I willing to give up in order to live peacefully with someone else?

> We got along though we were so different. We had different friends and lifestyles. She'd go to parties; I'd stay in my room and play my guitar or visit with a few friends. We painted our room together and that bonded us and we put silly things on

our door like—"we both throw up when we eat scallops, we
have so much in common." I think she thought I was odd, but
she liked me. But parts of me would disappear in order to get
along with her—maybe to avoid conflict. Parts of me were dor-
mant. I guess her side of the room influenced me.

Issues of competition arise as students measure themselves
against this live-in rival:

Why does he always have a girlfriend, and I can't get anyone
to go out with me?

Her parents give her anything she wants; she has so many fantastic clothes. I have a part-time job and wouldn't have the
time to shop even if I had the money.

I study constantly and get C's. He parties like an animal and
gets A's.

She's like a size two and keeps boxes of cookies in our room
for days. I'm always on a diet and having that food in the room
and looking at her skinny body drives me up the wall.

These are the daily problems confronting students as they
return home to the only private space available to them. Most
schools place freshmen in doubles or suites, and with the
current popularity of residence hall living three students often
are squeezed into a room meant for two. Those who do have
singles, and are outgoing and confident about initiating contact
with students in neighboring rooms, are delighted to have this
special place of their own. For the more introverted student,
single rooms can exacerbate the isolation and loneliness they
already feel . One problem is traded for another.

Throughout the freshman year, parents are likely to receive
unhappy phone calls about roommate and dormitory crises.
They may range from "He keeps messing with the things on
my desk!" to "She's talking of suicide and I don't know what
to do." Or from "She's the biggest slob!" to "He comes home
drunk several nights a week!"

Parents often react to these calls with a for or against
response. Some rally round with a familial Greek chorus,
fanning the flames by getting angry along with the student. Or
they call the residence director, the dean of students or the

president demanding a solution. Others, recalling sibling battles, may respond with a sarcastic "Well, now *you* know what it's like to live with a slob!" or "What did you do to provoke him?"—responses that tend to end any communication, leaving the student feeling that his or her one lifeline has been cut.

Many parents speak of their frustration and feelings of helplessness, the bubble of this carefully chosen expensive super-school burst by the reality of a difficult living situation and no administrator clamoring to fix it. Tossing their developing independence aside, some students plead with Mom and Dad to intervene so that they can rid themselves of the problem and get on with their lives. Under the circumstances, the temptation to do so is compelling, but this is a significant opportunity to encourage independent thought and action. College administrators agree that learning to live in a world full of differences is one of the most important lessons of the college years.

The most helpful parents are those who listen, acknowledge their child's feelings, and allow him or her to generate some options. Suggestions can be offered tentatively, as just one of several possible solutions, and students should be encouraged to seek out resources on campus such as counselors or student life personnel, who deal with similar situations routinely.

Parents can show support in more tangible ways as well. Survival kits of ear plugs, eye shades, or a Walkman to blot out sights and sounds can provide a lift for a student. These are simple gestures, but powerful reminders that those back at the home front care and send their support.

Often students help each other out or come up with their own creative solutions. A young woman who spent several months grappling with the problem of a roommate with a live-in boyfriend, rebuffed her parents' suggestion to talk to the RA, and worked out her own solution:

> I knew I had to live on that floor for the rest of the year, and I didn't want to tattle to the RA and have my roommate and her friends angry at me. I had some really good friends who lived at the end of my floor—and on the nights when Randy was spending the night, I took a sleeping bag and slept on their

floor. I did ask the RA to let me know of any room openings, and I moved second semester. It's funny—I was miserable at the time, but I'm sort of glad I went through it. I gained a lot of confidence just having to figure it all out.

And these comments from a woman at the University of Michigan:

My roommate had a lot of problems; she was bulimic, and she talked about it all the time. I was becoming more like a parent than a friend. I got too entangled—and at times, I needed to get away physically. My father told me to take her to the clinic to talk to someone, but I didn't. I needed to do it my way.

In some cases, parents may feel so concerned for their child's well-being that a call directly to a professional on the residence staff is warranted. A dean of freshmen cited this example:

We had a student who was being harassed by his suitemates. There was vandalism, theft, something was even set on fire. The student told his parents about it, and they told him to report it to the proper people in the residence halls. The parents had researched the proper procedures and encouraged their son to go through the appropriate channels. But he was unable to carry that out himself. He just wouldn't do it, or maybe I should say, couldn't do it. The parents realized that, and they took over. It was important that they did what they did.

Calls of this nature are most effective when they are collaborative rather than accusatory in spirit, in spite of the frustration and anger parents might feel. Dean Barbara Schmitter of Barnard reminds parents that "we are partners in this enterprise, not adversaries."

Friendships with roommates, floormates, and classmates begin to take shape in the first few months of school. Sorting out who will eventually emerge as good friends is part of the student's search for identity, and becomes an important focus for freshmen who, in fact, are recreating their lives in this new environment. There is a sense of promise and potential—an exhilaration accompanying the possibilities for new friendships with so many different kinds of people. At the same time there is a sense of profound loneliness and loss—an empty space left by old friends for whom no explanations are necessary. Students move back and forth between these two emotional states, now thriving on the excitement of new friendships—now retreating into times of quiet reflection and longing for the comfort of old, solid relationships.

After three months at Carleton, this young man made the following observation:

> Social life here is chaotic. So much is going on in reality and in your mind all at the same time. You're searching to have different levels of friendship—intimate, close and just plain acquaintances. You spend time hanging out with lots of different people at once. You look for people like you think you want to be—punk, intellectual, or whatever. And all the while you're questioning whether you want to make new friends at all or if that means turning your back on your high school friends.

And an Amherst freshman asserted:

> I had friends I'd met at a summer program, and they were really intellectual and my roommates weren't at all—that was a schizophrenic thing. My roommates didn't get along with these other people, and I didn't know who I wanted to be with and it was upsetting.

Perhaps this is another way of sorting out "who am I" questions—am I an intellectual or someone who likes *People* magazine and the Los Angeles Dodgers? Can I be both? Can I be friendly with different groups of people without losing out on both?

Some students find the identification with a group a secure substitute for missed family and friends. With their identity in such flux, it is not unusual for freshmen to stumble into a group simply based on its proximity. An Oberlin freshman, who had been adamantly disdainful of drug use in high school, found himself within three days of his arrival at college a member of a group of students who defined themselves by their marijuana use. As he reflected on his choice, it seemed almost arbitrary:

> Our floor quickly divided up into three or four cliques for the year. One clique was into country music and Karl Marx. My clique smoked marijuana a lot. We played a lot of cards. We

were really into games of any kind, mostly head games, I'd
say. Our conversations would be really twisted sometimes and
manipulative. Then there was the third group—the musicians.
Half of them were homosexuals and the other half straight.
And then there were some who hung out in limbo and went
from group to group.

Students speak of their floors as a family—often traveling
in packs, eating together, or going to a movie or a local hangout
as a group. Young people who come from fragmented families
seem particularly drawn to the bonding that takes place on
dormitory floors. They refer to individual friends by name, set
against a backdrop of characters on their floor, spoken of in the
college student vernacular as a "geek" or a "psycho," and yet,
with a tinge of affection, as if describing eccentric but beloved
extended family. Some who felt like outsiders in high school
now may experience a new sense of belonging to this accepting,
inclusive group.

The diversity of the college campus is apparent in the
microcosm of each residence hall floor. Students who have
traveled the globe share space with those who have just left
home for the first time. Some have been living "on their own"
for years; others are tightly bound to parents and siblings and
feel the stress of breaking away. Students who own BMWs
mingle with those brought up in factory towns and inner city
ghettos. Some students arrive on campus wise in the ways of
sex, drugs, and alcohol, while others have been sheltered and
are inexperienced. Whether sophisticated or naive when they
arrive, almost all students will be exposed during the course of
the freshman year to the problems of eating disorders and
clinical depression, to alcohol and drug abuse, to unfamiliar
religions and cultures, to gay men and women. Students become familiar with the intimacies of people's lives in a way
that they probably never will again outside the confines of
family and very close personal friends. Many learn a tolerance
of differences from these close associations that will last a
lifetime. Certainly, there is a loss of innocence, and with that
loss, a new maturity borne of questioning and introspection that
is often painful.

For many students, this environment is more disorienting than stimulating. Seeking the comfort of a familiar group identity, they may turn to Greek life or a religious, cultural, or political organization—a more homogeneous group whose identity is clearly associated with their own family values or perhaps just the opposite of those of their parents. Some may find at a later time that this group has become restricting, but initially it provides a feeling of stability to counteract the sense of uprootedness of the first semester:

> Initially the people I hung out with and found I had the most in common with were the more conservative. I took a turn toward a more conservative religion than my family's. My father's comments to my older sisters at college had been, "Are you studying and did you go to church on Sunday?"
>
> To me, it was, "Are you studying, and did you go to a Lutheran church on Sunday?" Ultimately I left the conservative church and went back to the Lutheran. As I became more comfortable, I started hanging out with a more diverse group of people.

> When I first got here I tended to hang out with a group of kids who were real involved in the Black Student Association, and I got involved too. I missed my friends from home and my culture. It helped knowing that group of kids. One of them, a senior girl, was like a mentor to me.

Students also form friendships through the camaraderie and absorption of shared projects—working on the newspaper, singing in the choir, playing on the soccer team. Especially on large university campuses, joining student activities provides a shortcut to finding others with common interests.

These shared experiences may offer moments of sheer delight. "It was like a Mountain Dew commercial!" exclaimed one student after a canoe trip with the outing club.

"Sometimes we stay up most of the night to get the paper to press on time," said another freshman. "I feel closer to the paper staff than to any other group of people on campus."

In the midst of all the people and activities, loneliness is as normal to the freshman experience as the common cold, mononucleosis, and the flu. Whereas most students feel lonely some of the time, there are others who are truly isolated and without friends. These are often students who lack social skills and have dealt with social isolation throughout their adolescence. Hoping that college will make a difference, they may project their unhappiness onto the school, complaining that "these are not my kind of people." Some students who were loners in high school do discover a whole new world of peers with common interests and talents that may not have been available to them before. But more than likely a young man or woman who has not been able to form friendships in earlier years will have difficulty once again. Most colleges and universities do provide free counseling or group experiences that deal with shyness or social skill building and support the development of the total student.

Cross-sex friendships are prevalent on today's campuses, a primary outgrowth of coed residence hall life. Though parents often worry about the repercussions of coed living, students are more likely to treat the members of the opposite sex on their floors as siblings, actually replicating the close relationships of missed family members, or perhaps enjoying the companionship of a "brother" or "sister" for the first time.

A young man who had just completed the first three months of his freshman year earnestly described to his parents the advantages of coed living:

> It lessens the tension between the sexes, and it eliminates all the locker room talk there was in high school. It makes for much closer friendships.

Unfortunately, parents are often uncomfortable with or disbelieving of such relationships. Platonic cross-sex friendships were not part of their own experience.

Some of these friendships do move into romantic relationships. The intimacy of shared late-night conversations about everything from future dreams to past traumas may lead to an intimacy borne of sexual and romantic stirrings. Developmentally, these are often healthy, affirming relationships, having grown out of caring and natural ties, but they bring up new questions and anxieties. What will this do to our friendship, which is so precious? What will happen if or when we break up? Will it mean too much togetherness?

There are some students who move quickly into romantic relationships, often for the first time. There may be an intensity about the involvement that suggests a mutual dependency more than a mature sexual relationship. These partners may cling to each other and provide a secure haven that keeps them from engaging fully in their new environment.

A University of Miami junior recalls:

> I began dating a graduate student the first week of school . I spent all my time with him and never got to know anyone. I barely even knew the people in the room next to me—I was just never around.

Most of these early relationships don't last much past freshman year, but they are still a vitally important part of that student's world and developing sexual identity. Some parents, suspecting that this may be just the first in a sequence of "serious relationships" dismiss it or minimize it. A freshman at Earlham describes her frustration when she calls home for support about her rocky relationship:

> At times when I call, they've tried to lessen what I'm saying. They think they're being really nice. They'll say, "Oh it's not that bad," and it *is* bad. I don't need to hear that. When they're good, they legitimize my feelings, but when they try to diminish a problem, I think they don't want to cope with the fact that their daughter's going through a rough time. All I want is some support and concern, not "Oh, it's just a college romance." It's not just a college romance. I'm having a nervous breakdown—don't you care? I'll end up calling my sister, but I like calling them first.

Some of these relationships evoke challenges to parental values as students become involved with classmates from different religions, races, and cultures. A freshman of Polish Catholic descent, and the first member of her family to go to college, refrained from telling her parents about a relationship she knew would upset them:

He was from Pakistan. They're going to kill me if the guy I marry isn't Catholic. If I told them I was involved with someone who's Islamic, it would just petrify them. They have a lot of racial prejudices. I just didn't want to inflict that on my relationship with them.

Students often talk about feeling torn and guilty, facing the dilemma of how to remain loyal to family while making independent decisions that are in conflict with established family norms. Sometimes these conflicts come as a surprise, as they did to a young woman from Philadelphia during her freshman year at Penn State:

I had met a guy over the summer who came to visit me in October. We decided to go to an inn for the weekend. It was a big problem with my parents. My mom was my rock and had always been so liberal and accepting. And now all of a sudden she was uptight about my spending a weekend with a guy. I learned something; I tested my boundaries and got to my mom's limit. When I was little and had an argument with a parent, I would end up thinking they were right. This time I felt they were wrong. She sounded like a bumbling idiot—this strong, liberal woman. I had always looked up to her. It was painful for me.

Unwittingly this young woman had tested her mother's limits and ran smack into a conflict. She stumbled into the need to make her own value judgments and to establish her own code of behavior.

Sex, Drugs, and Alcohol

Throughout the freshman year students face many puzzling moments of personal decisions, confronting previously established values, taking risks, and making compromises—all moments that sap energy and time and that provide fertile soil for leaps in personal growth. What are the unwritten rules of conduct in this place? Am I supposed to lose my virginity now that I'm in college? Am I supposed to pretend that I haven't lost it? Do I spend the weekend with my boyfriend in spite of what my parents think? Do I say "yes" to pot and "no" to coke? Do I go along to the fraternity parties where the action is even though I hate them, or do I look for alternatives, out of the mainstream?

Consider the dilemma of today's college freshman whose development has not progressed much beyond seeing things as either right or wrong. These young men and women are left to their own devices, in a place and time when the rules about drinking and drugs are often confusing and unenforced, and there are few norms about sexual behavior.

Many freshmen who "acted out" in high school and are experienced with sex, drugs, and alcohol reexamine their earlier choices within the new context of college life. With the freedom to do as they choose, some continue to experiment, stretching the boundaries to their institutional limits. Others, with no parents to bump up against, are not as involved as their classmates in the experimentation that is part of the freshman scene. "It is," said one student "a whole new ball game." The high school "boozer," "druggie," or "mover" arrives on campus without labels; fellow students carry no expectations, and there is a chance to try out a new identity.

Some students, who have lived in highly structured and restrictive environments at home and arrive at college with little experience, go haywire when they are left with no external constraints. Lacking internal controls and a sense of moderation, they experiment and try everything—usually to excess. As one young woman puts it:

> All of a sudden you can drink as much as you want, have sex with whomever you want, and do whatever drugs your heart desires. Your parents aren't there to check up on you and no one is telling you what to do. You are sleeping in a room where you can bring a guy or girl home and your mom is not going to hear you. She's three hundred miles away. That changed everything for me completely. You have complete freedom here. You can go to your room, his room—that made such a difference about sex. I went overboard with it. It was a blast, but sometimes I wondered just how much freedom one person could handle all at once.

Struggling to establish their own identities and to separate from their parents, some students take a blatantly rebellious stance. Their behavior sends a message that they are different from Mother and Dad; they are establishing their own moral turf. They may even tell their parents about their exploits. They call home and say, with the typical hyperbole of college freshmen, "Oh I'm totally out of it. I got completely wasted last night" or "I've been partying all week." One student described how much she liked to tell her mother shocking things. When asked why she enjoyed doing so, she replied, "Because Mom can't do a thing about it. She has no control over what I do."

Others try to hide their behavior, and their parents don't have a clue as to what is really going on. One Princeton student described what he called "a college student's nightmare—having your parents call when you're stoned":

> I remember having had several exams and coming back to a friend's room across the hall from mine and getting stoned. My phone rang, and I stumbled to it. It was my mother. It was the middle of the afternoon, and I was totally incoherent, and I knew it. The next day, my oldest brother called me because my mother had called him and said she thought I was studying too hard and would he talk to me. We had a good laugh when I told him what happened.

Actually most parents don't know what is really going on, and unsettling as this may be, it is a necessary part of the separation process. Students need privacy and an opportunity to establish their own limits and values. They need to experiment and handle the consequences. John Gardner, an associate vice provost at the University of South Carolina and founder of the National Center for the Study of the Freshman Year Experience, urges parents:

> Look at college as a laboratory for testing behaviors. Students have to figure out who they want to spend time with, what and when they want to eat, drink, and smoke—how much they want to sleep, socialize, and study. As students experiment, they are testing out the consequences of their behaviors. If they can't learn in an unfettered way, they'll test the same things out later when the stakes are much higher, when there aren't the built-in safety nets that exist in college.

There are times, of course, that students truly want their parents to be there for them or even to intervene. They send out signals that they are in trouble—a series of depressed phone calls home or aloof calls of the "everything's fine" variety; they may sound spacy or uncommunicative. Their grades may drop suddenly or their weight may change dramatically. They may be spending a lot of money they can't account for.

The director of student activities and orientation at a southern university comments:

> Parents need to look for signs, but they shouldn't jump to conclusions. If they have built a relationship through high school, they need to maintain it. Parents should confront their children in a positive way—express concern, not hysteria. They should ask about friends, about the weekend, about eating and sleeping. They should show that they care, but not interrogate.
>
> I think parents should confront their children if they find things that indicate drug use. They should take the time to explain their concern, but not cut off communication with a barrage of accusations. They shouldn't make assumptions, but should ask open-ended questions and listen. It's important to keep the lines of communication open. When parents know that their child is abusing drugs, they should seek professional help either at home or at a counseling center on or near campus. They shouldn't try to handle that kind of problem themselves.

A young woman who is now a sophomore at an east coast university found her parents' intervention during her freshman year particularly effective:

> One time last year my parents called me, and I was just really hung over. I wasn't bragging about it or happy about it, but that's just the way it was. I was in bed, and I said—look I can't talk to you right now. Let me call you back.
>
> When I called them back I was fine, and they didn't mention it. But then I did get a letter that said, we are really concerned that at 12:30, or whatever time it was, on a Sunday morning, you're hung over. And that was perfect! It didn't feel like they were bugging me. It was more like—hey, buddy—we're really worried about you. They were sort of acting like concerned friends.

I think I was relieved when my parents said something. I was already a little worried about myself. When they brought it up, that opened up a chance for us to discuss what was going on. We talked about it when I got home, and I don't know if it was a direct result of our talking, but I'm partying a lot less this year and have things much more under control.

Some parents have a tendency not to say anything, and then you start to wonder, don't they care? How come they don't say anything? I'm not sure how parents are supposed to know when there's really something wrong. But I think they should follow their instincts and at least say they're worried. They shouldn't ignore it.

Many students who choose to experiment with sex, drugs, and alcohol are motivated by the desire to be part of a group, by a search for intimacy with their peers. There is a compelling camaraderie that develops as students come together over beer or to share a joint while they listen to music and talk. Students often divide into groups according to their preferences in alcohol and drugs. The word gets around campus about who does what: one sorority is known for girls who "drink booze hard core," a fraternity is "into coke—it's part of the budget for the spring formal." One group "drinks and smokes pot and sits around playing head games," referring with pride to pot and hallucinogens as "the intellectual drug" and with disdain to the heavy use of alcohol or cocaine as the "drugs of the rich kids who are destructive and into the proving-you're-a-macho-man kind of nonsense."

Each group has an identity of its own, and as students wrestle with self-definition, the choice of a particular group reveals more than a simple preference for one substance over another. The lure of friendship and intimacy is powerful:

I hang out with a small group. We smoke quite a bit. Dope is an interest in itself—a social activity, and it brings about a state of mind that definitely is going to bring you together. And when you're with people who are smoking, a lot of times you'll do something together, like you'll smoke and go to a movie and then get together afterward and talk some more.

I'm kind of attracted to a crowd in the dorm next door. They hang out together and drink vodka and Kool-Aid and play

Pente. They're sort of pursuing me, but I'm not sure yet whether I want to spend a lot of time with them. I may have had enough of that.

People who smoke pot on campus know everybody else who smokes pot. You get to know a lot of people that way. We hang together. It's a self-protecting kind of culture. It's not the kind of thing that's broadcast.

I don't drink and I don't want to hang out with people who do. When I go to a party I sip a little beer—just enough so I feel kind of mellow. I call it "drinking for buzz maintenance."

Drug usage tends to be more private than alcohol and usually takes place behind closed doors. But on most campuses today, alcohol is everywhere. No matter what the college's official alcohol policy is, students are very resourceful when they want to drink. On weekends, parties seem to erupt spontaneously, and a keg is usually the main drawing card.

All students are affected when their hallmates or roommates overindulge. Said one freshman:

In high school I was used to seeing friends drink too much at parties. But I just went home to my nice quiet house. Now I have to deal with the rowdies in the hall every Friday and Saturday night. Sometimes just to get to the shower I have to step over the bodies of the kids who passed out.

Many students are overwhelmed by the party scene and the constant inducements to participate. A University of Michigan freshman admitted that she had a lot of anxiety about this part of college life.

I was scared 'cause I hadn't been a big party girl or sexually active. I found a lot of others in the same boat. Things move a lot faster than in high school and since we all live in such close quarters, we see a lot more. I saw a lot more drugs than in high school. I could walk down the hall and smell marijuana. I never did start smoking dope, but a lot of my friends did—and I was surprised to realize that I liked them anyway—that I was much less judgmental than I had been in high school.

Some students drink moderately or don't drink at all, and many of them say that they don't feel the overt peer pressure they felt in high school. "No one will make fun of you if you don't drink," explained one student," except during something like fraternity hazing. But there is a kind of self-imposed pressure. If you feel shy or awkward in the first place, it's kind of hard not to drink if you're at a party."

But for large numbers of students, the ethic is one of "work hard, play hard"—go to the library during the week and "get wasted" on the weekend. For most, drinking is a way to blow off steam, to get rid of social inhibitions, to prove that they are grown up. It is an integral part of their culture and inextricably tied up with their social life and their sexual behavior.

Though the sexual revolution appears to have peaked, there is still pressure on both men and women to be knowledgeable and comfortable with sex. Rarely are sexual encounters between college students as spontaneous, smooth, and carefree as their parents might think. Almost no one is immune to the agonies of sexual growth. Students worry about sexual attractiveness and performance, about finding a private place, and about the future of their relationship. They worry about the dangers of sexually-transmitted diseases and how to integrate these clinical intrusions into their lovemaking. Those who choose to remain virgins throughout their college years may question their own desirability or their sexual identity. "If everyone else is doing it, why aren't I? Is it simply that I'm not interested in sex without love, and I haven't fallen in love? Maybe there's something wrong with me." Those who feel sure of these choices based on moral or religious values may have to cope with the stigma of being different. And with the additional pressures brought to bear by the fear of AIDS, these decisions are more complex than ever.

In spite of the decline of sexual stereotypes, there is still more peer pressure on a man who remains a virgin than there is on a woman. And many women are now the initiators of sex, so that some young men find themselves saying no, which is incongruent with their messages about manliness and may cause them to feel off balance and bewildered.

Issues of confusion over sexual identity are also common among college students. The dean of arts and sciences at one selective university comments:

> This struggle often interferes with academic achievement. Students are sent to me because of academics, and then they start talking. They are not sure about their sexual identity; they can't talk to their parents; some of them feel uncomfortable going to gay groups. What I do is listen. I'm not sure what parents can do, but I think they should know that many students are questioning their sexuality. Their own kids may be and certainly they will be exposed to other kids who are.

Although homosexuality is far more open and aboveboard than in earlier generations, the stigma still remains. "Coming out" is usually a long and agonizing process. Some gay men and women who are clear about their sexual orientation before they come to college still have anxieties about how they will fit into this new environment.

The unfolding of a student's sexual identity and evolving comfort as a sexual being goes hand in hand with his or her total maturing process. One young man about to graduate looks back on that evolution with a new perspective and insight:

> My friends were mostly guys freshman year. At first it was like, oh, wow, college! It went from, girls and sex were something illicit, like drugs, or like alcohol, just going out of control and being really stupid and insensitive about it, to incorporating sex more and more into our personalities—having more respect for other people—respecting other people's lives and the way they behaved and learning how to live with people.
>
> I lived in a suite freshman year—and definitely we had problem times about that sort of thing—complete lack of respect for the other people around—for what people would think—like a group of us would be hanging out in the living room and a couple would come in and not even say hello—just go straight to the bedroom and the next thing, we'd hear the bedsprings and a lot of noise. That changed over time. People became a lot more conscious of other people and were able to be sociable about incorporating sex into their lives—becoming more social human beings.

This young man's remarks help put in perspective the sometimes outrageous behavior of freshmen. Bombarded with new freedoms and responsibilities, at a time when they are trying to figure out who they are and how they can live on their own, their actions are often disturbing to their peers as well as their parents. Their exhilaration is mixed with confusion, their experimentation tempered by responsibility. They are trying to incorporate new people and activities and interests into their lives.

So much seems to be happening at once. At times they appear very certain of who they are and what they think; at other times little about them seems to be integrated.

Macalester College's dean of students, Mary Ackerman, says:

> The freshman year is not primarily about academics—although academics are, of course, important. It's about separation from family and home. It's about the questions, "Who am I?" and "How do I fit in?" It's about maintaining one's ego in a strange environment, learning to live with a roommate and handling freedom and responsibility. It's about making friends and finding a niche.

Chapter 7
IN AND OUT OF YOUR LIFE

Carrie has that "New York look." Her clothes are from second-hand shops; they're always artfully arranged, never look studied, but seem a natural extension of her cameo face. She walks with assurance, her shoulders back, eyes straight ahead; she appears to know where she is going. A senior at Yale, she's a talented artist and enjoys exploring the rich resources of her hometown, New York City. She feels close to her parents, who have always supported her personal style and encouraged her independence.

It is obvious that Carrie's mother takes great delight in her daughter. She reminisces about Carrie's rocky start freshman year, and the unexpected ups and downs that followed:

> Carrie finished high school early and took courses at a college in the city in place of her senior year. She seemed ready to go away to school. In fact, she seemed more mature than most eighteen-year-olds and entered as a sophomore. My husband and I drove her to school. I remember that she was anxious and obviously disappointed by the posters of puppies and kittens that her roommate had already put up, but by the time we left she seemed to be cheerfully settling in. John and I drove home thinking, this is it, we're on to the next phase of life.
>
> The phone calls came as a surprise. There were lots of them, and they were always late at night. John slept through most of them, and I would listen for what seemed endless hours to her unhappiness. There were many tears and many tales of poor courses and loneliness. She was in one class with all seniors, the result of sloppy advising. It was way over her head, but she refused to change.
>
> Finally, when she came home for Thanksgiving, the dam burst. She became nearly hysterical, and the three of us talked most of the night. When she finally went to sleep, John and I decided . . . this is not worth it; we'll withdraw her from

school, send her for therapy, and she'll go to school here in the city.

The next morning when I began to tell Carrie what we had decided, I noticed the slightest flash of disappointment on her face. It was so tiny that only a mother would have seen it, and I knew instinctively that we were wrong, and that she was strong enough to get through this. She needed us to encourage her, not come to her rescue. I took a chance and said, "Carrie, this is all bullshit. You will go back. You can do it."

She looked shocked and relieved all at the same time. The next day she returned to school on the train. And now she's a senior and will probably graduate with honors. That first trip home was the turnaround. But it was also just the beginning. At times it's been a roller coaster existence. Carrie has been in and out of our lives in ways we never would have predicted three years ago when we blithely dropped her off in New Haven.

Throughout the freshman year and continuing through the rest of their college experience, young men and women move in and out of their parents' lives, often in fits and starts as crises or triumphs occur. When students become upperclassmen, the quantity and intensity of contacts usually lessen, as they shift their support systems from home to school and become more adept at discovering resources for themselves. But the vicissitudes of life at home and at school bring unexpected turns of events, and the reentry into each others' lives can be awkward and unsettling, as well as comforting and confirming.

During the course of a year, students experience losses and traumas and may turn to their parents for support. Parents, too, go through their own joys and sorrows, and occasionally will be the bearers of painful news from home.

For students who go to school a short distance from home, there is a sense of continuity as they drop back in for a quiet weekend, a family celebration, or a quick fix of TLC. Their parents, within a short drive of campus, may occasionally drop off a basket of fruit, post a brief note on the door of their child's room, or take their child's friends out for a much appreciated good meal.

But continuity of this sort inevitably diminishes for those who go to school far from home and whose contacts with family are reduced to vacations, occasional visits, and sporadic phone calls or letters. The experience of both students' and parents' lives during these years is reduced to images, frozen in time and often distorted and misunderstood like snapshots viewed out of context.

The impact of such slices of life reverberates across telephone wires every weekend as parents take stock of their children's progress, happiness, success—measuring their tone of voice and the contents that spill forth against an imaginary norm. How powerful these ten-minute calls or three-page letters are, pouring out the emotion of that particular moment. Exuberant accounts of recent events, successes, or a general sense of their child's well-being can brighten up a parent's day. On the other hand, complaints, distresses, disappointments, and depression are delivered in shrill staccato or flat, gloomy conversations that interrupt peaceful Sundays at home or invade an already overburdened parent's domain.

A successful surgeon, the father of four, acknowledges that on Sundays, when he and his wife routinely speak to each child at various locations across the country, "we are only as happy as our least happy child."

But what of the hours before or the days after his phone calls? Is his daughter who sounded sad or distraught rejuvenated an hour later? Is his son's happy voice genuine or a reaction to an unspoken, but imagined request to sound good-humored because Mom and Dad cannot tolerate sadness or depression?

A substantial number of students speak of protecting their parents from their disappointments and problems—some because they don't want to burden them when they are sacrificing so much for their education, some because they are protecting themselves from their parents' lack of understanding and support.

My Dad made it very clear that he didn't want to hear from me when I was complaining or depressed. He's got all kinds of problems with his wife and his stepdaughter, and if I sound down, he just gets mad and I end up feeling worse. So we have these stilted conversations because I have to pretend everything's fine.

Everytime I call home depressed, my Mom either starts sounding depressed herself, or she says maybe I should come home, like I obviously can't handle things. That's the last thing I want to hear.

When students are feeling down, parents often react too quickly; they have difficulty assessing from afar how much this depressed phone call or letter reflects the totality of their child's life. A Californian at an east coast university explains how frustrating it is when she simply wants some support and understanding, but her mother overreacts and responds as though her bad moments are the whole of her experience:

I'll say one thing on the phone, like I'm tired or down, and my mother makes such a production of it. She spends the whole day picking tangerines from our tree and wrapping them up individually to send to me. She encloses a note, telling me she's worried about me, and my sister tells me that's all she and my dad talk about for three weeks.

And a freshman at Trinity College in Connecticut has difficulty communicating her low times to her mother without getting what she considers an overreaction or an underreaction:

My mom is such a stoic, she just says, "you're fine," when I'm sick or depressed. It hurts her so much when there's something in my universe that she can't cure. All I want her to do when I'm depressed is to recognize it . . . to validate it. So when she says, "You don't sound too bad," I'll say, "You're not listening to me. I'm really, really down." And then she becomes convinced that I'm suicidal or deathly ill and starts calling every day. "Hi. Just calling to see if you're still alive."
I can't just have a cold . . . she either thinks it's nothing or its mono for sure. All I want her to say is, "I'm sorry you have a bad sore throat . . . I know how miserable that can be."

Many students admit that they call home when they want to complain and tend to share their good times with friends:

> There's only so much you can complain around here, because everyone complains so much. I have four papers due. My friends' attitudes are, "So what!" They'll be bitching about their own heavy load . . . so you call home for pity.

Even when students do attempt to communicate both the ups and the downs to their parents, they find it impossible to capture the day-to-day pleasures of their new world in such brief sketches. A Pomona student explains:

> I feel like my parents only know what upsets me, like when I call home and say I'm failing something or I had a fight with my roommate. But when I say I went to a party last night and had a lot of fun, I don't think they have any idea how wonderful my life is here . . . how wonderful my friends are. I think my life is pretty rich, and I'm very secure. This is more of a natural environment than even being at home was for me. I'm much more in my own element with people I'm comfortable with and have a lot in common with.
>
> I have two separate worlds. I have another life here that's as full and complete as my life was at home; they're separate and distinct. I'm made aware of it when I talk to my parents. Even though when I was home, they didn't know a lot about my life. We were close, but I didn't tell them very personal things . . . they saw it; they saw people I spent time with. When I talk to them on the phone now they really have no conception of what my life is like. It's so disconnected.

And for a young woman from India the physical distance, as well as the cultural differences implicit in her college experience, highlight the sense of disconnectedness:

> I've always shared everything with my parents. They're so far away now, I can't call them and tell them about everything. Especially when the work gets underway. I don't have the energy to sit down and write . . . what it would take is a ten-page letter every week. It's impossible to let them know what my life is really like here, so it tends to be post-cards or notes to my sister, letting them know that I'm okay. I realize I'm going to get out of here after four years without their ever having seen any of the rituals or the friends or anything that's become

such a part of me at this point, and they won't ever know that and that's hard, but there's nothing I can do about it.

I'm used to communicating with my mother on a very adult level. I am a friend to her. I'm the eldest, but once I came here I became her little girl. All she can think of is taking care of me. So, this very intelligent, interesting woman . . . all she can say is, "Are you all right? Are you drinking your orange juice? Are you praying every day?" That's the extent of our conversations. When she writes, she writes as to a child.

The fact is that college students *are* no longer a regular part of their parents' lives. For most students the reality of the ever-widening gap between their experience and the world of their parents is fraught with conflicting feelings. Young people, as well as their parents, struggle with letting go. At times college students revel in their separateness, keeping the delights and traumas of their lives at school to themselves. At other times they long to share their college world with the family at home, even as their worlds inevitably become more separate. Heady moments of independence and the adventure of expanding horizons give way to wistful desires to be taken care of and nurtured.

Keeping in Touch

How can parents keep in touch, yet still affirm their sons' and daughters' growing adulthood? There are a number of recommendations that students make again and again when they are asked what they would like their parents to do. Almost all students claim that they want attention and support from their parents—but not unsolicited advice. They want mail; the contents don't seem to matter as much as the simple, tangible connection to the life they have left behind. They want care packages, and they talk with childlike delight about receiving bundles of food at exam time and inexpensive decorations for their rooms at holidays. They appreciate phone calls, but not early in the morning. Most prefer to talk on the phone to one parent at a time, and especially enjoy private conversations with siblings.

Students talk also of their frustration with parents who call, "only when they're angry," and the pain of rejection by parents who always seem too preoccupied to communicate at all. They dislike getting caught in the middle between divorced parents, and sometimes can't remember what they told to which parent.

Many say they love it when their parents make their plane reservations home for them at the end of the semester, when they are overloaded with exams and papers. These same students, however, complain when their parents are "too helpful," sending immediate replacements for lost sweatpants or gloves, without being asked to do so, or sewing buttons on as soon as they arrive home for vacations. Though college students resent intrusions and parental attempts at control, they long to be understood, and contrary to their public claims, most of them do care what their parents think:

> When I call home excited to tell that I'm doing something independent, and I just want to tell them and they give me advice, it's deflating.

> I wish my Mom would be more in tune sometimes with what's going on with me. Mention my friends by name in letters; say hi to them so I know she's hearing what I'm telling her. I have my friends here, and she doesn't know as much about them as I'd like her to. That's hard. I guess it's part of growing up.

> Phone calls are very important to me. It's important that I have their approval, and even if they don't approve, it's important to have their understanding. They're not going to approve of everything I do, just like I don't approve of everything they do. We're different people with different ideas about things. But I want them to try to understand where I'm coming from, and why I'm doing what I'm doing.

> A lot of times you get the idea that professors don't believe in you. It's important for parents to let you know they care and believe in you.

> You want to share new experiences. Like one morning I called home and said, "I was at a party last night, and I was dancing right next to Brooke Shields." And the first thing my Dad said was, "A party? On Thursday night? What were you doing at a party on a Thursday night?"

> That was not what I wanted to hear! I didn't expect him to
> be as excited as I was, but I wanted him to be excited for me. I
> wanted him to say, "Wow, that's neat. Have a great day,
> honey."

> I called home full of complaints last night. Mom just listened
> and listened. At one point she said, "Isn't growing up a bitch?"
> That was just great!

Students want to be kept informed about the changes at
home, from superficial alterations in household decor to more
substantive changes in the health and well-being of family
members. They are particularly vehement about being told
about major crises and feel betrayed when parents, hoping to
spare them, withhold information. "I want the privilege to
worry over someone I love," one young woman exclaimed
angrily after learning of her father's serious illness when she
arrived home for spring break. "It's a violation of trust not to
tell me. I'll always be anxious about what might be happening
that I don't know about. And it makes me feel very isolated and
remote from everyone at home. What I know about, I can
handle."

Though students make it clear that they want to know what
is going on, parents still have to wrestle with how much to say
and when to say it: Can the news wait until exams are over or
is it important to tell her right away? Can I let him know what
is happening without burdening him with details and my own
anxiety? Should I call some official at the college? How can I
use the system that is already in place to provide support during
this troubled time?

One mother received the traumatic diagnosis of a malignan-
cy and impending surgery several days after her freshman
daughter's arrival at William and Mary. Her sensitivity to her
daughter's needs in the midst of her own crisis helped to ease
this difficult time:

> Amanda went to school early for preseason hockey practice, so
> she was in an empty dorm with just her head resident. I told her
> I wanted her to tell people what was going on at home, and she
> agreed to talk to her head resident. I called the head resident

myself and also her coach, the two people I knew she was having the most contact with.

She wanted to come home, but I said, "No, you need to get started." I suggested she come home in early November after the surgery, after people had flocked around, and when I knew I'd need cheering up.

In their concern for their children's happiness, parents unwittingly may focus on their vulnerabilities. When the father of a young woman who has a tendency to procrastinate keeps asking her if she has had a productive week, or a shy young man's mother asks repeatedly if he's made any friends, the students' attempts to cope independently are undermined. By constantly bringing up a sensitive topic, the parent is sending the unspoken message: "I'm worried about you and don't think you can manage on your own." The student may become more anxious or, in an attempt to break the parental bond, engage in the very behavior the parent is worried about. A sophomore at Emory comments:

> Everyone in our family has a weight problem. Before I came here my mother teased me about the freshman forty instead of the freshman ten. When there is a weight problem in your family and the last thing your mother says before you go away is "Watch out for the freshman forty," that's really not a good thing.
>
> When I first got here I was paranoid about food. The first few weeks of school my mother asked at every phone conversation, "How is your weight doing?" Parents should be careful, because the number of bulimics at school seems to be amazingly large.

Parents may wonder why at times their children seem so accessible and at others, so distant. Moments of understanding and tenderness between them are treasured by both. And yet, as parents and children temporarily bridge the gap between their worlds, their sense of connection is tenuous. Although comforting for students, it can also feel threatening—a flashback to earlier times of childhood dependence.

Sometimes after periods of intense and intimate contact with parents, students pull back abruptly. Ambivalent about

their own ability to be independent, they act out this ambivalence through bouts of silence or antagonism. They may
stop calling or writing for weeks on end and be unresponsive
to family attempts to communicate, claiming uncharacteristically that they have nothing to say. Some fight their separation
battles on an intellectual level, haggling with parents over the
phone about politics or values, testing themselves and establishing their autonomy. Some silently retreat in an attempt to
extricate themselves from the knots that bind them to an alcoholic family member, or from battling parents who are vying
for their allegiance. Or, simply finding it stressful to switch
gears abruptly from being an independent college student to the
kid in the family, some decide to stay at school over brief
vacations such as fall break or Thanksgiving.

Students may seem unpredictably elusive and remote for
months at a time when college life takes them into realms never
experienced by their parents. A young woman whose parents
live in a working-class Irish enclave and have never left their
home state, talks about feeling guilty and frustrated as she tries
to share with them the diversity of her college friends and the
travels they have enjoyed together. Another student returns to
his ghetto neighborhood in East St. Louis and tries to imagine
what it would be like to bring his neighborhood friends and
college roommates together. He often feels like a stranger in
both worlds, but he can't explain any of this to his parents, who
wonder why their formerly gregarious son is suddenly so quiet.

A lesbian from an upper middle class, competitive, and
traditional Long Island community deliberates over how to stay
close to the family she loves and admires while rejecting their
community and lifestyle. Though she goes to school less than
two hundred miles away, she rarely goes home, but worries that
she is hurting her parents as she wrestles with redefining her
relationship with them.

And still another student from a Puerto Rican immigrant
family talks about the anger she felt toward her parents, espe-

cially during her freshman and sophomore years, because they didn't understand her life. She resented what she considered their limited aspirations and their attempts to limit her. She withdrew from them emotionally and physically. Now, as a senior, she has come to a renewed appreciation of her parents, and the realization that if they hadn't done certain things, she never would have gone to college . . . that her own life would have been much more narrow. After a painful withdrawal, she has reclaimed her past and reentered their lives.

When Something Goes Wrong at School

The unexpected bombshells from campus that suddenly invade the daily routine of a family back home range from bouts of homesickness to serious illness. It is not easy for parents to assess the severity of a problem from afar, but students do send them signals and clues, some of which are indirect pleas for attention.

During the first few months of school, homesickness calls are routine interruptions in many homes. In most cases they eventually wane, only to erupt once in a while at particularly stressful times. A divorced mother of five recalls her middle child's grueling first semester:

> At first she called nightly wanting to come home. I told her she couldn't, but could come for a weekend. She cried every night. She was really scared and kept telling me she missed the rainbows in her room and that she wanted to stay with me forever. I finally told her she could call two times a week unless there was an emergency and after the first semester, we would talk about whether she would stay. She made it through the semester . . . we both did; it was tough. By second semester she had made a commitment to stay and had three and a half pretty good years after that.

There are, of course, the few exceptional cases that deans and counseling centers deal with each year when the rupture of leaving home is simply too great and the panic increases with each passing day. With the help of college administrators and counselors, parents and their children may have to come to the disappointing, but not irrevocable, decision that a student should go home. Most youngsters will be able to separate from their parents eventually in their own way and at their own pace, some with the additional help of therapy. Many return to college after a year or two of either working or going to school closer to home.

It is bound to be difficult for parents when their children come home unexpectedly. This sudden switching of gears throws a wrench into the whole family system. Parents may feel let down or burdened by having to cope with their children's problems on a daily basis. While trying to provide their children with emotional support, parents are likely to be struggling themselves with a sense of remorse as they question what went wrong. This return to the fold certainly was not part of the original plan when, full of dreams and expectations, they sent their children off to college.

As they try to separate, young adults often test their parents' limits in painful and destructive ways. The more emotionally dependent they feel, the more dramatic the rupture is likely to be. "In our darkest moments, we felt vilified as parents," said one mother whose daughter left school abruptly during her freshman year. "We turned to our friends for support. It was comforting to be told that we were just human, that we'd done the best we could."

And from the father of a student who returned home halfway through his first semester:

> We had to keep letting Josh know that we cared about him. He got an apartment near where we live. He was belligerent and very hostile. When we heard from him we had to listen to the melody, not the words. The melody said, "I need to know you're around." The words said, "I don't need you."
>
> We all got into family therapy. It was important for us to have an outside person to bring us together when the ferment was so chaotic.

During the course of their college careers all students inevitably face bouts of minor illness. When they become run down and suffer from colds and the flu, they understandably miss the comforts of home, the privacy, the chicken soup, or coddling they may have been used to. They are likely to call when they are feeling their absolute worst, seeking a bit of mothering. The first time this happens the parents may be caught off guard. The mother of a Creighton University freshman says with a smile:

> The second or third week of school, he called and said, "Mom, what do you do for a really bad earache?" What I wanted to say was, "You put the phone down and wait for your mother, and I'll be there in four hours."

Of course, she didn't say that, but told him instead to go to the health service, which on all campuses is equipped to handle common illnesses and injuries. Some students simply need—in addition to expressions of sympathy—a bit of encouragement from their parents to use these services and to take responsibility for their own well-being.

The calls that all parents dread are those that bring news of a child's serious illness or accident. Most parents expect the college to keep them informed of serious medical problems. The notion of what constitutes something serious, however, is a matter of opinion. It's not unusual for parents to find out about episodes such as a skateboard accident or a case of mononucleosis long after the fact. They may be upset by this, but as one health service director explains, "Students are in the process of passing from dependence to independence, and we try to foster that."

If students are coping well with the problem and have not been hospitalized, most colleges will not call home on their behalf. They may encourage the students to do so, but will treat them as adults.

When students do encounter serious medical problems, parents face the difficult situation of having to place their trust in unfamiliar medical caretakers and their child's own ability to follow through. In the course of the academic year a certain number of students will have to be hospitalized with either a physical or psychological illness. Anne Schroer, associate dean at Washington and Lee, firmly recommends that at such times, unless the hospital stay is brief and not traumatic, one or both parents should come. Many students are hesitant to ask, but usually want their parents with them, even if they don't say so directly. This is a time when parents can work in tandem with administrators to give the support and encouragement a student will need. Adjustments will have to be made; perhaps a lighter courseload or leave of absence will be in order. When a serious accident or illness temporarily sends a college student back to childlike dependency on parents, it may take a special effort for the family to separate again after the student has recovered.

Less dramatic than hospitalization, but equally demanding of a parent's attention, are students' comments, either direct or indirect, that they are worried about their own behavior. Students who hint at or tell their parents of eating disorders, alcohol and drug dependency, and other self-destructive and compulsive behavior want their parents to respond. They don't want them to panic or nag, but to know they are in trouble and to take them seriously, as this student from Ohio State asserts:

> It took me two years to get up the courage to tell my mother that I was bulimic. By that time I was frantic. She hardly responded—kind of blew it off—and never mentioned it again. I'm not sure if she just couldn't handle it or if she really just thought it was a phase and didn't realize how serious it is.

Another student, a sophomore at Columbia, describes her parents' head-on approach:

> When I came home over break, it was obvious that I had gained weight and wasn't keeping in shape or doing any sports like I usually do. And during the first week I was back, I was hung over two or three times. My parents were really worried about this drinking thing with me to the point where they made me see somebody about it. They sent me to my doctor, who discovered that I'd gained twelve pounds, which is a lot on a small frame. He also said I had an iron deficiency, which can happen from drinking.
>
> Maybe I was lucky that my parents picked up the signals, and that my doctor discovered I had anemia. Once my doctor figured out what was going on, I talked mostly to him. When

my parents and doctor intervened it was kind of like I was pulling back from being totally responsible for myself. I guess I wasn't doing a very good job of it. There had to be some help.

Doctors in college clinics see an abundance of symptoms related to stress. When a student comes in four or five times complaining of headaches, stomach aches, or sleep difficulties and no organic problem surfaces, the physician is likely to view the symptom as a functional problem and may talk with the student about it, perhaps making a referral to a counselor or psychiatrist for evaluation.

Psychological concerns are often insidious, developing over time and perhaps not clearly problematic until well under way. College students are often mercurial; they use the word depressed when they simply mean tired or lonely, and they tend toward hyperbole, especially when describing their own moods. So it is particularly difficult for a parent to distinguish normal ups and downs from psychological distress that needs attention.

Just as parents are beginning to relax and enjoy the pleasure of thinking about their son as an independent, capable, well-functioning adult, they receive a frantic phone call from him— now anxious and frazzled, having lost all sense of perspective. Or, they get a disturbing late night call from a despondent daughter who is questioning the meaning of her life. After a sleepless night, the parents anxiously call back the next day only to find the same daughter about to leave for a touch football game, irritated by their overreaction.

Brief episodes of depression and anxiety are common among college students; most will feel the extreme pressure of some aspect of college life sooner or later. Always another book to read, another paper to write, another exam to take, another set of problems to do—it never seems to go away. Add to this a broken love affair, disappointing grades, the threat of losing a scholarship, being rejected by a fraternity—all losses that take their toll. Most youngsters will cope with their fears and disappointments and, given the time to grieve for their losses, will pick themselves up with remarkable resilience.

Letting go of dreams, coming to terms with one's own limitations is, after all, part of the reality of being an adult. But losses
may be particularly powerful at this stage of development.
Noted psychiatrist Robert Arnstein comments on this
phenomenon in a 1986 book on suicide and depression in
adolescents and young adults:

> The developmental issue of separation may be especially im-
> portant in vulnerability to a depressive disorder. Depression is
> often precipitated by a loss or separation; because loss and
> separation are part of psychological development at this life
> stage, a late adolescent-young adult may be peculiarly vul-
> nerable to depression. There are several events that are charac-
> teristic of this period. First, going to college may be
> experienced as a separation from parental ties; and, although
> this is presumably a desirable step in the process of develop-
> ment, not everyone is emotionally ready and some may be over-
> come by depressed feelings. Second, romantic attachments and
> detachments are frequent occurrences in this period, and the
> detachment phase may be especially painful for the late adoles-
> cents. Although pain probably always accompanies a loss, the
> superimposition of the actual loss of an attachment to parental
> figures may multiply the feelings of depression and lead to a
> state of hopelessness.[1]

Dr. Arnstein's observations may help parents to understand
the intensity of some depressive episodes when there seems to
be no momentous precipitating cause. Why does a young man
become suicidal when he gets a C in physics? How can the
ending of a two-month fling bring on such feelings of
worthlessness and hopelessness? These are the young people
who don't bounce back from their bouts of anxiety or depression, but who continue to sink deeper into a period of increasing
despair.

Depression is a complex topic, and its causes are still being
debated. College students whose identities are shaky live in a
highly charged and demanding environment. Some bring with
them the added burden of family problems; some may have a
predisposition to depression. It is no wonder that depression is
the most common psychological problem among college students.

Janet Loxley of the University of California at Irvine's counseling center acknowledges that many of the typical signs of depression may simply be normal behavior among college-age students. Changes in eating and sleeping patterns, withdrawal, low energy, and flat affect in conversation, are a few of the common symptoms that may or may not signal trouble.

Dr. Loxley believes, however, that if parents notice a cluster of these kinds of changes in their child's behavior, they should pay attention:

> In addition to the other patterns I mentioned, a marked change in hygiene, not just long hair or weird clothing, is something I'd be concerned about. Other things of note are forced cheer—trying hard to look happy—a sense of apathy and lack of interest in peers, waking up early and not being able to go back to sleep. Contrary to what some people might expect, depressed people are unlikely to be sitting around crying all the time. It's more subtle than that; they often just demonstrate little energy or interest in the world around them.
>
> If parents are concerned that their son or daughter is depressed, they might start by asking a simple open-ended question such as, "What's going on?"
>
> When a kid says to a parent, "It's not going well; I don't have friends," the parent wants to make the kid feel better fast and is tempted to say things like, "Don't worry. It will get better." Or "I know how you feel. I went through the same thing. Everyone does."
>
> What the kid needs instead is to know that he or she has been heard, that the parents heard that these things are problems. A parent might say, "I'm not 100 percent sure but you sound kind of down to me. Do you want to talk about it?" Let the kid feel as though he has some room.

Dr. Loxley believes that it is fine for parents who are worried about a noncommunicative and seemingly depressed child to call up a housing official or dean and tentatively express concern, though their son or daughter will be initially displeased by their intervention. Parents shouldn't, however, try to get the university officials to collude with them without telling their child. That's not what any young person needs. Dr. Loxley asserts:

It's one thing to call the head resident in the dorm and say, "My daughter has been sleeping late every day, and I want to make sure she's up by eight each day—and don't tell her I called."

It's a totally different matter to call and say, "I'm not certain that there's a problem, but I'm concerned about my daughter and told her I was going to call you. I'd appreciate it if you'd keep an eye on her and encourage her to use whatever resources you and she think might help her."

A number of students suffer severe psychological illnesses that require them to be hospitalized, and some eventually have to leave college. This is devastating to parents and activates intense feelings, from guilt and self-doubt to anger and resentment. These families suddenly find themselves catapulted into a world of mental health professionals that is foreign and frightening. It is not within the purview of this book to examine in depth the onset of serious psychological illness during the college years. However, a number of parents who have experienced this kind of crisis have found the book, *You Are Not Alone* by Clara Claiborne Park and Leon N. Shapiro, especially helpful and informative. It is comprehensive in scope and filled with clinical information that is well within the grasp of the layperson. Parents are encouraged also to reach out to friends, counselors, or clergy at such a draining time so that they can get support for themselves and still be emotionally available to their child.

Phone calls bringing news of unexpected traumatic experiences are likely to catch parents off guard. When a son calls to report that he has been mugged on his way home from the library or a daughter describes a sexual assault by a date, parents may respond out of their own anxiety rather than in ways that would be helpful to their child.

Though date rape and crime on campus are common topics for the headlines, nothing really prepares us to handle these situations with aplomb when they happen to our own children. Startling evidence of our sons' and daughters' vulnerability is likely to stir up all of our most protective parental instincts. We're thrown off balance ourselves—frightened, sad, and angry about what has happened. We'd like to think that there's some way we can prevent something like this from ever happening again. And that's when we start asking the kind of questions that one student labeled the "why did you? why didn't you?" variety.

A young woman who had been forced to have sex with a classmate after a party explains what happened when she finally got up the nerve to call home and tell her mother about it.

> The first thing my mother hit me with, after she asked if I was o.k., was "why was he in your room? Were you drunk? Was he drunk?" I was raped, for God's sake!
>
> And then I had to deal with my father who called me back that night and wanted the name of the guy. He wanted to call the dean and find out what the college was going to do about it.
>
> They just didn't get it! At that point, I didn't know exactly what I wanted, but I knew I didn't want to be blamed or rescued ... just listened to and supported. I needed someone to help me figure out what *I* wanted to do.

Having experienced the helplessness, violation, and betrayal of a date rape, a woman needs to regain control over her life—to make her own decision about reporting the incident or pressing charges. It's not unusual for a woman to wait weeks or even months before she labels an act of unwanted intercourse as rape, and it may take even longer for her to reveal it to someone else. Recovery from rape, or indeed, from an attempted rape, is a long process. Most campuses now employ counselors who are equipped to help students who have suffered this trauma.

When a young woman calls home to talk about what has happened to her, parents can help by encouraging her to use campus resources. Though times such as these may stretch us to our emotional limits as parents, our children need us to listen, not judge; to be patient, understanding, and supportive.

Julie Steiner, Director of the University of Michigan's Sexual Assault Prevention and Awareness Center, offers parents the following advice:

> The first thing you should do is take two deep breaths, and then tell your daughter you have faith in her, and that you're really sorry this has happened. Emphasize that it's not her fault, and that the decisions about what to do are hers, and that you'll support her through this.
>
> Then I think you should go get support yourself. The feeling of helplessness, especially for parents who live far from their daughter's school is overwhelming. Supporting your daughter through this is very painful, and you're probably going to need help yourself.
>
> In addition to counseling and support from friends, I highly recommend Linda Ledray's sensitive and informative book, *Recovering from Rape.*

Students often respond intensely to the problems and tragedies that occur around them. A fellow student's attempted suicide, a rape, a fatal accident—any tragedy that powerfully shatters the illusion of invulnerability that cloaks the lives of college students—is likely to create ripples of distress throughout the campus. "I used to feel so invincible," said one student after the death of a classmate in a car accident. "Now it's never going to be the same again."

College faculty and administrators are on the alert when there is a suicide on campus. Such an event triggers thoughts of suicide in other students, and there is often an increase in attempts during the weeks following. Though many colleges don't report—or even keep—suicide statistics, suicide has been deemed the second leading cause of death among college-age people.

Students react, also, to the losses their classmates suffer. When one student's parents decide to get a divorce, his or her friends may start to feel anxious about the relationship of their own mother and father. And when the parent of a classmate becomes seriously ill or dies, intimate friends, and even acquaintances who happen to live in close quarters, feel the reverberations of the loss.

Some students become so entrenched in the problems of their friends that they feel virtually overtaken by a sense of responsibility to them—more responsibility than they can realistically handle. Although students often can help and support each other through difficulties, some problems do require professional intervention. In their concern for each other and desire to be helpful, young people often are unable to set appropriate boundaries. When parents become concerned about their child's overinvolvement with a depressed or suicidal friend, they might point out that their constant availability is impeding him or her from getting the professional help that is actually needed.

When Parents Visit School

Visits to students on their own turf have the potential for bringing new perspectives and delights—if parents are sensitive to their child's needs and agendas.

Some parents choose to visit on Parents' Weekends, specially planned occasions orchestrated to show off the college at its most hospitable. Others opt for a visit that fits more easily into their child's schedule or one that coincides with a particular event involving their youngster, such as a soccer game or a musical performance.

Most freshmen look forward to showing off their new home, new friends, and new selves to their families. They may look like the same young people who left home so recently, but the first few months of college seem like an eternity to them and they'd like their parents to take note and understand their lives. They may act surprisingly remote at first, suddenly feeling the vulnerability of their emerging independence. Or they may take charge, frenetically trying to introduce their parents to everyone and everything on campus.

A freshman at a small New England college describes how she felt about her parents' first visit to campus:

> I was nervous and excited when my parents said they were coming for Parents' Weekend. I wanted to show them my world, to show them where I go biking and where I take people on admissions tours. It's my home. I wanted them to see it and like it.
>
> I wanted them to meet my friends, but not for too long—like I didn't want them to hang out in my room. I wanted them to see the faces behind the names I'd been talking about. But I

was used to acting a certain way and kidding around with the guys next door. I was afraid Andrew and Rick would do something embarrassing in front of my parents—or that my parents would tell a dumb joke or tell a story about when I was little. At first it felt kind of weird to suddenly have all these parents around. But it all worked out fine. We kind of got back together as a family and had a fantastic time.

Not every freshman is this enthusiastic about parental visits. A senior from the Midwest recalls:

My mom kept asking me about Parents' Weekend freshman year. And I kept putting her off. I guess I just wasn't ready for her to come visit yet—maybe because I'd only been there a few months, and it still didn't feel like my place. I wasn't sure what I wanted, but she must have picked up my uncertainty, and I'm grateful for that. She waited until sophomore year to visit, and by then it was great to have her here.

Bubbles can burst when parents comment on the state of their child's room or clothes or shaggy hair. The weekend can turn sour if the visiting parent demands instant maturity and constant attention. Students expect to be able to continue their studying and social lives when their parents are in town. A delightful dinner together may deteriorate if parents are disappointed or angry when their child leaves for a party soon after the coffee has been served:

I learned the hard way that Parents' Weekend didn't mean that Doug would be with me the whole time. He had a paper to work on, and he slept in for the parent breakfast Sunday morning.

Tom and I realized that just as we had some rules and expectations when Heather came home for vacations, she had expectations of her own for us when we went to see her. We decided ahead of time that we were going to try to tune into her agenda instead of sticking to our own. For example, we were hoping to go to a class with her, but that clearly and emphatically was not o.k. with her. Once we got past the initial awkwardness, I felt almost euphoric seeing her in her world. I got a new sense of how in charge she is, of how much she feels at home there. Before we went I had questioned whether we could justify the

cost of the trip. Now it's a high priority for us to visit her at
school once a year.

Both divorced and married parents talk about the particular
pleasure of a solo visit to campus. A woman who recently spent
a day with her son while on a business trip to Boston reflects:

> I ended up going on a long afternoon walk with Dan and his
> girlfriend, making a couple of stops along the way for ice
> cream and a cappuccino. Then Dan and I went biking along the
> Charles and topped off the evening at his apartment, where he
> cooked dinner and his apartment mates wandered in and out.
> The music was blaring and the phone kept ringing, and I
> soaked in the whole scene in a way that just wouldn't have hap-
> pened if my husband had been with us. When I came home and
> told Steve about our day, he was jealous and decided that he's
> going to treat himself to his own visit sometime during the year.

Students who live off campus talk with pride of sprucing up
apartments and cooking meals for visiting dads and moms. It's
an opportunity for them to show off firsthand another step in
their growing competence. Although visits to college are
wonderful opportunities for students to share their world with
parents, most students still take great pleasure in old stand-by
parental pampering, such as a care package from home or a
special dinner out for them and their friends.

When Students Come Back Home

Visits home and long-awaited vacations often crystallize the
changes taking place across the miles. They evoke questions
about relationships and highlight a student's growing independence and separation. They may be particularly complicated
for the large number of students whose divorced parents live
in different households, sometimes in separate cities. Even
parents who have worked out custody and visitation arrangements long ago may suddenly find themselves locking horns
over where their son or daughter will spend most of their brief
college vacations.

And if parents divorce while their child is away at college,
the student has to grapple with questions of allegiances at the

same time he or she is trying to separate. It is a difficult combination. In the turmoil of their own distress, parents often minimize the blow of this news to their college-age children and may be surprised by the emotional fallout. College students still define themselves as part of a family, and the rupture to that family unit is usually a major jolt. They may be angry at their parents for splitting and although they may act cool about the whole situation, parents should not assume that their external reaction represents what they are feeling inside. It is important for parents to keep their antennae out for emotional reactions and to refrain from involving their child in their own conflicts.

"I've seen parents pull at a kid like a Gumby doll," said one director of residential life. "One kid who didn't want to face making the choice between the two of them went back to his home town for Thanksgiving and checked into a hotel with his brother."

A move to a new city can also be wrenching for college students, especially at vacation times. It makes separating more complicated and often has more of an impact on a youngster living away at school than parents realize. College students are at loose ends when returning home for vacations to a city without friends or familiar landmarks. Family rituals and traditions provide a sense of continuity and may be particularly important at such times. But young people may feel displaced when parents are their only link to this alien community. At a time when they are trying to separate, coming to a new home may throw them into an uncomfortable position of dependence. They may be testy or restless; they may want to leave and return to familiar places and high school friends. A sensitive and understanding parent will be flexible about vacation plans to accommodate this conflict.

A junior whose divorced parents have each moved twice since she started college comments:

> The worst time was freshman year when my mother moved out of the house I grew up in. I felt like a visitor when I went home. My mother's next move was to a whole different part of the country. After that move I did a lot of visiting over the

vacation; I went to my boyfriend's house. My parents didn't care, but my grandparents did.

Moving is a pain in the neck. Most of my stuff at my mother's place is in boxes. Things that are real important to me are here at school. School is more of a home than my official permanent address is.

Home is wherever I am at this point. In a lot of ways it's at school cause that's where my closest friends are. If any place really feels like home, it's where my grandparents are. I think of them as family and spend part of each of my vacations with them.

The first vacations of a student's college career are usually the most intense for everyone involved. Students and parents, eager to see each other, feel an unfamiliar tentativeness as the family comes together again. A junior at Tufts recalls:

I didn't go home until Christmas freshman year. It was really awful. I remember lying in bed crying the first night and thinking, Sara, you're not the same Sara who left here. I had come home with a bad cold and I was up half the night feeling terrible and confused. The next morning Mom looked at me kind of sad and asked why I wasn't happy to be home. She looked so let down.

Another student remembers wandering around his house, thinking, "I'm supposed to be different, but I don't really feel different."

And from the father of a Colby freshman:

We picked Andy up at the airport the day before Thanksgiving and, after the initial greetings and hugs, he just kept staring at us. As he got in the car, he looked at it and said, "Wow, our car—our same old car." He kept making remarks like that about all the familiar landmarks on the road back home, fast food restaurants he had frequented, even gas stations—anything he'd ever had any connection to.

His first few hours at home, he kept walking around the house, noticing every detail. He kept saying how quiet it was, and how weird it was to have all this space for four people. It was like he was trying to drink it all in, like he was trying to convince himself that it was all real. It took a while before we could just settle in and be with each other.

When students return home, most of them expect to find everything just the way they left it, as though time had stopped while they were gone. They prefer to find their rooms untouched and their siblings and parents just the way they always were. Yet, they also want their parents to recognize and respect that they have changed, that they have been living on their own and have become more independent. All this calls for a sense of balance—not to mention a sense of humor. And it is the rare family whose members do not find themselves trying to renegotiate relationships and expectations during these weeks between semesters.

Young people look at their families with the discerning eyes of outsiders, seeing, sometimes for the first time, qualities and dynamics they had never noticed before. They may be disillusioned at the less than perfect scene they see; it is likely to have been idealized during their months apart. Or, after observing the way their college friends or roommates interact with their families, they may appreciate aspects of their own home life that they previously had taken for granted. They cast disdainful glances at household changes, even simple improvements.

The mother of a Yale sophomore recalls:

> When Jeff came home freshman year, he was taken aback to find we had a computer and a microwave. He joked about it and said, "Hey! I'm the one who's supposed to go away to college and change, and now you've come into the twentieth century."
>
> We've had a family myth that we're not a technological family. That was part of Jeff's identity and we took it away from him. This year he came home and we had a VCR.

Some students react by being outwardly critical of family habits and patterns that have long been taken for granted: "Why do we have to eat dinner at such an uncivilized hour? Why don't the women in this family stand up for themselves? Why do we have to go to church? So what if you and Dad are divorced—can't you at least be civil to each other?"

They often bait their parents with newly learned, but as yet unintegrated, bits of philosophy and social consciousness.

They bristle at parental attempts to control their comings and goings, their behavior, or their schedules. Having been used to the independence of college life, yet feeling uncertain about their adult status within the context of the family, they may take rigid stances and balk at any suggestions offered:

> It hadn't entered my mind that I'd have to ask to use the car or answer so many questions like "Where are you going?" "What time will you be home?" "Who will you be with?" "Call if you're not home by 12:30." It was a chore.

> Can you believe it? My mother started getting upset about my shoes being left on the stairs? I mean, who cares!

> It's so weird after being independent to go home and have to be a son. What do you mean, clean up my room?

> My freshman year winter break, it was ten or ten-thirty at night, and I wanted to go out and get some coffee, and my mother said she didn't think it would be a good idea. We live in suburbia, not exactly dangerous. My mother said, "It's kind of late." I said, "It's ten-thirty. Are you insane?" And I walked out the door.

Parents may find it tricky to strike a balance between respecting their son or daughter's emerging independence, and wanting to run their household with some degree of order. They may need to modify some of their old rules in light of the increased independence their child has become accustomed to. Everything becomes even more complicated when divorced parents have conflicting sets of guidelines in their separate homes. Each family has to negotiate its own set of expectations, but says one freshman dean:

> There's bound to be some tension about rules and what needs to be said and done. Students are used to coming and going without reporting to anyone. I think it is fair for parents to expect the same things from their children that they would expect from a courteous guest. It's reasonable to expect them to pick up after themselves, and let you know whether or not they will be home for dinner and approximately when they will be in at night.

Students, too, talk of setting new guidelines with their parents after having lived away from home. One young woman describes how she convinced her mother to respect her need for quiet in the morning:

> I'm really in a foul mood when I get up. Unless it's an emergency, I'd rather not have people talk to me, and that was something I'd gotten used to at school. My roommate and I had made quiet pacts and didn't say a word to each other for the first hour we were up. When I told my mother I wanted to do that at home she was surprised, but it worked out okay.

In some households there's a sense of self-consciousness about how to reenter each others' lives. Students describe parents who suddenly treat them so much as equals that they lose the special quality of their relationship:

> All of a sudden I'm just another person in the house. My parents think I want to be treated as an adult, like their equal. I'm tired of all this independence. I really needed to go home to my mom and have her be a mom. Instead she wants to be my pal.

Others say they feel smothered and long for more parental recognition of their evolving independence:

> I want my parents to treat me as an equal. They baby me and don't seem to realize that I don't want them to do everything for me.

And one young man tells with an amused grin how his parents, each trying to welcome him home, acted like caricatures of their good intentions:

> I went home to a nursemaid and Buddy Hackett. My mom started washing my clothes and folding them for me. My dad started telling me dirty jokes, slapped me on the back, and said, "Hey, you want a beer, kid?"

By their very nature vacations are times of relaxation and pleasure, and many people approach them with anticipation and heightened expectations. Parents who take their cues from their returning college offspring report delightful moments of rediscovery and joy. Recognizing that this is, in fact, their son's or daughter's vacation, not theirs, they take pleasure in watching their youngster get together with friends and do not mind when he or she spends endless hours just unwinding around the house.

But as students arrive home geared up for rest and reconnecting with high school friends, many parents have their own, very different agendas . . . fantasies of special family outings, three weeks of unscheduled time for productive summer job-hunting, intimate moments alone with a maturing son or daughter. Such expectations are a trap and may lead to disappointed parents and resentful offspring.

Some parents save up their serious conversations for vacation times; they have plans of heart-to-heart talks with their child about excessive partying, poor grades, summer plans, or, perhaps the most stressful subject of all, their child's future. All of these are legitimate concerns, but timing is important and, without caution, discussions can become lectures that will turn off even the most receptive young person.

Often a simple open-ended question such as, "What's happening in your life?" or "How are things going?" gives students just the opportunity they've been waiting for to talk about what's on their minds. A young woman from Scripps remarks:

> It's tricky. I want my parents to know about my friends and what's going on with me, but if they ask too much it might feel intrusive. I think the best thing is for parents and kids to take some of the time when they're together over vacation to try to catch up. My father did that last semester when I was home. I was dating someone, and I had always brought it up on the phone and my parents had always let the subject drop. I can understand that. He's only the second guy I'd ever talked about seriously, and they probably didn't like handling that too much. I think that's a big deal for a parent.
>
> Anyway, over vacation my father made the biggest move he's ever made. He said, "So what's going on?" I let out a big sigh of relief and said, "I'm glad you asked. Let me tell you."
>
> We talked about four or five of my friends at school including the guy I was dating, and we had never done that before in the year and a half I had been there. We had discussed what courses I was taking and extracurriculars, but we hadn't dis-

cussed social life, which is a big part of my life. It's difficult to
have those kinds of conversations over the phone. I think vacations are really the best time when you can just sit after dinner
and talk. For me it was the ideal situation; my mom and sisters
had gone to the movies, and Dad and I were sitting by ourselves. It was just the two of us, and it's easier for me to talk to
my parents one on one. They have different styles and different
responses to what I say.

Some students plan to talk to their parents about issues of
major concern during vacations rather than by letter or phone.
A gay student from Iowa describes the painful process of
coming out to his father during the winter vacation of his
sophomore year.

I'd always known I wasn't attracted to females, but I kept praying it would change. I kept hoping when I got to college I'd
start over and things would be different. I did become very attracted to someone, but that someone was a male; I realized I
couldn't fool myself anymore.

My mother died when I was in high school. My Dad and I
have always been very close—which, by the way, destroys the
stereotype about homosexuals having cold, distant, or absent
fathers. I wanted to tell him, and I knew eventually that he
would accept it, but I was still worried about his reaction.

During Christmas break, I got my courage up and told him.
Initially, he was very accepting, calm, and supportive. He said,
"You're my son. I still love you. Nothing changes. I just want
you to be happy."

The first time I became involved with someone, however,
he reversed a bit. He was very upset that I was comfortable
with it and that I was really planning to go ahead and live my
life this way. I hesitated bringing my friend home at spring
vacation. After several phone conversations, my Dad seemed
to have become more resolved. He said, "Of course come
home and bring him. If he's someone you care about, I want to
meet him."

This young man acknowledged that he had the "near-perfect
coming out" and that many of his friends went through a much
more traumatic time. Some have been banished from their
families; the parents of others desperately try to find ways to
"cure" their children through psychotherapy, religion, or by

actively encouraging heterosexual relationships. And still others pretend they do not know and make it clear they do not want to talk about it. All of these negative responses lead to alienation and distancing between parent and child.

The student quoted above was sensitive to the shock and pain his father would go through. Both father and son had built a strong foundation of trust and communication, which allowed them to get through some tension-filled times and to become closer. They recognized that these first awkward conversations are part of an ongoing process—a process that began long ago with their evolving relationship and will continue as each moves through his own difficult journey ahead.

Parents often need information and support when their children confront them with the news that they are gay. And the students, themselves, find it encouraging when their parents take it upon themselves to become informed. *Beyond Acceptance* by Carolyn Griffin and Marian and Arthur Wirth and *Coming Out to Parents* by Mary Borhek are among several sensitive and informative books on the subject. And the national self-help organization, Parents and Friends of Lesbians and Gays (Parents FLAG) has groups in all parts of the United States that have helped provide information as well as support for those in need.

For many parents vacations are a bittersweet time. Just when they thought they had gotten used to a quieter household, it fills up again with the music and laughter and exuberance of college students. Their children's friends drop by and reminisce about their old childhood capers, and share tales of their current college exploits. Suddenly there isn't enough milk in the refrigerator and the phone rings every five minutes as plans for the evening are made and remade. The dinner table crackles with the excitement of newly discovered passions, academic and otherwise, and everything seems a bit livelier than it had been. Of course, the dinner table is also the setting for the replay of sibling bickering and volatile outbursts about trivial matters: Who gets the car tonight? What TV shows do we watch? What do you mean, borrowing my sweater without asking? For most parents, however, the squabbles and the McDonald's wrappers in the car and the pile of towels on the bathroom floor seem a small burden to bear compared to the joy of reconnecting as a family.

"But," says a Wisconsin mother of a sophomore and a senior, "even though it's great to have them back, there's a certain sadness. You realize that it will never be the same again; they are not totally home. They have a whole different world that is part of them, and they are only temporary visitors."

And, indeed, most parents do find that as their children progress through their college years and become more separate, their visits home take on a distinctly different quality. Students' eagerness to return home and reconnect with family and friends freshman year typically gives way to a more tempered reentry in the years that follow. As upperclassmen, they may become more distant, more protective of their separateness. Many say they don't feel as though they really belong anywhere. School isn't home, and home is no longer the center of their lives.

A Hawaiian woman whose only child attends the University of Santa Clara in California found herself facing a whole new level of adjustment between her daughter's sophomore and junior years:

> It hit me during the summer that this may be her last summer home, the last time she'll be with us for a whole three months. The reality is that there are very few jobs here, and she probably won't be coming back here for a long period of time again.

Students may return less often or set clearer boundaries of separateness when they do come back. Sometimes their behavior is confusing, sometimes humorous, and sometimes painful. Many go through periods of strident distancing before they can reconnect comfortably with their parents on more mutual terms.

The father of a sophomore describes a discrepancy between the way his son relates to him over the phone and the way he wants to interact when he comes home for vacations:

> Kevin calls a lot from school when things aren't going well. He calls to complain about courses or girls who gave him the cold shoulder, almost anything that's on his mind; he describes how

he's feeling—if he's depressed or anxious or questioning what he's doing there.

Then when he gets home, all the things he needs to talk to us about when he's at school suddenly seem not to be issues anymore. But of course they still are. It's just, I think that he feels safer talking about them when he's at school. We can be a long-distance sounding board. But when he's in our house, he might be swallowed up by us. It's too threatening. He's very quiet here, and I think we need to respect that.

And the mother of an in-town student who lives in the residence halls reports:

When Abby was a freshman, she used to come home every week to do her laundry, and she'd spend a lot of time talking to me. She said the washing machines weren't very good. This year she's a sophomore, and she never comes home to do her laundry. It's funny; they're the same washing machines as last year.

A divorced mother of two describes the abrupt change in her older daughter's behavior during the summer between her junior and senior years:

Libby used to tell me everything. Sometimes I worried that she was too dependent on me as a confidante. Her father left home when she was thirteen, and she and I had some rocky years together. Anyway, we were very close. But last summer when she came home it was as though she put a curtain down between us. She barely spoke to me. I knew she'd been going through a hard time at school, but she didn't want to talk about that or anything else. It was really a strain having her around all summer and getting the silent treatment. But I kept telling myself that there was a method to her madness, that she really needed to pull back from me.

Now that she's back at school, we've had a few good talks over the phone. It's not the same as it used to be, but at least we're talking again.

As students mature they increasingly look at their parents as separate people, not just Mom and Dad. After a long absence, they may see signs of aging they had never noticed before. They shed their self-absorption and begin to feel more empathy for the stresses and struggles of their parents' lives. A young woman, a junior at Washington University, observes:

> I've noticed changes in my parents lately, especially my dad. I think he's changing as he's watching his parents get old and is responding to things differently. My dad is going through the kind of changes my mom went through a few years ago when her parents died. Right now my dad's mother is very sick and his father is not doing so well either. In the last six months my dad has had to take over the role of taking care of both of them. I think he feels the burden of a lot of responsibility. I also think he's analyzing what happened in his parents' lives and the way they dealt with him. I'm not sure what the outcome of that will be, but I've already seen a change. I think he's becoming more sensitive. I also think he's feeling very pressured, watching his parents get old before his eyes, and sometimes I feel some of that pressure. For instance, if I come home from school with an incomplete, it feels like a disappointment to him. I think he needs as few problems as possible. I think he needs nurturing. He's having to nurture his parents and his kids, and I think he needs some of that nurturing back.

The pleasures and pains of parenthood are highlighted during the periods throughout the college years when children reenter the household. There is the joy of seeing a child develop—listening to her describe the way she is going to improve the school literary magazine, or watching him explain to his little brother what archaeology is and why he is so excited about it. It is rewarding to see evidence of burgeoning intellectual capacities and self-confidence that may have been apparent in letters and phone calls, but bring a more poignant delight to parents in the course of daily interaction.

When children return home with problems, however, their disappointments and pain become part of their parents' day-to-day existence too. It hurts to see a child in the throes of misery from a broken romance, or filled with self-doubt, or struggling with a weight problem. It is more difficult to separate your pain from theirs when they are at home; their unhappiness is a constant presence.

And parents are reminded, also, of bothersome traits in their children—traits that had faded temporarily from their memories in the glow of eagerly awaited letters and phone calls from their distant college offspring. They may find themselves worrying about behaviors they hadn't thought about for a while and wondering, "How can this budding engineer consistently leave the gas tank on empty and never replace the toilet paper on the roll?" Or, "She doesn't know how to lose an argument. How will she ever sustain a relationship or hold down a job?"

Parental anxiety often gives way to renewed attempts to control, to take another stab at trying to "set this kid on the right track." In their more rational moments parents know, of course, that such attempts are doomed to failure.

As students move through their college years, their early experiments begin to turn into commitments—and these commitments may be in conflict with parents' own dreams and values. The mother who was amused by her son's "granola stage" freshman year now has to come to terms with the fact that he has decided to become a forest ranger rather than a lawyer as originally planned. The father who hardly gave a second glance to the silent, sulking boyfriend his daughter brought home freshman and sophomore years begins to wonder if he is going to be a permanent fixture in the family. As they decide who they are and how they want to live their lives, students make choices about their majors and careers, about religion and values, about sexual preference and intimate partners. When they return home, these loaded issues leap to the forefront and parents come face to face with the essence of letting go.

Chapter 8
SOPHOMORE SLUMP
AND THE YEARS BEYOND

Did you feel when you first came to college that it all was so new and exciting, such a big change from home? By spring it began to be a little routine, and this fall here you are taking these courses and it's much the same and you don't really know what you're here for and you don't know why you're taking *these* courses rather than any other courses. You're sleeping a lot, but still always seem to feel tired. Maybe you're just blowing off—sitting in the library, staring at the same page for forty minutes; maybe you're going out and eating pizza when you know you should be doing your problem sets, but you just can't focus your attention.

"That sounds like me," a bewildered sophomore responds, wondering how his dean knows so much about his lethargic state these past few months. This dean of a highly respected and academically rigorous university is not a psychic, nor does she have informants waiting in the wings. She has just described the common phenomenon known as "sophomore slump" to a student she had summoned to her office for a discussion about a failing grade.

The sophomore slump doesn't always happen sophomore year; some experience a similar state during the second half of their freshman year or when they are juniors or seniors, and some don't experience it at all. But the sophomore year has particular characteristics that make it an unsettling time of self-doubt and vulnerability for many students.

What happens to the energetic and enthusiastic freshmen of just a year before? What happens to their intense and often quixotic responses to the college environment, that beckoning world with new intellectual vistas and few social restraints?

One might expect the second year of college to be a repetition of the first, perhaps a bit more stable since the sophomore has the advantage of knowing the ropes. The sophomore slump, though a common colloquialism, comes as a surprise to both parents and their children.

Sophomores return to school without the anxiety and hoopla of orientation that launched them the year before. Most are happy to be back and eagerly seek out friends and old haunts. They bask in their sense of belonging as they watch the glassy-eyed freshmen stumble by. Once school is under way, the peaks and valleys of the academic year—marked off by exams, vacations, and traditional college events—are reassuringly familiar. But the second college year intrudes with new choices, new responsibilities, and new problems to solve. The worlds of college sophomores are substantially different from their freshmen counterparts.

Sophomores, no longer the "new kids" on the block, are responsible for themselves in ways that they hadn't been the year before. They don't have a freshman advisor holding their hands while picking courses. They are expected to know the system by now, and they are often embarrassed to let others know when they don't. No one is eagerly showing them how to use the library or computer center or guiding them to the remote corners of the campus. Campus groups are no longer clamoring for their membership; and everyone assumes that sophomores know from their own experience what it means to belong to a particular fraternity, team, or club. No one assigns them a roommate; the choices and the consequences are their own. If they don't get along, they can't chalk it up to a glitch in the computer matching system or the misguided whims of the residential life staff. They may feel both comforted and confined by their friends from the previous year, but the potential for making new friends no longer seems unlimited. And intimate relationships may suffer the strain of unexpected changes after a summer apart. Some sophomores move off-campus into an apartment, especially in large, overcrowded universities, undertaking a whole new range of tasks and responsibilities.

As one administrator put it, "No one is loving you up anymore, whether it is the RA, an advisor, or your parents; and at the same time you're betwixt and between in your academic life."

Academically, sophomores know enough to recognize how little they know. Though they are developing the tools that will allow them to do the more creative work later on, they wonder if they will ever be able to master anything—whether they have what it takes to be as competent and knowledgeable as the juniors and seniors they admire. They haven't yet delved into the meat of the substantive, specialized courses, and in many schools they are still relegated to large lecture classes. If they haven't picked a major and affiliated with a particular department, they have no academic home. The few who have collected enough advanced placement credits to move into upper-level courses may have difficulty competing with the juniors and seniors who already know the academic ropes and can handle what one dean refers to as the "rapier cut and thrust of the classroom discussion and the put-downs that accompany it." These gifted students find their upper-level courses stimulating, but may feel like failures and question their own ability, perhaps for the first time.

The freedoms that sophomores celebrated the previous year haunt them now. The choices still seem endless—choices of courses, friends, and activities; choices of politics, religion, and lifestyle; choices of stopping out, transferring, or a year abroad. But they think more about the consequences of their choices than they used to. Making one choice means relinquishing others; choosing means taking responsibility for the choice. All the while, time is running out. In most colleges and universities, by the end of sophomore year, students are expected to choose a major, and the pressure of career choice is not far behind.

The Slump—More or Less

> I felt like the character in the roadrunner cartoon—you know, running frantically full speed ahead, straight off of a cliff—and that awful moment when he looks down and realizes there's no

ground under him—that he's just out there by himself in the
middle of the air. That's how I felt most of sophomore year.

Forging ahead with enthusiasm and eagerness, students may
discard—though often temporarily—the values their parents
hold dear. Now, as they are pressured to make decisions about
their own futures, many become aware of the void that is left.
Though some youngsters attend religious or culturally
homogeneous institutions that confirm family values, the
majority of today's college students are surrounded by the
diverse points of view of their classmates and professors. For
them college functions, in large part, as culture shock. They are
exposed to many so-called right answers all backed up by
rational arguments. How can all these answers be true?

Many sophomores not only question their parents' values
and choices, but the very possibility of making rational choices
at all. As they move beyond a dualistic view of the world, one
idea seems as worthwhile as the next. They feel off balance and
disoriented; nothing seems solid. Seeking answers, they find
only questions. "Why am I taking this course?" "How can
behaviorists and Freudians both be valid?" "I always thought
physics was great, but why is physics better than philosophy?"
"Why am I at this school?" "What difference will it make if I
stay or transfer?" "What is the purpose of education?" "What
is the meaning of my life?"

They describe their experience as "tenuous," "arbitrary,"
"meaningless." They describe themselves as "fragmented,"
"seasick," "rootless." Frequently students look inside themselves and feel lost and immobilized. Their reactions range
from hedonistic escape to existential angst.

A Brandeis student recalls:

Sophomore year everyone collapsed—or at least my friends
and I did. It was a year of questioning. What's the point of
doing anything in life? What does it all mean? What is this all
about? "Being and Nothingness" was the name of the game.

Parents may be taken aback by unexpected phone calls from a normally upbeat child who is suddenly questioning the meaning of life. Said the mother of one sophomore:

> Madeline called at midnight talking about God and death. She's taking a course about aging and death, and she was distraught. After forty-five minutes of listening, I finally told her I just had to get some sleep. I suggested that she talk to someone there—a chaplain or counselor—and I'd call her the next day after I got home from work.

When asked about his sophomore year, a University of Chicago student responds:

> All through my sophomore year I was unhappy. I was losing sight of what it all meant. It was kind of a masturbatory philosophical question, because there really wasn't any answer to it. It was just, where am I headed—what does this mean? I got so wrapped up in trying to solve that one that I neglected the present. I was real unsure of myself. There weren't a whole lot of black and white standards to deal with. Nothing was concrete.
>
> It seemed like I was spinning my wheels with school work. Nothing seemed to make much difference. I would turn in the token paper for the token class, making the points that they grade on. It wasn't doing me any good. It just seemed really trivial at the time, like a big spoon of cough medicine that everyone has to take at some time.

Some students, such as this young man, become paralyzed by their own introspection. Caught like a gerbil continually spinning the wheel in his cage, they may try to alleviate their anxiety with numbing devices: drugs, alcohol, or a series of meaningless sexual liaisons. Some look outside themselves and impulsively grab hold of a group or ideology for support—a fraternity, a women's center, a political group or, for a few, the rigid structure of a cult. Others, aware of a general malaise but unable to pinpoint the source, decide to transfer or take time off, hoping to find solutions elsewhere. Even those sophomores who continue to be actively engaged in their studies and social environment are often caught off guard by periods of confusion and disenchantment.

A young woman from Ohio, now a vibrant and self-confident junior, looks back on her sophomore year:

> I had done really well second semester freshman year, and I came back to school thinking I know how the system works now. But it was a real struggle. I thought, now I'm just going to sail through with A's and B's the whole way. But I took classes I had no background in—a computer class, accounting, Spanish. They were all tedious and time-consuming, and I felt very inadequate. Spanish was the first class I ever took where I studied and didn't see results. The only thing that kept me studying was the fear that if I didn't, I was going to fail. At one point that almost sounded better. If you fail, at least you can say that it's impossible, that you just can't do it. If you get C's and D's you always question if you could do better.
>
> I had already decided to major in English, but I had a bad experience in the first E. Lit course I actually took. My professor's comments on my first paper basically said—learn to write or get out. I felt outclassed because there were a lot of seniors in the class. I felt there was a gaping hole between what I needed to know and what I knew. I went to talk to my professor, and he wasn't very reassuring about it.
>
> On top of this, I had been invited to participate in a Women's Leadership Training Institute. We met monthly and it brought up a lot of issues I was ready to deal with. Thank God for WLTI! But it also brought up problems in a relationship I was in. I became angry at my boyfriend as I became more aware of things. I started thinking, I'm a woman first, what does that mean?
>
> I started looking at what I wanted to do with my life. And how does my English major fit in? I think I spent the year saying, is this what I'm cut out for? Does this tap into some wonderful resource I have in me, or am I just going to struggle along like this the whole way? I remember feeling tired a lot.

In the midst of all this questioning, students wonder whether the financial commitment they and their parents are making is worth it. Financial sacrifices and the specter of loans to be repaid weigh heavily on students who feel unmotivated and unproductive:

> My sophomore year was a very tenuous time for me. I was very frightened. I was afraid I was drifting apart from my friends at home. I wasn't quite sure where I was going, what

direction. I had no solid ground to pin myself to intellectually. I was aware of time flying by. Tuition was going up each year. What did I have to show for it?

Some sophomores who don't feel the unsettling ennui of the slump describe an almost manic sense of excitement that can be unsettling in its own right. Each new course they take uncovers another academic possibility, another world waiting to be discovered. They ask themselves, "Is this the department I want to settle in? Is this the subject I want to master?" Or, stimulated by the interests of their classmates, they take up one hobby after another—playing the guitar five hours a day, then turning with equal intensity to ultimate frisbee or lyric poetry.

A sophomore at Dartmouth describes her second year there as "fantastic," but adds:

> Sometimes my head is reeling from all the choices. When I look at the catalogue before registration I get excited—and confused. There's so much I want to study. My parents probably think I'm nuts each time I call home with a different idea about what I want to major in. Right now I'm into philosophy—eighteenth century. And 1 love Italian. Maybe I'll combine that with art history and spend time in Italy next year.

While all this is happening at school, students continue to loosen the ties to home. Loyalties shift from family and high school friends to college friends, suitemates, and lovers. Students who conscientiously used up their roll of one hundred postage stamps freshman year barely make it to the mailbox as sophomores. Though new connections are beginning to replace the old, sophomores often talk about feeling lonely and adrift. They describe their feeling as a sense of aloneness in the world rather than a dearth of friends.

Many college students live in a world devoid of meaningful contact with adults. As sophomores they are unlikely to have developed the close relationships with faculty that are usually the purview of juniors and seniors who have immersed themselves in the seminars and research projects of their major department. Even in small schools that pride themselves on their accessible faculty, underclassmen are often too shy and intimidated to seek them out. It is not unusual for sophomores to go through the whole year without ever having an intimate conversation with someone over twenty-two years of age. No benevolent housemother is hovering over them; for adult relationships they must take initiative to seek out head residents, deans, faculty, student activities personnel, or chaplains.

Disturbed by a feeling of rootlessness, students reach out to one another. Friendships that were formed freshman year may begin to deepen and thrive. Some unravel, however, as students continue to develop new interests and venture forth from the pack:

> I moved into a suite sophomore year. We were all good friends and we thought, this is going to be so much fun living together. And the first two weeks were fun, but then each person got singled out—"be mean to Sue week." It was a mess. We had a huge fight at the end.
>
> We'd been so similar freshman year. We were all freshmen in the same boat, all gained ten pounds, all were homesick. We came back and we started to choose majors and meet more people and expand our circle of friends, and we didn't like each other's friends or the habit of smoking that one picked up—a lot of petty things—but we were establishing our own identities. Sophomore year I started solidifying the me that people know and the me that I know.

Longing for intimacy and continuity as well as new adventures, many students talk about their dashed expectations. From a University of Pennsylvania sophomore:

> I thought when I started my sophomore year, now I can choose my roommate and where I'm going to live and I know people. It's going to be great. But I found out things were pretty much the same. I wanted to meet new people, do new activities, study in new places. I was intimidated by people already having friends. The friendships I have here seem so artificial and unsatisfying. I haven't really found something yet that's for me, and the older guys are checking out the freshmen girls now.

Questions of identity and intimacy are intertwined, as young men and women refine their definitions of themselves through their relationships with each other. They treasure the intimacy of being a couple, yet strive to protect themselves from getting lost in the twosome. Particularly those who live in the same dorm, sometimes even on the same floor, struggle to be identified as individuals instead of one half of a whole. The constant, "Where's Becky?" that he hears as he walks down the hall, the guilt that she feels as she moves quickly past his door without stopping in—these incessant reminders echo in the thoughts of committed couples, and as a result, they may start to pull away from each other.

In all arenas of their lives, there is pressure on sophomores to define themselves and begin to take a stand. Marion Hyson, associate professor of individual and family studies at the University of Delaware believes that the issue of control is at the crux of a lot of problems students face during sophomore year:

> Many feel little sense of control over their own destinies. They feel trapped by the choices they made freshman year—choices about friends, fraternities or sororities, roommates, and courses. They have to declare a major, but feel constrained by family and social agendas. They are pulled in different directions, asked to make choices and live with the consequences.

Those not ready to make commitments are most vulnerable to the sophomore slump. For some this is an important though painful time. In an article for a Princeton parents newsletter, a junior describes the unexpected slump he experienced and the effect it had on him:

> In my case, and I think in most cases, the slump did not result in disastrous grades. Underneath the decent marks, however, lay an academic dissatisfaction and a temporary lack of desire to learn. Curiosity waned, and reading became a task rather than a joy. If I took anything from the aimlessness of sophomore year, it was the insight that comes from having no direction. . . .
>
> In retrospect, it may have been necessary to waste time. For many Princetonians, high school was an intense, harried experience. Freshman year at college is a matter of survival. Total confusion forces new students to be on their toes.

Sophomore year is the transition between wide-eyed awe and upperclass confidence. The slump may not be as much a sin as a temporary hibernation, a time for the mind to sleep and to wake up refreshed.

At this vital and energetic stage of life, standing still and feeling stuck can be almost unbearable. Kenneth Keniston, noted author and social psychologist, writes of the "enormous value placed upon change, transformation and movement" of young men and women, and their panic, "when confronted with the feeling of 'getting nowhere,' of 'being stuck in a rut,' or of 'not moving.' " [1]

In the past, young people projected their desire for motion outward toward social and political causes—the women's movement, the peace movement, the civil rights movement. The restlessness of youth was captured in books and film, from *On the Road* to *Easy Rider,* and in the alteration of self through transcendental meditation or psychedelic drugs. Today's generation of students channels its need for movement primarily into the world of upward mobility, the fast track of career, status, and power—a world of adulthood that some sophomores view as the ultimate trap. And so they procrastinate, stagnate, spin their wheels, until they find it intolerable and begin to make decisions.

The Major Decision

I declared my English major in September and then spent the rest of my sophomore year investigating it.

I changed from architecture to urban studies and sociology. I'd wanted to be an architect since sixth grade. It was hard to change. It was hard to lose the identity I'd built up over all those years. I didn't tell my parents about it until first semester junior year.

Horrendous, horrifying! Here at Harvard, we call them fields of concentration and most of us change at least six times.

In high school I was president of the computer club. When I got to Oberlin, I hated math. I took an anthropology course and loved it and decided to major in it. There was a lot of pressure from my parents to make a choice, to choose a road. My parents didn't care what I majored in as long as I chose something.

Working as an engineer seems great, but I'm not wild about engineering school so far. I love metalsmithing in the Fine Arts School more than anything else I've done here. But switching doesn't seem practical.

The pressure to choose a major starts as early as the sophomore and junior years in high school when students fill out the forms for the Preliminary Scholastic Aptitude Tests. Fifteen- and sixteen-year-olds are asked to indicate their academic and career interests, and the computer code for undecided always seems to be double zero. Most college admissions offices request similar information from applicants, conveying the message that before students even come to college they are supposed to know what they want to study and what career they wish to pursue.

It is not unusual for parents to apologize to admissions officers on behalf of a child who "hasn't decided what he wants to do yet," as though being open to all kinds of possibilities is some sort of deficiency. In response to this parental anxiety, one admissions officer always replies by asking the parent how old the child is, knowing full well that a prospective college student is likely to be seventeen or eighteen. He then says incredulously, "Well, that seems perfectly normal to me. Most people don't know what they want to do with the rest of their lives when they are seventeen. Did you?"

There are, of course, those rare young people, driven by their talents and passions, who know they are destined to become musicians or computer jocks or entrepreneurs. When one such student was asked by a professor if she still wanted to be a dancer, she looked at him with eyes flashing and said, "It's not a matter of what I *want*. It's what I *am!*"

But such commitment and certainty is exceptional among the young, and despite the careerist era in which we live, most entering college students are not sure what they want to study. And even those who claim they know are likely to change their minds. Dean Anne Schroer of Washington and Lee, for instance, estimates that only 15 percent of freshmen really know what they want to pursue. And in a 1986 survey of University of Virginia alumni, fewer than 10 percent said they had a very clear direction when they graduated.

But on most college campuses the mythology prevails among sophomores that, "everybody else seems to know what they want to major in and what they want to do for the rest of their lives." Rumors run rampant about which departments are good, and what the future holds in store for its graduates. Each campus has particular departments that are held in high esteem by students, and others that command little respect. Some schools are stridently preprofessional; others are more supportive of the liberal arts. Everywhere, stereotypes abound. Choosing a major not only means choosing a course of study, it means selecting a niche on campus—assuming an identity as "an intellectual philosopher," "a no-nonsense computer scientist," or "a far-out artist." When students meet each other, one of the first questions they ask is, "What's your major?" And the response elicits a set of assumptions, an initial code for sizing each other up.

A young woman may feel defensive about picking a traditionally female field such as social work or education. On some campuses she is likely to catch flak from her peers who have more respect for the hard sciences and preparation for the high status professions than they do for the humanities and helping professions. Jokes about majoring in "play dough" or "sandbox" quickly wear thin, and some education and child development students even contemplate changing majors as a result of repeated taunting.

Today's business and engineering students complain about being stereotyped by their peers in the humanities and social sciences who make assumptions about their motivation: "I get tired of everyone making comments about me going for the big bucks," said a sophomore in mechanical engineering. "I'm in engineering because that's what I'm good at and that's what I like."

In making a decision about a major, students weigh their own interests with concerns about status and image and future opportunities. They may feel pulled in different directions by parents and peers and faculty, all trying to help—all sure that they know what's best for the student.

In an ironic twist of the women's movement, mothers pressure their daughters to stick to architecture or engineering, or other fields that used to be the realm of male students twenty-five or thirty years ago. Urging their daughters to take advantage of opportunities they never had themselves, they unwittingly present them with a new set of constraints that make independent choices stressful.

Those students who enter the university with a specific and pragmatic career goal in mind pick the major that fits their career choice. That seems simple enough, but often the career goal of an eighteen-year-old is based more on image than a realistic understanding of the demands of the course of study and the career itself. When a physical therapy student who wants to help people, but doesn't like science, looks ahead to the long sequence of required science courses; or an engineering student realizes that an aptitude for mathematics isn't necessarily synonymous with an interest in engineering, a change is in the offing. That change can be upsetting, particularly when the student is uncertain about what to study instead. And parents are often upset when their child makes an alternative choice based more on passion for the subject than pragmatic career preparation. Students and parents worry about time lost, about getting "off the track" when time is precious and tuition costs are high.

Premeds who change their minds—and many of them do—often have a particularly difficult time giving up their identity as a premed. Long after they've decided that they're not interested in the studies or the career, or they've realized that they simply don't stand a chance of gaining admissions to medical school, many students struggle with finding new academic and career goals.

Some of these students, referred to by one administrator as "prenatal premeds," had never actually made a choice to be premed in the first place. They may have been successful in high school science and, swept along by the enthusiasm of their teachers and parents, they began to think of themselves as premed. Or they may have come from a family of physicians and merely assumed that they would follow in the family tradition. When these students decide to change, they are taking a big step in separating from their parents and asserting their independence. Unfortunately, some parents make it difficult for them to do so. Perhaps finding it painful to give up the dream of "my child the doctor," and failing to separate their own goals from those of their son or daughter, they refuse to accept the impending change of plans. Some parents respond with accusations or sighs of disappointment; others go as far as threatening not to pay tuition for any course of study except one leading to medical school.

A former premed describes her change of heart and her father's subsequent disappointment:

> I was a gung ho premed, but I started changing my mind first semester. Competition here was really fierce. I think that little spark in me started to dull and when I'd go to these classes with two or three hundred people, half had already had AP chemistry, and I was struggling for the first time.
>
> I had a couple of so-called friends tell me the wrong way to do problems before first semester finals. They thought it was funny and said, "Oh well, we're cutthroat premeds." I started realizing that part of my excitement about premed was connected to my father's thrill that I had decided to go preprofessional. I started realizing I wasn't totally doing this for myself. I started looking around and began to realize I'd enjoy and do better in psychology and sociology. And that's what I've double-majored in, much to my father's chagrin. He still keeps telling me I'd make a good psychiatrist.

Many parents, wanting to assure their son or daughter a secure and satisfying life, exert a tremendous pressure on students to follow a clear-cut professional route. Even parents who simply give offhand suggestions have more influence than they realize. Students often experience their comments as demands. Aside from explicit expectations, there are often implicit family norms. If the parents are successful in a particular field, they set expectations by their example. So do older siblings, whether they realize it or not.

According to Ernest Boyer's report of the Carnegie Foundation study, 90 percent of college-bound high school students and 88 percent of their parents rank "to have a more satisfying career" as a very important reason for going to college. So it is not surprising that discussions about majors inevitably lead to the question: What are you going to *do* with *that?* And when the proposed major is a subject like comparative literature or history, the question often is asked with an air of obvious skepticism. Indeed many students who become enamored of a liberal arts discipline, ask the question of themselves.

They are, in a sense, asking themselves the wrong question. They might ask instead, "What kind of an impact will these studies have on me? Who might I become, how might I view the world, and what skills might I develop if I begin to master this particular discipline?"

President Mary Patterson McPherson of Bryn Mawr College urges parents not to worry if their daughter calls home and says that she is going to major in Latin, or any other subject. She says:

> In my view, it doesn't matter a hoot what your daughter majors in. What matters is that she loves the subject; that she can work creatively and freely in it; that she's learning what we have to teach her. And what we have to teach her is not content. We teach her approach, methodology. We're honing her faculties, her skills. We're letting her find her intellectual strengths and measure her own weaknesses, and it doesn't matter what we're doing it in. And the fact that she does it in Latin may mean she'll be a much better lawyer or a much better doctor, which many of them go on to be anyway, not professors of Latin, though excellent professors of Latin are needed as well.

Nevertheless, students tend to attach an enormous importance to choice of a major. They are reluctant to believe it when their deans or advisors tell them that there is no *right* major, and that in most cases their major will not determine their career. In a University of Virginia survey of arts and sciences alumni, seven out of ten reported that, "no matter what their major, the broad educational background of liberal arts was much more important on the job than any specific educational training."[2]

Dean Linda Salamon of George Washington University comments:

> It really doesn't matter what students major in. But it's important for a student to major in something. An important part of intellectual development is beginning to have some sense of mastery over a body of material, to be able to get your arms around a discipline. You get a sense of the variety of analytical tools that are brought to bear in this discipline, the kinds of questions it asks and those it doesn't. With luck, with good faculty, you learn some of its mistakes and dead ends.
>
> You can get that kind of sense from English, political science, or geology. You'll get some idea of causation, some sense that things can be divided into component parts. In any discipline you will learn to make reasoned judgments, to develop fundamental intellectual skills—to analyze, synthesize, and express yourself. What we are giving students is power, the tools to teach themselves a new subject during the rest of their lives, the ability to approach a new mass of material and say, okay, how do I start? That's the real world skill that a major is all about.

Some students are comfortable with exploring. They may take a long time to decide on a major and enjoy the academic journey. Others are so anxious about making their choice that they are reluctant to experiment. Says University of Delaware professor, Marion Hyson:

> Many of our students find it hard to justify to themselves or their parents the value of taking anthropology or musicology. I wish they could see that the period of time they're settling on a major is not just spinning wheels. They're developing skills of pursuing certain kinds of inquiry and self-expression. As sophomores, some start to make connections in their minds between different fields of studies and disciplines. That can be very exciting in itself.

For some students, however, lack of a focus is so uncomfortable that they may find it hard to concentrate on their studies. They complain about being unmotivated and may consider

leaving school. They desperately want to make a decision, to
have a goal. George Washington University's Dean Salamon
suggests that these students invest in temporary choices. She
urges them to "try out" their interests and tells them,

> If you think you're interested in psychology, try it out. Get
> into it. Really get into it. Take several psych courses. Work in
> a child development center. If you don't like it, come back
> and we'll talk about it.
>
> Negative choices are terribly important. Being able to
> shut doors is just wonderful. Sometimes when we close doors,
> we open others. Sometimes when we narrow the perspective
> somewhat, we can move on.

With all this talk about majors, it is important to remember
that a major usually constitutes about a third of the courses a
student will take in college. For most students, especially in
liberal arts, there is plenty of opportunity to plan a curriculum
that complements and supplements the courses in the major
department. More students today are choosing double majors,
or a combination major and minor. They are combining business and English literature, French and international development, sociology and computer science. They are straddling the
humanities and technology; they are pursuing their intellectual
passions and pragmatic skills.

Most colleges and universities, mindful of the liberal arts/
preprofessional dichotomy, have introduced numerous opportunities to combine the two. Internships and cooperative education programs offer students hands-on experience while still
in school. And career-related part-time and summer jobs supplement many students' traditional academic fare.

A junior math major at Duke, who was actively involved
in the performing arts, had no idea what she was planning to
do after graduation, until she stumbled upon a summer job in
the education department of a major symphony orchestra, and
loved it. Arts administration seemed to combine her organiza-
tional skills and facility with numbers with her interest in the
arts. Upon her return to school in her senior year, she was able
to gain administrative experience by doing an internship with

a local dance festival and producing the campus fall musical rather than acting in it. By using her imagination and initiative, along with the resources of the university and the community, this young woman was free to immerse herself in the intellectual challenge of higher mathematics while developing marketable skills for a career in arts administration.

This kind of inventiveness is increasingly common among today's students. An English major who capitalized on her experience as an orientation leader eventually wrote a handbook for parents' orientation and was sent to the National Orientation Directors' Conference by her college. A double major in Spanish and international relations did a summer internship at the International Trade Administration in Washington, and was invited to do research for them the following academic year. An economics major, who took a year off to work at the Chicago Stock Exchange, returned to finish his academic work while interning in the production department of a public television station.

The anxieties that students feel about entering the job market can't be dismissed. For those whose academic interests lean toward the humanities and social sciences, internships, jobs, and student activities provide a means of developing career-related experience. These opportunities free students to pursue majors that truly interest them and to make an academic commitment.

More Decisions

It was February—cold and bleak outside. I was cooking a pot roast when the phone rang. It was Betsy calling from Skidmore.

"Are you okay?" I had just talked to her two days before.

"Yes, fine. But I forgot to talk to you about a few things."
She sounded exuberant. I relaxed.

"I've decided about next year, but I don't think you'll like it."

So much for relaxing.

"Instead of spending my junior year in England,"—she plans on majoring in English—"I want to go to Italy and study art. I talked to someone in the Syracuse program and she loves it, and you get the language training and live with an Italian family."

I was both jealous and concerned.

"It's your choice, of course, but you've always had so much trouble with languages, and what about your require-ments for your English major?" I hated my words which were bursting her bubble.

"I'll take care of that. Don't worry. And another thing—spring vacation? I could come home or stay here and ski or Les invited me to New York to stay with him." Was this the time to mention that she still hadn't gotten a job to pay for her living expenses? Better leave it alone. "I think I want to work on a ranch this summer."

"What about the camp job you interviewed for?"

"It's not enough money, and I really want to work on a ranch."

"Did you have any particular ranch in mind?" My mind was beginning to swirl and the pot roast was burning.

"Well no, but I'm talking to people."

"You'd better check that out soon because if you wait you'll end up like last summer."

"What was wrong with last summer?"

"You didn't make much money and you were bored with your job."

"I was not!" The exuberance was definitely gone.

When I hung up the phone I wondered where I went wrong.

When I repeated the conversation to her father, he said, "Terrific. That's Betsy! England was safe. Italy's an adven-ture—the same with this summer."

He responded to her spirit. *I* kept placing barriers in her way.

And by the way, she did go to Italy, she never mentioned the ranch again, and she came home for spring vacation.

This is one mother's account of a typical conversation with her sophomore daughter. Overwhelmed and disconcerted by her daughter's barrage of options, she was reeling by the time she hung up the phone. Although she thinks of herself as a supportive and encouraging mother, her instinctive reaction had been to pull back in face of the onslaught and to point out all the potential pitfalls of her daughter's list of possibilities. Not a particularly helpful response, but one that many parents succumb to at some time during their child's college career.

Sophomores often call home with an ever-changing set of ideas and plans that may seem like the "whim of the week" to their bewildered parents. Just as parents have gotten used to the idea that their son is going to spend second semester in Washington on a political science internship, he calls home and says he has scratched that idea and is now planning to stay at school and switch his major to Spanish. Last week's request for permission to take a semester off turns into this week's decision to transfer to a larger school instead.

Summer vacations are also filled with possibilities. Today's career-anxious students want to fill their résumés with meaningful summer experiences, and many eschew the traditional jobs of the lawn care and lifeguard genre for positions in banks and research labs or pursue exotic alternatives such as picking fruit in the south of France or canning fish in Alaska.

The plethora of choices that face today's college students is often overwhelming to their parents as well as themselves: from summer internships in Africa to a semester at sea; double majors and joint degrees; stopping out and dropping out; a year abroad or an exchange at another university; graduating in three years or a fifth year of undergraduate study; staying put and making do or transferring to a different school.

Many parents assume that their child will go off to college for four years, pick a major and stick with it, come home and work in the summer, and graduate at the end of the fourth year, moving directly to graduate school or a professional job. But just as the typical nuclear family of working father, housewife, and two or more children represents only a small fraction of the population, so too the typical linear progression through college is more the exception than the rule. Many of today's students are approaching their education with a creativity that reflects their own needs and the demands of the society in which they live.

Stopping Out

"Stopping out" is not a euphemism for "dropping out" or running away, but a viable alternative for many students who want to spend a semester or year away from school. According to a National Center for Education Statistics report, one in four students takes longer than four years to earn an undergraduate degree. A student may take time off or stop out for any number of reasons—to find an academic focus or sense of purpose, to earn money, to contribute something to others, to get experience that will be valuable later on. Although the most common time for stopping out is during junior year, students may decide to take time off at any time in their college career.

Many colleges and universities have begun to acknowledge these periods of time out in an institutional way. At Harvard approximately 25 percent of the undergraduates take a leave from school, and the university assists them in their plans to do so. A Williams College handbook for parents states,

> The college urges that such time off be for the duration of an academic year and hopes that it will be spent positively and planned constructively. Such time away, perhaps as a period of reassessment and self-evaluation, often proves more beneficial than a half-hearted commitment to academics.

Parents may view the decision to take time off as a failure, a deviation from the norm. And those parents who feel constrained by the financial and emotional obligations of their middle years may find it difficult to listen with patience to the many enticing choices their child is contemplating. When parents haven't taken a vacation in years because of college expenses or obligations to an aging parent, their son or daughter's dilemma about whether to spend a year in Germany or to take time off to prospect for gold in California may seem like a frivolous indulgence.

In spite of her father's skepticism, a sophomore at Brown exudes a dazzling sense of possibility as she describes a string of alternative routes for the coming year:

> My Dad denies this, but I think he and my Mom have an "ownership philosophy." You know, "We're paying for your education . . ." "When you're living in our house . . ." "Because I'm your father, that's the reason."
> I feel they're not supportive about what I want to do and don't take it seriously. I wanted to go abroad with the American Field Service for a year after high school. They

didn't want me to. I'm definitely going to do something different after my sophomore year. I go crazy when I feel like I'm
just a student and not "living." It's so frustrating. I'd like to
take a semester at home at Case Western. I know Cleveland
and I can integrate being a student with my volunteer work in
the community. Or maybe I can go to Bryn Mawr. I almost
went there and I'd like to see what it would be like. I'd like to
drive or bike across the country. I'd like to go to Central or
South America. I'd like to have a significant job.

This young woman, excited and unfocused, needs a calm
and patient listener who might help her begin to channel her
energy. She may not yet realize that there is no best answer, but
in finding the better answer she will learn to make commitments and to live with the regrets of roads not taken. She will
certainly be more motivated to follow her own path than the
one chosen by her parents.

Parents who came of age in the sixties or seventies might
be tolerant of their children's plea to stop out if they plan to
devote themselves to a cause. But most students today are not
leaving school to rally for or protest against anything. Many
feel the personal pressure to succeed, to produce, to be responsible, to pay off loans, but are not quite ready to face such
grown-up commitments. Some, like the woman above, see their
education through a wider lens and want to grasp opportunities
that are now available to them. Many have a hard time articu-
lating why they want to leave. Using the college-age vernacular
of "splitting to get my head together" or needing time to "hang
out," these young people often turn parents off before any
discussion begins. Their own language trivializes whatever
legitimate insight lies behind it. "At more than a thousand-dol-
lar increase in tuition each year, he can go 'find himself' after
he finishes!" one father exclaimed.

Parents who give an unqualified no to a request for time
off without an opportunity to explore alternatives may stymie
their child's growth inadvertently rather than encourage it. A
job or internship is just what some students need to find the sense
of direction that eludes them on campus. For others, merely

having unpressured time for reflection is enough for them to become refreshed and clearer about their personal and professional goals. There is, of course, a fine line between bumming around and doing nothing, and pausing for some time to gain self-understanding. Financial pressures are of concern to most families, and a student who is serious about taking time off should be prepared to grapple with the dollars-and-cents aspects of this decision. By assuming financial responsibility, even through a mindless job, students enjoy an increased sense of independence, while stepping back from the academic world to get a new perspective.

A University of Michigan student describes what happened when he took a break from school and moved back home:

> Living at home this semester really hasn't been the big exclamation point in the book of life by any means. Living with my parents again is a weird thing. From their point of view I came home because I had something I wanted them to help me out with. I think they thought I'd be sitting down and talking to them for hours at a time. They were apprehensive; they worried about me. But I just wanted to get a job and hang out by myself for a while. I needed to clean out my system and get reoriented—to stop and think. A degree is something to work for; it's not an end in itself. But it does figure significantly. Like you have to do the work in order to get it. I'd been kind of missing that crucial point.
>
> When I was at school, I really didn't spend much time by myself except when I was sleeping. At home, when I'm not with my family, I'm on my own. It just gives me a lot of latitude for thinking and ironing out things—coming up with new ideas and perspectives. It's a good feeling to wash all this excess off the top of your skull. I'm enjoying it. I like figuring out things about myself. I think stopping out was probably the best thing I could have done. I'd go as far as to recommend it to other people who need to clear the air. There's no social stigma attached to it.

Setting aside time for thoughtful face-to-face conversations about taking time off can clarify the issues at hand for both parent and child. And without such discussions, parents may find that their attempts to direct their son or daughter on the traditional four-year path backfire.

A senior in his fifth year at a midwestern university recounts his experiences:

> I wanted to split school to get my head together, and my parents wouldn't allow it, which was a stupid mistake on their part. I wish I would have been able to convince my parents to let me do it' but they simply wouldn't listen. I felt definitely that I wasn't able to take advantage of what the university had to offer, and what they were putting their money down for. It was just not the right time for me. I was just too messed up. There was a lot of time that I wasted in college being stoned. Being in school was a kind of ideal model for them. My parents have the idea that everybody finishes college in four years. But it wasn't happening. I didn't finish some of my courses and had a bunch of incompletes. I blew the stuff off, and I felt bad about it. But I thought it was stupid that they had this idea about the number four.
>
> Last year I finally laid it on the line with them. I told them I wasn't going to graduate, that I had more stuff to do as far as the university was concerned. I knew there was a lot more I could get out of it now, and I wanted to go back. They agreed, and I'm very glad that I came back here. It's been very positive so far.

Sometimes open, flexible discussions about taking time off lead to a change of heart on the part of the student. The mother of a University of Wisconsin sophomore relates:

> My son was rooming with someone first semester this year who didn't like school. He clearly had an influence on Peter who called home right after he returned to Madison in January and said, "I think I'm going to leave school for a while."
>
> I told him I didn't think it made sense or was practical to leave school in the middle of sophomore year. I put my foot down, knowing that he was probably looking for some kind of limits at that point. If my daughter had called and said the same thing, I might have reacted differently. I threw out some options and said, "You might want to take off next year and work, or try photography which you love, or transfer to another school." I tried to give him some reasons for my opinions and some options to consider. I tried to combine the guidelines with leeway, so he could eventually make the best decision for himself.

I also knew that like so many sophomores he was concerned about picking a major. It had gotten to be a joke over winter break. Everyone who saw him asked the same question, "What are you going to major in?" He got really fed up with the repetition of that question, and eventually started to answer very fliply—to smart off by saying, "Sanskrit" or some such thing. The truth was he really didn't know.

I suggested he go to the counseling center to talk about choosing a major. He started to get a handle on his interests and before long it became quite clear to him that he wanted to major in journalism. The counselor he talked to suggested that he start to work on the newspaper, which he did. After that we never heard any more about his desire to leave school. We weren't against his taking time off; we just didn't want him to do it for the
wrong reasons.

The mother of a Lafayette student who stopped out cautions:

The original reasons they give may not be the real ones. Our son told us what he thought we'd want to hear. "I'm wasting your money; I don't have a sense of purpose."

True, he hadn't been very happy there; he had no idea what he wanted to do, and he had to declare a major by the end of sophomore year. But he also wanted to earn enough money to buy some expensive musical equipment. And underneath that goal was his need to establish his independence.

He lived at home, because it wasn't financially feasible for him not to, but he paid much of his way, gas for the car, the phone bill, that sort of thing. He worked two jobs and found them boring. And he missed Lafayette and visited there several different weekends. He began to appreciate college more. And he realized that his college degree is a union card. That's the hard and fast reality, and he doesn't want to go through life without one.

Of course, many parents fear that once their youngster leaves school, he or she may never return to graduate. Although this is always a possibility, most students who do return after a leave of absence perform at higher levels than they did before they left. The change of pace triggers renewed enthusiasm and a sense of purpose and commitment to their formal education when they return.

The dean of a highly competitive liberal arts college comments:

> I think I have never known a case where the student took time off and returned to the same institution and didn't do better. I think they find out it's no fun to work in an unskilled job. They return more mature, with a better sense of who they are and about the world of work.

In retrospect, many parents who had originally opposed the idea, look back at their children's time off positively. A Brandeis senior recalls with a wry grin:

> I took a year off—worked on construction for six months and then went to Europe with the money I'd earned. My father was desperate about it. He was so afraid I would never finish. Now he thinks it was wonderful. He tells all his friends about this adventuresome thing I did.

Some students don't finish. A college education is not for everyone, and some youngsters make the decision to turn their sights to other pursuits—part-time study, vocational or technical training, apprenticeships or opportunities to develop artistic talents, to name a few. Others who feel locked into the university or a particular field of study because of parental pressure, may go through the motions of getting an education but, lacking the interest or talent, ultimately fail or leave. For them college has not been a rich, expansive field of knowledge, but a confining prison that has rendered them unmotivated and thwarted. Most students who leave school don't make the decision lightly. They still want and need their parents' emotional support at the same time that they long for acknowledgment of their separateness. This is often a challenge for parents who must let go of their own dreams for their child, and accept, instead, the alternative route he or she has chosen.

Moving Off-Campus

Though living in the residence halls is back in vogue, a lot of upperclassmen contemplate moving to an apartment off-campus. At many universities apartment living has become as much a part of campus life as pizza and beer.

Some students make the move because they have to; there simply isn't enough room for them in the dormitories. Others, discovering that sharing an apartment and cooking one's own meals can be cheaper than the room and board plan on campus, make the move to save money. Some who are tired of the lack of privacy in the residence halls, seek space and quiet and a haven from the constant social scene. Still others crave the independence that apartment living symbolizes and see the move as another step toward the adult world.

Parents who spent four years at a residential college, where everyone lived on-campus, may be surprised when their son or daughter calls with the news that a move to an apartment is in the offing. The next surprise comes with the mention of a roommate of the opposite sex, since coed living is common off-campus as well as on. Though parents may have difficulty believing it, most of these arrangements are based on friendship, practicality, and serendipity. Women often feel safer and worry less about security when there are men in the apartment. For many, sharing apartment space with the opposite sex simply seems a natural extension of coed dormitory living.

When students who live off-campus talk about their roommates or apartment mates, they are referring to the people who share their apartment. When they use the term "the man—or woman—I live with," that usually means they are in a relationship. Neither arrangement is unusual today. And the difference in phraseology is a subtle but commonly understood part of the campus vernacular.

Sometimes the decision to move into an apartment is based on a student's commitment to a small group of friends. These groups usually come together with high expectations of community and intimacy, hoping to create their own home away from home. Other students who barely know each other join together in haphazard ways, united only by their common desire to share space. They expect little more of each other than basic civility.

All students who make the switch from dormitory to apartment life face the daily challenges of independent living. Paying rent on time, keeping the common living spaces clean, and buying food for a relatively balanced diet require time, thought, and action. At a time when much of their world seems tenuous and unsettled, taking care of themselves in the most basic pedestrian ways can help students assume more control of their lives.

Many students muddle through and feel increasingly self-reliant. No lecture on nutrition from a parent is as likely to change a student's eating habits as opening the refrigerator once again to find it stocked only with diet soda, beer, and leftover spaghetti. And after seeing their funds erode at the campus cafeteria, students begin to plan ahead and pack lunches for themselves. Arguments with roommates must be worked out without the help of an RA, and students learn to negotiate and share household responsibilities. Seniors often remark that the experience of living in an apartment reduces their pregraduation jitters, that it makes the transition into the real world look a bit less traumatic.

But apartment living requires adjustments that may add to an already overloaded schedule. The freedom of living on one's own is accompanied by the burden of responsibility. And if a student is weighed down with schoolwork, extracurricular pursuits, or a part-time job, the additional responsibility of taking care of an apartment may prove to be too much. Some students enjoy the space of off-campus housing, but feel isolated and cut off from college life. They miss the easy availability of friends and the ever-present stimulation that dormitory life provides. The decision about whether to move off-campus has to be weighed in the context of everything else going on in the student's life at the same time.

A vivacious young woman, now in her junior year, remarks:

> I moved into an apartment sophomore year. I had opted for an apartment because I wanted my own room. I'd never had a room of my own. I'm a vegetarian, and I thought meals would be easier for me if I could cook myself, and I wanted the adventure of an apartment.

But I felt really isolated. I met no one. By the end of the year, I was working at a snail's pace in my architecture classes. I had gotten more involved in outside activities, and I was in a stressful, serious relationship. So this year I decided to become an RA and move back into the dorms. The money I save by being an RA takes some of the financial pressure off as well.

Transferring and Other Alternatives

Almost all students contemplate transferring at some point during their first two years of college—some fleetingly, others giving it serious thought. Disappointing classes, broken friendships or romances, the sheer exhaustion of a demanding schedule all lead to periods of confusion and doubt. A change of scenery, a fresh start, is a tempting solution—a magical "right" answer to a complicated question. The grass and the ivy look greener somewhere else. How do students sort out the inevitable imperfections of their college experience from a legitimate mismatch?

An assistant dean advises:

It becomes a question of, are you running away from something here—loneliness or confusion—or are you moving toward something that isn't available here. Much of what I ask them revolves around what kind of a person they are and what kind of a person they want to be. Being bored isn't an acceptable answer; it's up to them to change this.

Some students stay simply out of a sense of obligation. They don't do anything to change the situation, and they're the ones I call the "what ifs." What if I had done this instead? What if I had gone there? Others go through the questioning period and then really make a niche for themselves here. They get involved in the newspaper or a committee, go to lectures, seek out the community at large. They have a successful time.

Sometimes it is clear that transferring will answer a specific need. Discovering an interest in occupational therapy at a school without an OT department, feeling overwhelmed and lost at a large university and longing for the sense of community that a small campus affords, missing the stimulation of an urban center after time spent in a rural setting—these are clearly concerns that can be rectified by going to a different school.

But when students speak of transferring to a school that is a rubber stamp of the one they are in, chances are they are seeking solutions that exist right under their noses, or that they are searching for a nonexistent perfect place. Parents can help by asking open-ended questions, listening patiently, and allowing their child to discover his or her own solution.

A New Jersey father talks with pride of his son's growth as he wrestled with the decision about whether to transfer:

> Gordon complained a lot about St. Lawrence. The kids weren't "like him"; he didn't like his classes. He was convinced that he had made the wrong decision and that there was a right school somewhere out there for him; he just had to find it. But his sophomore year he moved into a theme house; it was a political awareness house, and it gave him a niche. He had housemates with similar interests. He also really got into skiing. It was a turning point for him. The school still wasn't all that he had hoped for, but he began to see that he could make the difference.

Parents' reactions to a talk of transferring are often proportional to the amount of time and investment they spent in the original college selection process. One mother recalls:

> She came home and said, "I hate this place." I'd been telling everyone how much she loved it. I guess when I think about it, she hadn't really said much.
>
> I was angry. I thought, here we go again. I'd put all that energy into helping her get into what I thought was the right place, and now I was wrong. I felt one of the reasons she had ended up there was because of me.
>
> I told her, "Okay. If you can find a school that will take you, and you make the arrangements, do it." And this time around she did everything herself.

The process of transferring offers another opportunity for a young person to make an independent, reasoned, and informed decision. The mother above insisted that her child take the initiative this time. When her daughter went to a school of her own choosing, she found that she was in for a big adjustment, but one that she was willing to tackle.

Some students decide not to transfer, but opt for a semester or a year in a different setting or different kind of institution. A young woman from Wellesley College was able to look at her all-woman institution with new and appreciative eyes after a year at coed Williams. A Beloit student, feeling confined by her small, sheltered surroundings, chose to study at an urban university on the east coast, and returned from her adventure to enjoy the familiarity and warmth of her friendly campus for the last year. Students have opportunities of enormous variety, ranging from semesters of study with policymakers and lobbyists in Washington to programs in urban education in major cities or wilderness field station studies in remote locations. The most popular choice of alternative study still seems to be study abroad, usually in the junior year. It is an option that affords yet another confusing but tempting array of possibilities.

Junior Year Abroad

Bolstered by a spirit of adventure, more and more students are taking advantage of the unique opportunities for international study. Over 150,000 Americans annually enroll in about 2,000 foreign programs. Some of these students study in summer and graduate programs; but academic-year programs for undergraduates are available for credit at more than a thousand schools.

The experience of a semester or a year abroad provides the opportunity to enlarge young people's vision of the world, of the United States, and of themselves. It proves to be a pivotal life experience for some, a splendid adventure for others, but it is not for everyone. Before students decide *where* to go, they face the dilemma of *whether* to go.

In some cases, the decision is made for them. Many programs and universities require a minimum grade point average; in certain disciplines, such as engineering and business, a prescribed study in sequence makes it difficult, if not impossible, to take the time during the academic year for a credited period of study abroad. Language requirements eliminate many underprepared students; family obligations and financial restraints prevent others from going. For some, especially language or international relations majors, study abroad is an integral part of the curriculum.

For many students, the decision presents a tug-of-war. They weigh the alternatives, and ask themselves, "Should I grab this once-in-a-lifetime opportunity? If I go, I can't transfer; should I transfer instead? If I stay, I'll have a good shot at being editor of the paper senior year, or maybe president of the fraternity. Do I want to give that up? Studying abroad will look good on my résumé, but will I fall behind in the job search? Can I afford it? Will my financial aid transfer? What's going to happen to Jane and me if we're so far apart for a year? Do I have the guts to go?"

Some students have the misguided notion that study abroad will magically solve academic or social problems, that the added stimulation of exotic new cultures will cure the state of confusion, stagnation, or ennui that they are currently experiencing. It is true that many students find study abroad programs stimulating and the catalyst for personal growth, but those who choose them to escape from unhappy circumstances are likely to bring their problems with them or simply postpone them for another time.

Students need not make this decision to study abroad in a vacuum. They talk to friends, faculty, and advisors. And upperclassmen who have spent a semester or year abroad are usually delighted to share the pleasures or disappointments of their own experience. For information about the programs themselves they turn to a Study Abroad Office or an Overseas Program Advisor, who has been designated to provide this service. These offices and campus libraries offer informative books and pamphlets. A starting point for anyone considering study abroad is the free comprehensive leaflet put out by the Institute of International Education, "Basic Facts on Foreign Study."

All programs are not created equal, and beckoning brochures can be misleading. Study abroad counselors can help point the way to tried and true programs or guide the more adventuresome student to apply directly to a foreign university—a less costly alternative and one that promises an integrated experience. Students are often surprised to learn that some study abroad experiences are less expensive than a year at their home college.

The decision to go abroad stirs up feelings reminiscent of the initial departure for college. Parents, as well as their children, get caught up in the anticipation and anxiety of the upcoming journey:

> He's refusing to figure out if all the stuff fits into a backpack for four weeks of travel before school starts. He says, "I don't need to test. I've got everything under control." The last four days that control has dissolved. He's bouncing off the walls. His confidence is shaken and so is mine. And my husband has been living on Tums.

> No, I'm not worried about the terrorists. I'm worried that she'll lose her passport or mess up her money or miss her train—the same things I always worried about with Nancy.

> He is so much more into getting ready for this than when he went to college—scattered, but much more organized. But he seems like such a naive little kid sometimes. My fear is that he will not pay attention to his surroundings and something dangerous will happen.

These are the voices of parents as their children leave home again, but this time for distant and unknown places. Thrown into a heightened state of anxiety and excitement, families play out the themes of separation once more, the discordant tensions of disengagement and the unexpected pangs of loss:

> My intense reaction to Christy's leaving for a full year abroad in Paris came as a big surprise to me. I thought, "We've been through this passage when she went to college and we weathered it so well. Why am I feeling so much anxiety and loss?" I think it's partly because she's so much more wonderful to be with at twenty than she was at seventeen. I feel like no sooner had I gotten to know her as a young adult this summer without so many of the tensions we've had in the past then she's off once again. So I will genuinely miss her. And I also know she doesn't need me as much anymore. Somehow her

determination to go on this adventure, so far away, confirms what I already know—that she has grown up.

Once the initial weeks of study abroad are under way, some parents discover a new relationship with their offspring. Overseas phone calls are outside of many students' budgets. Those who have never written before yearn to share the excitement of their new lives and so discover the art of letter writing. Their letters are often unself-conscious and revealing in ways that long-distance phone calls seldom are. They are full of vivid impressions of places and sights and expressive discoveries about themselves and the world. Paradoxically, the distance of an ocean provides a safe cushion for intimacy.

A UCLA senior from New York reminisces about her correspondence home during her year in Israel:

> I could kind of say anything when I was six thousand miles away, and I wrote things I would never say when I was with them. I told them a lot that I loved them and how much I appreciated having this opportunity, which they never had.

And a Miami University junior wrote from Denmark, "Would you please send me any bits of advice for when I get lonely and depressed. Don't worry. I can handle it from this far away."

As the months go by, many parents describe a growing sense of liberation, as they experience a new level of separation. The vast distances make it virtually impossible to remain entrenched in a son or daughter's life, and as a result, students are left to their own devices, and in most situations, they rise to the occasion.

> As much as I missed her, I also knew that I had very little control or input into her life. I didn't know the customs, the rules, or the dangers. I had to defer to the resource people in her program who did.
>
> I always feel freed up when the kids go back to school after vacations. They may go out partying until all hours of the morning, but I don't know about it so I don't worry. Well, having her in England was like this only tenfold. I didn't speak to her by phone. By time her letters arrived, they were an-

cient history. I had no choice but to let her struggle through the hard parts, the loneliness, the homesickness. This was the first time I felt really free of the pull to make things okay for her.

Students' growing self-assurance breeds a new respect from their parents. Young men and women speak of the confidence born of weeks of traveling on their own, of the capacity to manage their own finances in a foreign currency and of the uphill struggle to master another language—often a lonely and arduous task. A junior in an English-speaking program in Madrid lived with a local family and learned the language slowly and tediously:

> When people talk to me, I have to watch them, their gestures, anything I can pick up. Every time I have a conversation, I first have to translate what's being said into English and then go through it again before I speak. I have to plan out whatever I say, a meal or a favor; it can't be spontaneous. I have to have complete concentration all the time. I'm so tired at night, I just flop into bed.

By the middle of her second semester, however, her confidence grew along with her competence, and her letters home were joyful:

> All of a sudden, everything is beginning to click, and if it continues like this, all those months of struggling and shyness will be worth it to say the least. God, it's the most amazing feeling to achieve something like this and to have fun doing it.

Parents who are able to go abroad for a visit have the pleasure of witnessing firsthand their child's growing language skill, maturity, and cultural immersion. These are treasured times when the tables are turned and their son or daughter becomes a much appreciated and admired guide, interpreter, or art historian.

The students who thrive the most seem to be those who are receptive to the culture, without too many preconceived expectations. An ability to make friends easily, to be uninhibited in trying out an imperfect command of a foreign language, to be able to tolerate occasional periods of intense loneliness—these capacities all tend to enhance the study abroad experience. And those who stay for the full year describe a feeling of mastery the second semester that surpasses the romance and stimulation of the first:

> I've graduated from frenetic energy to lazy relaxation; that is to say, life is much more normal now and I'm enjoying the increasing feeling of *being* a Florentine more than observing the culture as a foreigner as I did last semester.

> After one semester, you can say, I spent a semester in England. After a year, it's like home. You know how things work. You get a much fuller picture.

> I went into an Army basic training program for foreign students during the few weeks between semesters. All my Israeli fellow students had already been in the army for two or three years, and I decided if I wanted to understand them better, I had to do something that was key in their life. After that, I was much happier second semester. I made more Israeli friends and could identify a lot more.

Identity issues broaden from "myself as a woman" or an engineering student or an advocate for social causes to "myself as an American," an American who has discovered Norwegian roots, an American Jew committed to the state of Israel, a Japanese American devoted to Japanese heritage or an American who is part of a world community. Just as students discover the flaws in their own families when they see them from a distance, many young people view the United States through the critical eyes of their new international friends.

Students return home with remnants of a new culture—a British accent, a Parisian style of dressing, a subscription to the *Jerusalem Post*, or a zest for Renaissance art. They miss the friends and families and lovers who had become a part of their lives in another land. A student returning from South America recalls:

> I was gone for a year in Colombia, and I had really assimilated. I had a life there and I felt Colombian. I didn't just change countries. I changed identities. The last two weeks there were

terribly emotional. I couldn't bear the thought of leaving my country.

Many suffer culture shock when they are reunited with their families and their friends at school. A senior describes the period of reentry after spending a year in Norway:

I felt so totally alone; it was a terrible loneliness until October or November. No one could understand what I had been through—what my life was like. I was a different person there from who I was when I left sophomore year. And when I came back to school, I expected the world had stopped because I wasn't here. And to think my friends here lived without me and they have their friends and everyone else is doing their own thing and I don't have my niche anymore.

But more longlasting than the adjustments of reentry, they return with a new perspective, a world view that replaces the self-absorption of their e. ● ier identity quest, and a new sense of their own ability to handle life on their own.

Commitments on Campus: Junior and Senior Years

After getting through sophomore year—it was horrendous—I came back to school with the attitude that I can make it for sure.

I see a big difference between sophomore and junior years. The main thing for me is I know how to solve problems. I know how to dig deeper and find resources. That goes for academics too. I know how to approach academic problems.

Juniors and seniors have made a place for themselves. We've got a major and a definite set of friends we'll be calling up in forty years and asking, "How are the grandchildren?"

I trust my own opinions a lot more than I did freshman or sophomore years. I feel freer to disagree with faculty or drop a class if I want to.

I'm more realistic about what I can and can't do. I've channeled my commitments and don't try to do everything. I manage my time better and make sure I eat and sleep right. Sometimes my work comes second. My main priority right now is the lighting for the spring production.

Junior and senior years are a time of consolidation. No longer trying on a series of roles, juniors and seniors have a more solid sense of their own identity. Most have settled into a social niche on campus that confirms who they are and what they value. They have staked out an academic home in their major department. And now it is their turn to assume the campus leadership positions they may have aspired to as freshmen and sophomores.

As they become more aware of their own limits and talents, they wrestle with trade-offs, with the pros and cons of one choice over another. Whereas their earlier choices were made in the spirit of exploration, rebellion, or testing extremes, the commitments of upperclassmen are those they claim for themselves. Some opt for a balanced lifestyle, measuring their time among part-time jobs and academic, social, and extracurricular pursuits. Others choose to put most of their energy into one arena of campus life and narrow their focus.

Those who immerse themselves in academics discover the rewards of scholarship. Their sense of self-confidence grows along with their insight and competence in their discipline. They develop the skills of critical inquiry and delve into research and analysis. No longer satisfied by the "right answer" of an external authority, they respond to the challenge of ambiguity. They read original sources and struggle to form and justify their own viewpoints. They measure their success in academic terms, and their scholarly pursuits are an essential part of their identity.

Some "hang out" in departmental lounges, endlessly drinking coffee and testing their emerging skills in discussion and debate with their classmates. They may become involved in departmental politics or undergraduate organizations that revolve around an academic discipline. Relationships with faculty change, as students leave behind the formality of the large lecture halls for the more intimate seminar rooms of upper-level classes. Some seize the chance to work as a research assistant for an admired professor; if they are fortunate, the professor takes on the role of mentor, guiding and encouraging their intellectual growth.

Although extracurricular involvement is meant to supplement academic life, for many upperclassmen, what goes on
beyond the walls of the classroom has become their first
priority. The sports editor of the college paper dashing to meet
a deadline feels the rush of excitement as he joins his coterie
of fellow journalists in a common pursuit. No journalism class
could measure up to this laboratory of learning. No fraternity
bond could be stronger than the one he feels in this community.
A junior who had enjoyed singing in a campus choir in prior
years, now spends many evenings at rehearsals with a small
madrigal group and is taking lessons in the flute as a result of
her growing interest in early music. As a computer science
major, she has found the complexities of sophisticated
programming intriguing, but she considers the friends who
share her passion for music to be her college family.

Sometimes campus activities give students their first taste
of a potential for leadership. Whether their commitment is to a
sorority, a religious group, or a service organization, they have
the chance to develop lifelong skills and a sense of themselves
as people who can effect change. A senior from Portland,
Oregon, looks back at the impact that campus involvement has
had on her:

> I joined the undergraduate English society sophomore year. I
> liked going to its poetry readings and figured I might as well
> get involved. Before I knew it I was in charge of pulling
> together a panel for one of the meetings. I had to call alumni
> and ask them if they'd be willing to participate. I was scared to
> death calling all those important people. But I did it, and then
> on the night of the program I introduced them and moderated
> the panel. It was the first time I thought of myself as a leader,
> and I liked it. That was just the beginning.
>
> By junior year it all started to come together. I was elected
> president of the English society and got involved in campus
> politics. I was invited to participate in a retreat for campus
> leaders run by the student affairs staff, and I was knocked out
> by it. We learned everything from assertion skills to how to
> lead a meeting. I got to know kids I never would have met
> otherwise. And I got to know the guy who's the director of stu-
> dent activities and he's had a big influence on me ever since.
> They kept talking about empowerment, and I understood what

they meant because I was starting to feel it. Right now I'm running for president of student government. It's the first time in a long time that a woman has run for the top office.

Whether this young woman wins her election is less important than the process that got her there. There is only one student government president at every school, but all students have an opportunity to learn through their involvement in campus and community life.

The journey from the fragmented and disconnected state of the sophomore slump to the engagement and commitments a year or two later is not the same for everyone. But by the time they are seniors, most students have a greater sense of their own competence in and out of the classroom. They know more about who they are and what they believe in. They have found a place in the community that has become their home.

Chapter 9
THE END IS THE BEGINNING

The familiar ritual of departure in early fall—the journey back to campus, reentry one more time—the beginning of senior year. By now it seems so natural, this coming and going, this moving in and out of the family orbit. Students casually pack their life's belongings into the back of a car and drive off to school. Or they hop on a bus or a plane with the confidence of those who know where they are heading.

Seniors are at the top of the heap now. They are the team captains and newspaper editors, the leaders of campus organizations, and the enlightened voices in the classroom. Though some revel in that knowledge for the entire year, most are acutely aware that their position is tenuous. At some point they are struck by the realization that, "I'm a senior. This is it—the end."

The year is filled with a series of last times, the last convocation, homecoming, basketball game, fraternity rush, winter term, midterm, final. Never will life be quite so ritualized again. And the dawning of the reality that "this is it" evokes a flurry of "last chance" activity. There is a sense of urgency, of time running out. Some students throw themselves into a host of endeavors as they try to make the most of college opportunities. They spend precious time with their circle of friends, hang out with professors, explore the city or countryside that surrounds them. And with graduation a mere eight or ten courses away, encounters with the academic catalogue take on a new significance. As they juggle their schedules, they no longer are just choosing courses; they are relinquishing possibilities of taking that seminar in Shakespeare's sonnets or a fantastic course on film, or a once-in-a-lifetime chance to study with a renowned professor.

Some seniors use this year to take an assortment of courses they have always wanted to take—courses they consider fun. Some fill in their liberal arts curriculum with accounting and computer programming, pragmatic courses they see as an entry to the job market. And others streamline their academic and extracurricular involvements, focusing on an honors thesis or an engineering final project, a music recital or a drama production. This represents the culmination of years of effort and for these students, the sense of accomplishment has a tangible by-product.

A graduating civil engineering student beams with pride when describing the final structural design project that he did with a team of three students:

> We were told by the faculty, "You will design a bridge over the Mississippi River and you will design everything. You will design every bolt, every plate, every girder, every beam, every cable, every piece of cement. You will design the whole thing, and then you will present it to us, and we will tell you if it is good."
>
> This is the one class that pulls it all together. For the past two or three years I've been saying, all this theory, all this pragmatic, dogmatic stuff—as long as I can put out a good structural design project, I'll be satisfied. Now I know I can do this. Look at this bridge! You present this thing, and you have a professional engineer saying, "That's a good bridge."

George Washington University's Dean Linda Salamon is a proponent of honors theses and senior projects:

> No matter what the field, I see value in a sustained piece of work over a long period of time. A research effort and synthesis demonstrates to students, not so much that they can master a particular discipline, but that they can use skills of inquiry, analysis, and sometimes creative imagination as well. It's a culminating experience for students who do it. When they call their parents in the midst of it, moaning "I'll never finish," or "This is a giant monster," parents shouldn't worry. They should just encourage them.

For some students the sense of mastery is not tied to a thesis or particular project; it is more internal, less accessible to public display. They exude a sense of joy in their intellectual development. A Chinese studies major at Middlebury exclaims:

> I feel on top of the world. Academically it is my best year. I feel as though I can do anything. My professors agree with what I say, or if they disagree, I realize I can argue with them. I've taken lots of classes specific to my field, and I've spent a year studying and traveling in China. I don't depend on gut feelings anymore; I can back up what I say with sources and cogent reasoning. Whatever I say has some validity to it. I know I can say something without making a fool of myself.

And a graduating history major, while enjoying the richness of his senior studies, realizes that the end of his college experience marks the beginning of his commitment to learning for the rest of his life:

> Since I've found something that interests me, that I want to learn about, this year has been incredible for me academically. I want to take classes on my own until I'm sixty or eighty because now I realize there's so much more to learn, and I'll study because I enjoy it and not because I have to. There's a reason for it. It won't be for a distribution requirement; it won't be for my major or for my minor; it will be because I'm interested and I really want to know.

Lacking a crystal ball to predict their future, seniors look back, sometimes wistfully, often with amazement, at the accrued accomplishments and changing perspectives of past months and years.

> I keep having these total flashbacks of four years. I can just picture myself waiting in line as a freshman, not knowing what to do next, staring at the map, trying to figure it out. I've done so many things, been so many places, met so many people. I've done some really crazy things. I think about how it's all progressed and how much I've matured.

> College opened my eyes to life and what happens—good and bad. I had no idea how bad things could get—or how good—or how different people can be. In high school it was almost like a mold that everyone fits into. Last year my floor had a lot of international students and I lived with people from countries I didn't even know existed. I learned about everything from

food—like how Latin people don't eat much peanut butter—to how Pakistani people get married, to dances and clothing and a little bit of language. It's made me much more tolerant—more open-minded. Not many things surprise me anymore.

Somewhere I had this assumption that things would be taken care of at this stage—that I would cancel the newspaper and cancel the phone service and pack up all my personal problems and blithely move on to start life anew in another city. All of a sudden I realized that it was not going to be quite so simple. I see the complexities of things so much more now. It's not that my life is more complex. I guess I'm just more aware of the complexities. No more good, bad—right, wrong. It's harder this way. My mom says it's all just part of growing up.

Many express frustration, and regrets as well—thoughts of lost opportunity and squandered time. They often describe such thoughts, however, with a newly acquired perspective on their total college experience:

At the beginning of the year and part of this semester, I would kick myself about, oh God, I wish I'd done that, and I did so much wrong in college—but I guess part of growing up is knowing there are going to be regrets. There are things you're going to mess up—then realizing why you didn't do things as well as you could have and learning from that.

Some students have to come to terms with the fact that they haven't done well in college. Occasionally students who've scraped by with C's and D's fail in their final semester. Unable to graduate with their class, they face summer school and an anti-climactic finish. This is a difficult scenario for everyone involved. An academic dean who deals with this each spring reminds parents:

The student knows this is a failure—it's a failure in the biggest task he's undertaken in life to date. And he needs his parents to be there for him. Parents should remember, it's not their own failure.

Senior year is a time of intensity and contradiction—of the highs of accomplishments and the lows of dreams unfulfilled— of the comfort of familiarity and the anxiety of the unknown looming ahead. For many, there is a sense of things coming together, of goals reached, of efforts rewarded. And yet, standing on the top of the mountain, there is scarcely time to admire the view. Self-confidence becomes shaky as thoughts of the future invade the present.

As seniors make forays into the world beyond the campus, the question, "What's next?" is never far from their thoughts. Some do internships in a brokerage house or TV station, in a juvenile court or an art gallery, wondering throughout—is this what I want to do next year? For as long as they can remember, their occupation has been student, and September has meant going back to school. But now September conjures up either a blank, a void, or shifting images of where they will be, whom they'll be with, or what they'll be doing a year from now. Some hedge their bets and apply to graduate school and for jobs simultaneously. Some become immobilized and do nothing. Still others make a conscious decision to concentrate on school and postpone the search until after graduation.

The number of students planning to go directly into the job market rather than to graduate school has increased substantially in the last twenty years. Although many eventually will seek advanced degrees, the majority of today's college seniors face the tensions and uncertainties of searching for their first job in a shaky economy. Dressed in their interview suits, future bankers and corporate trainees run—or wobble on newly purchased high heels—from an oriental philosophy class to a meeting with a recruiter from Chase Manhattan Bank. They write résumés and practice their interviewing skills in front of a video camera.

Those aspiring to graduate or professional schools write applications and take entrance exams, comparing their scores with an intensity reminiscent of their former bouts with SATs. Those who have no idea what they want to do are sure that everyone else does. Waves of panic sweep over most seniors periodically, sometimes triggered by a friend's job offer—or their own rejection letter.

At just the time that students may be feeling vulnerable and looking to their parents for reassurance, many parents become anxious as well. Instead of providing a calming perspective, they often inadvertently add their own worries to those of their children. Separation issues resurface as they look forward to the end of tuition bills, but wonder if these will be replaced by other burdens, financial and emotional. What if he doesn't get a job? What if she doesn't get a fellowship? What if he wants to come back home to live?

Even those who have been avid supporters of a broad liberal arts education may get the jitters about job prospects as the end is in sight. Fathers who had been uninvolved in the brouhaha of "getting in" four years before, suddenly call inquiring about on-campus interviews by major corporations, "I know you don't want to work for IBM, but perhaps you should have a contingency plan in case newspaper writing doesn't work out." Mothers give unsolicited advice about how to dress and act in interviews. Parents, who just months before bragged of their daughter's independent travel on another continent, now worry that she will be unable to figure out the next step in her own future.

Parents who forge ahead as if the job hunt is their own are often puzzled by their offspring's negative reaction when they call to announce that they have set up an interview for him with a friend or client. Others are more subtle, hinting, "I saw a great new book on résumé writing in the book store."

A senior from Dallas describes the added burden of her parents' interrogating phone calls:

> My parents have been more involved than ever this year. They call wanting information. "How's it going? How're you doing? Have you heard from this school? Have you heard from that school? What are you doing this summer? Do you have a job? Do you have a place to stay?"
>
> It's hard. I already expect a lot of myself. Then to be bombarded with questions by them makes it harder. I want to say, "Look Mom, look Dad, I know how important this all is." They don't seem to understand that I *am* aware, that I *do* know what's important. I wish they'd say stuff like, "We know that you're going through a lot. We know it's tough." Or ask, "Are

you nervous? Are you scared?" They seem to just be concerned
with the facts.

Robert Thirsk, director of the Placement Center at the
University of Washington in Seattle, urges parents to acknowledge the development that has taken place in their son or
daughter:

> Though parents want the best for their children, they're not
> helping when they try to control them. The world is *their*
> universe. They may feel overwhelmed, but they do want to
> make their own decisions. A lot has changed since they were
> freshmen.

Although every senior seems to have at least one friend who
has landed the "perfect" job in the "perfect" place at a higher-
than-hoped-for salary, the majority of students do not have
everything wrapped up by graduation. It is not unusual for
seniors to leave campus after commencement stating as one
student did, "My life is one big *if*. Nothing is solid right now."

"The growth in today's job market is in small and medium-
sized firms that don't recruit on campus," says Jim Case,
assistant vice president at the American Graduate School of
International Management:

> It's a myth that most people work for large multinational cor-
> porations. Though students can get started while still in school,
> and can certainly learn about strategies and resources at their
> campus career center, most will have to wait until after their
> diploma is in hand before they can devote adequate time to a
> job campaign. As all the career literature suggests, looking for
> a job is a full-time job.

The ambiguity and uncertainty of not knowing, however, is
frustrating, and students appreciate parents who acknowledge
this without trying to rush in and solve the problem for them or
prod them into instant action.

Understanding and encouragement does not imply a light
dismissal of the problem either. An engineering student who,
much to his surprise and disappointment was without a job at
graduation, found his parents' buoyant optimism more stressful

than helpful: "They don't seem to understand that I'm really scared about not having a job. And it doesn't help when they tell me it's no big deal."

Knowing that they will soon be on their own, seniors are emphatic about maintaining their sense of autonomy. A former premed who discovered Spanish and international relations during her sophomore year called home with excitement when offered an opportunity to do an internship for Amnesty International after graduation—unpaid. Her mother, a nurse, was shocked and mystified at the news that her talented and bright daughter was planning to return home to live, and work at a menial job to pay expenses, so that she could support herself while participating in an unpaid internship:

> To my mom, this internship is kind of a black hole. When I called her and told her about it, there was silence at the other end of the phone. I knew she was upset. To her, it's no payoff for all the work I've done. To me, it is the foundation for moving on to something else. It's very important.
>
> When I switched from premed to Spanish in the middle of sophomore year, that was a hard thing to do because Mom wasn't happy about it. When I went away to Mexico junior year, it was the first major thing I did without her approval. And it was the best year I've ever had.
>
> Now this internship is an opportunity to build a foundation for what I want to do in international relations. For my mom, it's a culmination of all the changes I've made. She's realizing that I'm going to be doing stuff like this forever, and that's hard for her to handle. She doesn't understand the international opportunities of jobs, and what I can do and why I want to travel. My mom grew up in Cleveland and never left; it was an environment where you either went to nursing school or you became a teacher—something traditional with a name or a title. And I'm never going to have that. I don't want to have it. She was divorced and worries about my security. If I'm not something with a title, that's very insecure to her. To me, it's not. To me, it's exciting.

Though this young woman longed to maintain the close, loving relationship she and her mother had always enjoyed, she was determined to pursue her own goals. The week after she had called her mother about the internship she wrote to her and essentially laid it on the line. Her confidence in her own identity, in who she has become, is evident:

> I wrote an intense letter, spilled my guts, and said, basically, accept me as I am. I said, would you like me to come home to the suburbs and become a secretary and live there for the rest of my life? That won't be me. It's not me; it's not who I've become. You sent me off to college to do well, and I have—and I took advantage of the opportunities, and I grew, and I traveled, and I learned. And now here I am at the point of graduating. I am who I am because of what college has done to me and what I've done during college, and it's too late now. I can't change that. College is in me.

What a tribute to all college can and should be—the sheer joy of a student's discovery of the expansive world around her and, ultimately, of her own expanding self. But as parents, we often cringe when it is our own child who is taking the more adventuresome, less traveled path—or any path that differs from our hopes and expectations. We carry our own agendas— a dentist, whose real passion has been an involvement in Jewish volunteer activities, has a strong investment in his daughter becoming a rabbi. A mother of the sixties drums into her daughter time and time again that she should take advantage of today's opportunities for women and not settle for the traditional teaching or social service job. The doctor who sees a medical career as the only acceptable route for his son; the bus driver who makes sacrifices for the dream of his daughter, the engineer. But the would-be engineer discovers TV production, and the doctor's son opts for a graduate degree in classics. The dentist's daughter forgoes rabbinical school for a career as a Jewish educator, and the young woman whose mother had visions of law school makes a commitment to medical social work.

Our children will go their separate ways, and so they should. They have become who they are, not who we would have them be. As graduation draws near and students declare their financial independence, both parents and children feel the balance of power shifting between them. Money has, after all, been the one tie that has continued to bind, often unacknowledged, but inevitably present in the background. With plans to enter a bank training program in Chicago, a Hamilton College senior rejoices in the prospect of his impending financial freedom:

> I've got my own Visa card now! I have my independence. My folks can give me advice; they always have. But they can't tell me what to do anymore. It's not that I've always listened to them, but up 'til now there's been this feeling of obligation.

In many families, issues of money are still under negotiation. Some students have put themselves through college and are facing substantial debts. Others worry about building a financial base so that they can go to graduate school in the future. Still others are in the throes of a job hunt. And questions arise for both parents and their children. "Who will pay off the loans?" "Can I retain my independence and live at home?" "How long am I willing to help subsidize my kid?" "Who's going to pay for graduate school?" "If he lives at home, should I charge him room and board?"

Each family has to weigh its own financial realities, values, and needs. Those who talk openly about money matters—expectations and limits—avoid disappointment and resentment at a later date. There are, of course, no hard and fast rules. One student who supported herself all through college decides to live at home so that she can pay off her loans. She is confident and secure in her independence, and her parents, who were unable to pay for college, welcome the chance to be of help. Another senior turns down his parents' offer to pay for graduate school, even though he knows it will be several years before he can pay for it himself. He's convinced that the financial ties are too threatening to his autonomy.

By the time they are seniors, most students have stopped turning to their parents for their primary emotional support, and turn first to their friends and lovers. For many, the heart of college life, especially during these last months, centers around a cherished group of friends. Much of their undergraduate experience is tied up in a mutual history of heartaches and treasured memories.

As the school year comes to a close, students are aware of the impending separation from those who have become so central to their lives. They plan outings and weekend getaways; some look forward to traveling together before settling into the routine of a job or graduate school; others hope to keep a thread of continuity in their lives by joining forces to live together after graduation.

They look to these trusted friends for confirmation of their decisions and validation of their identity. An about-to-graduate senior from the University of Wisconsin confides:

> I went through a stage three months ago of being very remorse-ful about leaving my security blanket, which this university has become. My friends know Lisa. They know what she stands for, what she does. I'm accepted here. I dread going out into the real world and having to reestablish myself and reintroduce myself. My self-confidence is wavering. I've decided to stay in Madison for the summer, live with a good friend, and send out applications.

Those whose plans will clearly take them far away from friends anticipate the grieving process that lies ahead. A young woman who intends to return home to Minnesota before entering divinity school notes:

> Part of me dreads after graduation, when I've left all my friends and I go home and get depressed and my parents are going to say, "It's not that bad—get yourself together"—and I'm going to say, "No, let me be depressed. It's okay for me to feel bad."

Those who plan to work after graduation worry about leaving behind a world in which they have been surrounded by people their own age—where "it's always easy to find someone to talk to about politics or music or whatever. And there's always something to do—parties, lectures, concerts. And they're usually free!" As the time to part approaches, they make plans to keep in touch and joke about the reunions they'll have in the as yet unimaginable future. Those who have stayed in close touch with high school friends reassure themselves that they'll do the same with their friends from college. A senior on her way to medical school says laughingly:

> I know I'll keep up with my friends here. And I know that if I get married, my little kids are going to meet their little kids. There's no doubt in my mind that's going to happen. And now I understand that anywhere I go, I'll be able to make friends, but that it's going to take time.

The unspoken intentions of romantic partnerships must now be addressed. Graduation brings a convenient end to some of these twosomes; commitment was only to this time and place. But for many students, conflicts of identity and intimacy are brought clearly into focus at this juncture. Choices are many, and decisions are often painful and poignant: "Should I give up the chance to work on Wall Street and pick up whatever I can in Ann Arbor while she goes to grad school?" "Will our relationship withstand the strain if he's in D.C. and I'm in Tampa?" "If we compromise and go to the only law school that accepted both of us, will we end up resenting each other?"

Parents are often surprised to find that couples who appear to be very much in love put career priorities ahead of personal ones. Old assumptions about relationships no longer hold true. Women do not drop everything automatically to "put him through medical school." Some men make compromises in their own career aspirations to follow the woman in their life. Some couples develop a sequential plan and take turns making career compromises for each other.

Many young men and women acknowledge that their priority is to establish a more solid sense of themselves beyond the campus world before they make a long-term commitment to someone else. After an intense year-and-a-half relationship, a future graduate student in education finds herself at a crossroads:

> The past twenty years I've been my parents' child, and even at college, you're not a full adult. And I'm getting out and here I have a chance to be me and that's most important. I love Sean a lot, but after twenty years, it's time for *me* now; it's time for me to do what's best for me. And if what's best for him is

going to coincide with that, well that's great, that's fantastic.
But he's not the most important thing in my life right now. I
don't expect to be the most important thing in his life either.

Parents may be caught off guard when they find that their
child is making plans to live with a partner. What may look like
impulsive, cavalier behavior may actually represent a carefully
thought out decision. A senior at Dartmouth explains that his
parents were taken aback when he called to tell them that he
and his girlfriend were moving to San Francisco together:

> I had intentionally not told my parents much about our relation-
> ship. I didn't tell them anything until it was a fait accompli. It
> ended up being more of a scene than it would have been other-
> wise. They were very upset because they had no idea how im-
> portant she was to me. I hadn't told them. In trying to avoid
> confrontation earlier in the year, I brought on more. I underes-
> timated them. After all, I'm the fifth child, and nothing I could
> have done would have been a surprise. If I had to do it over, I
> would have let them know more along the way.

In the midst of all this planning for the future, saying
goodbye to dear friends, wrapping up the last round of papers
and finals, the pressure mounts. A chemistry major from Puerto
Rico recounts:

> This is probably the most confusing time in my life. Everything
> is up in the air. I haven't heard yet from med school in Puerto
> Rico or if I have a job here. I'm packing up four years worth of
> stuff, but I don't know where I'm going to be. I'm still under
> pressure in one class—a take-home exam I have to finish by
> tomorrow. My parents have a new house. Nothing's solid past
> or future. It's nine days before graduation, and I never thought
> it'd be like this.

Even those with definitive plans begin to feel disoriented,
to experience waves of highs and lows as the countdown to
graduation begins. When they finish their last exams, everything comes to a halt. "It's like coming off of drugs," said an
engineering student from a highly competitive university:

> You've spent four years of intense pressure, day in and day
> out, and your body has become used to such an incredibly high

level of stress. I keep thinking, what do I have to do? What's my homework? I've got to race to get this done. And then I remember, it's over.

His girlfriend added:

I finished up yesterday and I thought, I'm going out to lunch and get drunk. And I'm going to be so happy, and my life is going to be so perfect now.

We had lunch, and I was kind of let down. It was like—well—I'm going to go home and take a nap now. It wasn't what I thought it would be.

An anthropology major from Minnesota shares his thoughts:

I'm leaving everyone I love here, all my supports, all the people who love me. It's like leaving home all over again.

On the brink of adulthood, these young men and women retreat to realms of childlike playfulness. "I've done a lot of crazy things with my friends," said a business student in his final weeks. "Nothing harmful. Just absurd, like walking six miles to White Castle for a hamburger last weekend." The campus takes on an air of celebration, a spontaneous round of parties and picnics, barefoot smiling students cavorting with friends among the ubiquitous campus canines chasing sticks and frisbees, scantily clad seniors lazing in the sun—a week's hiatus before the finale.

Students put finishing touches on plans for the big day—graduation. Groups of friends make arrangements for cocktail parties and brunches and look forward to introducing their parents to each other on their own turf. For a number of students from divorced families, graduation stirs up the pain of unresolved family conflicts. Some of them anticipate having to orchestrate the comings and goings of parents, stepparents, and grandparents who barely speak to each other. They talk about feeling trapped and resent the burden of having to hold things together on their special day. For many children of divorced parents, however, this isn't a problem. Their parents put their own conflicts aside, and come together to share the joy of this milestone in their child's life.

When graduation day finally arrives, the campus is at its most resplendent. Lawns clipped and bushes pruned, instant gardens have sprung up in newly planted flower beds. The carillon rings out familiar tunes, and with luck the weather cooperates to produce the picture-book aura of the admissions office's most enticing brochure.

Parents, some with young children in tow or with grandparents on their arm, view the proceedings through the eyes of omnipresent video cameras and the more traditional thirty-five millimeter variety. Reflecting the diversity of the graduating class, the assembled guests sport turbans and veils, three-piece suits, cowboy boots.

The students congregate, a sea of black robes and mortarboards. Beneath the solemnity of academic garb, they express their individuality with Hawaiian shirts and shorts, purple sandals and red hightops, sunglasses of every imaginable color. Atop their mortarboards they have taped champagne glasses, pinwheels, a mysterious Chinese symbol, a sign that says "Hire me." They carry everything from bottles of champagne, balloons, and flowers, to a stuffed Snoopy dressed in full graduation regalia. As they line up for the processional, groups of friends join each other, expressing disbelief that this day has finally come. Their irreverent humor hints at their anxiety and belies the formality of the ritual: "I was once a waiter. I can do it again!" "I think I'll pick my grad school by what nifty color robes and hoods they have; I like the Stanford hoods myself." "It's with all of you guys that I got my best education. Good luck. We're getting out of here!"

The ceremony starts with a roll of drums or flair of trumpets, followed by the color and pageantry of a medieval academic procession. The music builds to the familiar strains of "Pomp and Circumstance"—guaranteed to send chills up the spines of even the most jaded of graduation-goers.

Among the speeches and musical interludes and conferring of honorary degrees, there are the familiar phrases that invite the assembled graduates to "enter the company of educated men and women." The final words are greeted with cheers, popping champagne corks, tossed mortar boards, the release of balloons into the sky.

The grandeur and pageantry of this final college ritual is ephemeral; it remains only in memory and faded family albums. What endures is less dramatic and unfolds over time.

In the words of a brand new graduate:

> It's not like right after graduation time stops and you just stand there and look at this big event—and this big white light comes out of the sky and says—"Sandy you're twenty-one! Look into the past at your life. Look forward at your future."
>
> You just take off your cap and gown and it's still the quad.
>
> The place hasn't changed but I have. Four years ago I wouldn't have understood this, but I feel like I'm leaving college with so many more questions than when I came in—and that's great. I know what the questions are and how to go about finding the answers.

As the recessional sounds, our children march out with arms around each other. We stand aside and watch them from a distance, catching a glimpse of the world that has been theirs for four years. We feel pride and joy and tenderness—but we also know that this is *their* moment, that they are creating their own futures.

NOTES

Chapter 1: Some Things Never Change: The Search for Identity, Independence, and Intimacy

1. Margaret Mahler's pioneering research on the development of young children has provided countless insights into the preverbal period of childhood and the movement from oneness with mother to psychological separateness. Trained as a pediatrician, Mahler later became an eminent child psychoanalyst and researcher. As a result of thirty years of painstaking daily observation of children interacting with their mothers during the first three years of life, Mahler and her associates describe a normal but complex developmental sequence, which they named "separation-individuation." These are seen as two separate, but complementary interweaving themes. Separation refers to the young child's emergence from a symbiotic relationship with his or her mother. Through individuation the child develops unique personality characteristics and the ability to retain a consistent mental image of mother and self.

Mahler adopts the biological term, "symbiosis" to describe the early bond between mother and infant. This close tie provides a foundation of basic trust from which the infant can begin to separate. The separation unfolds gradually over time in a mutually adaptive interplay.

The first signs of this process are the specific smiles that a baby reserves for its mother at about four or five months, signs of recognition of her as a separate and special person. Through the next two and a half years, the child will go through the sometimes exhilarating, sometimes painful process of moving away from mother to become a separate person in his or her own right. From a "practicing phase," when a toddler, who has just learned how to walk, feels all-powerful and in love with the world, to a "rapprochement phase," when with increasing separation anxiety, he or she becomes aware of his or her vulnerability and help-lessness, Mahler describes the often contradictory behaviors of the separating child. An empathic and helpful mother responds to her child's natural pull to venture forth with encouragement and support.

By about three years old, the healthy child will have the capacity to hold in his or her mind a loving, positive representation of mother as well as a consistent and clearly separate self-image. This positive "internal mother" image is available for comfort at those difficult times when mother is away or when she is frustrating or disappointing. It is a remarkable and complex achievement for a three-year-old and one that requires both trust and confidence as well as physical and cognitive maturity.

2. Psychologist Peter Blos has written extensively about the tumultuous years of adolescence. In his classic work, *On Adolescence,* he borrows the term a "second individuation" from Mahler to describe this chaotic time, which leads finally to a consolidation of individual identity.

> The oppositional, rebellious, and resistive strivings, the stages of experimentation, the testing of the self by going to excess—all these have a positive usefulness in the process of self-definition. "This is not me" represents an important step in the achievement of individuation and in the establishment of autonomy; at an earlier age, it is condensed into a single word "No."

3. Psychoanalyst and developmental theorist Erik Erikson points to this critical time as part of the natural evolution of human psychosocial development. His "eight stages of man" extend through the life cycle. Each stage is characterized by a crisis or turning point with polar opposite possible resolutions, one leading to growth and the other to difficulties. (Basic trust versus basic mistrust; autonomy versus shame and doubt; initiative versus guilt; industry versus inferiority; identity versus identity diffusion; intimacy versus isolation; generativity versus stagnation; ego integrity versus despair.) At each stage, there is a crossroads, a shifting in perspective, which leads to disequilibrium and vulnerability. The positive resolution of one stage makes moving to the next one possible. The child who has negotiated successfully earlier stages of trust, autonomy, initiative, and industry will have an easier time becoming a confident and self-reliant young adult, discovering the answers to the question, "Who am I?."

Erickson's stages are not neatly packaged, clearly defined time periods. Moreover his clinical observations were based on a male model of development. The more recent research of theorists Nancy Chodorow and Carol Gilligan has pointed to significant differences between identity development for men and women. Whereas men's identity is defined primarily in individual achievement and autonomy, women's identity is formed in the context of relationships. Gilligan's positive acknowledgment of the "woman's voice" of empathy, responsibility, and care adds a provocative dimension to the study of human development, which is only beginning to unfold.

Other theorists are examining the subtleties in the identity formation of specific minority groups. What is it like to be black in a white world? A homosexual in a world that values heterosexuality? A young man or woman from a culture that values close ties and obligations to extended family living in a western society that promotes individualism and independence? All pose questions that challenge or may simply broaden

Erikson's original observations.

4. Based on a study in the fifties and sixties involving a series of interviews with Harvard undergraduates across their college years, William Perry and his associates postulated a theory of intellectual and ethical development that has had a far-reaching impact on our understanding of the college student. Perry's scheme describes how students think in increasingly complex ways as they move through their college years. Many educators and researchers have found the material relevant and useful in tracing the development of critical thinking of the college student. Perry's research was done primarily on male subjects, and recently as an outgrowth of the work of Carol Gilligan, others are expanding on Perry's original work to incorporate "women's ways of knowing."

Perry described nine positions moving from an early stage of basic duality, when students see things in black and white terms, to a more complex relativistic view of the world, and finally to a point at which they are ready to make personal commitments.

5. According to Erik Erikson, it is essential to develop a solid sense of identity before moving on to the next task in his developmental scheme, forming intimate relationships. He writes in *Identity: Youth and Crisis:*

> It is only when identity formation is well on its way that true intimacy—which is really a counterpointing as well as a fusing of identities—is possible. Sexual intimacy, is only part of what I have in mind, for it is obvious that sexual intimacies often precede the capacity to develop a true and mutual psychosocial intimacy with another person, be it in friendship, in erotic encounters or in joint inspiration.

Chodorow and Gilligan challenge Erikson's assumption, claiming that his linear scheme is not representative of women's experience. For women the formation of identity and a capacity for intimacy are much more likely to be intertwined.

Chapter 2: Some Things Do Change: College Life Today

1. Alexander W. Astin, Kenneth C. Green, and William S. Korn, *The American Freshman: Twenty Year Trends* (Los Angeles: The Higher Education Research Institute of UCLA, 1987), 7.

2. Alexander W. Astin, William S. Korn, and Ellyne R. Berz, *The American Freshman: National Norms for Fall 1990* (Los Angeles: The Higher Education Research Institute of UCLA, 1990), 4.

3. Colin Campbell, "Campus Scenes: Seeing the Light at the End of the Liberal Arts Tunnel," *The New York Times,* 17 November, 1986, 14.

4. Helen Lefkowitz Horowitz, *Campus Life* (New York: Alfred A. Knopf, 1987), 289.

5. *Friends and Lovers in the College Years,* Formulated by the Committee on the College Student Group for the Advancement of Psychiatry (New York: Mental Health Materials Center, 1983), 71.

6. *The Cult Awareness Network,* 2421 West Pratt Boulevard, Suite 1173, Chicago, Illinois 60645. Hotline: (312) 267–7777.

International Cult Education Program, P.O. Box 1232 Gracie Station, New York, New York 10028. Hotline: (212) 439–1550. Marcia R. Rudin, Director.

International Cult Education Program is sponsored by the American Family Foundation and the Cult Awareness Network. ICEP provides educational forums and materials about cults and psychological manipulation. The director, Marcia Rudin, is a knowledgeable resource for parents.

7. Ethan J. Felson, quoted by Elizabeth Greene, "Conservative Activists Eye Politics; Leftists, Focus on Campus Issues," *The Chronicle of Higher Education,* 2 September, 1987, 84.

8. Ernest Boyer quoted by Edward B. Fiske, "Wave of Curriculum Change Sweeping American Colleges," *The New York Times,* 10 March, 1985.

Chapter 4: Ready, Set, Go: The Departure

1. Gail Sheehy, *Spirit of Survival* (New York: William Morrow and Company, Inc., 1986), 26.

Chapter 5: Orientation and Disorientation

1. Ellen Goodman, "When Students Fly from the Empty Nest," *The Philadelphia Inquirer*, 17 September, 1986.

Chapter 7: In and Out of Your Life

1. Robert Arnstein, M.D., "The Place of College Health Services in the Prevention of Suicide and Affective Disorders," *Suicide and Depression Among Adolescents and Young Adults*. ed. Gerald L. Klerman, M.D. (Washington D.C.: American Psychiatric Press, Inc., 1986), 350.

Chapter 8: Sophomore Slump and the Years Beyond

1. Kenneth Keniston, "Youth: A New Stage of Life," In *Readings in Adult Psychology: Contemporary Perspectives*, edited by Lawrence R. Allman and Dennis T. Jaffe (New York: Harper & Row, 1977), 133.

2. Richard S. Benner and Susan Tyler Hitchcock, *Life After Liberal Arts* (Charlottesville: University of Virginia, 1986), 10.

BIBLIOGRAPHY

Alper, Joseph. "Depression at an Early Age." *Science* (May 1986): 45–50.

Anderson, Harry. "God Goes Back to College." *Newsweek on Campus* (November 1986): 10–16.

Apter, Terri. *Altered Loves: Mothers and Daughters during Adolescence.* New York: Ballantine Books, 1990.

Arnstein, Robert, M.D. "Development Issues for College Students." *Psychiatric Annals, 14 (September 1984): 9.*

———. "The Place of College Health Services in the Prevention of Suicide and Affective Disorders." In *Suicide and Depression Among Adolescents and Young Adults.* Ed. Gerald L. Klerman, M.D. Washington, D.C.: American Psychiatric Press, Inc., 1986.

Ascher, Carol. "Ensuring a Rainbow after the Storm: Recent Initiatives to Institutionalize Pluralism on Predominantly White Campuses." *Review* (Higher Education Extension Service at Yale University and ERIC Clearinghouse on Urban Education, Teachers College, Columbia) (Spring, 1991): 1–11.

Astin, Alexander W., William Korn, and Ellyne R. Berz. *The American Freshman: National Norms for Fall 1990.* Los Angeles, California: The Higher Education Research Institute of UCLA, 1990.

Astin, Alexander W., Kenneth C. Green, William S. Korn, *The American Freshman: Twenty Year Trends, 1966-1985.* Los Angeles, California: The Higher Education Research Institute of UCLA, 1987.

Begley, Sharon. "When Food is the Enemy." *Newsweek on Campus* (March 1987): 18–19.

Belenky, Mary F., Blythe M. Clinchy, Nancy Rule Goldberger, Jill M. Tarule. *Women's Ways of Knowing.* New York: Basic Books, Inc., 1986.

Benner, Richard S., and Susan Tyler Hitchcock. *Life After Liberal Arts: Information and Advice for Students from the University of Virginia's College of Arts and Sciences Alumni Career Survey.* Charlottesville: University of Virginia, 1986.

Bloom, Allen. *The Closing of the American Mind.* New York: Simon and Schuster, 1987.

Bloom, Michael V. *Adolescent Parental Separation.* New York: Gardner Press, Inc., 1980.

Blos, Peter. *On Adolescence: A Psychoanalytic Interpretation.* New York: The Free Press of Glencoe, 1962.

―――. *The Adolescent Passage.* New York: International Universities Press, 1979.

Borhek, Mary V. *Coming Out to Parents: A Two-Way Survival Guide for Lesbians and Gay Men and Their Parents.* New York: The Pilgrim Press, 1983.

Boyer, Ernest L. *Campus Life: In Search of Community.* Princeton, New Jersey: The Carnegie Foundation for the Advancement of Teaching, 1990.

――― *College: The Undergraduate Experience in America.* New York: Harper and Row, 1987.

―――. *The Condition of the Professoriate: Attitudes and Trends, 1989.* Princeton, New Jersey: The Carnegie Foundation for the Advancement of Teaching, 1989.

Brans, J. *Mother, I Have Something To Tell You.* Garden City, New York: Doubleday & Company, Inc., 1987.

Cahn, Victor L. *A Thinking Student's Guide to College.* Norwell, Massachusetts: The Christopher Publishing House, 1988.

Cammer, Leonard, M.D. *Up from Depression.* New York: Pocket Books, 1969.

Campbell, Colin. "Campus Scenes: Seeing the Light at the End of the Liberal Arts Tunnel." *The New York Times,* 17 November, 1986.

Chodorow, Nancy. *The Reproduction of Mothering: Psychoanalysis and the Sociology of Gender.* Berkeley, California: University of California Press, 1978.

Cohen, Robert D., ed. *Working with the Parents of College Students.* San Francisco: Jossey-Bass Inc., 1985.

Colarusso, Calvin, A.M.D., and Robert Nemiroff, A.M.D. *Adult Development.* New York: Plenum Press, 1981.

Colt, George Howe. "Suicide." *Harvard Magazine* (September-October 1983): 47–66.

D'Souza, Dinesh. *Illiberal Education: The Politics of Sex and Race on Campus.* New York: Free Press, 1991.

DeBuono, B.A., S.H. Zinner, M. Daamen, and W.M. McCormack. "Sexual Behavior of College Women in 1975, 1986, and 1989." *The New England Journal of Medicine* (March 22, 1990): 821–25.

DePalma, Anthony. "Separate Ethnic Worlds Grow on Campus." *New York Times* (May 18, 1991): 1, 7.

Donovan, Bruce, and John Robinson. "A Letter to Parents and Guardians of Members of the Class of 1989." (Pamphlet published and distributed by Brown University, August 1985).

Edmiston, Andrew J. "Life at Lehigh: A Conversation with Parents." (Pamphlet published and distributed by Lehigh University).

Edward, Joyce, Nathene Ruskin, and Patsy Turrini. *Separation-In-dividuation Theory and Application*. New York: Gardner Press, Inc., 1981.

Ehrhart, Julie K., and Bernice R. Sandler. *Campus Gang Rape: Party Games?* Washington, D.C.: Project on the Status and Education of Women, Association of American Colleges. 1985.

Eichenbaum, Luise, and Susie Orbach. *Understanding Women: A Feminist Psychoanalytic Approach*. New York: Basic Books, Inc., 1983.

El-Khawas, Elaine. "Campus Trends, 1986." *Higher Education Panel Report Number 73*. Washington, D.C.: American Council on Education, August, 1986.

Engram, Barbara. *The Roommate Negotiation Workbook* (Hood College).

Erikson, Erik H. *Childhood and Society*. 2nd ed. New York: W. W. Norton, 1963.

———. *Identity, Youth and Crisis*. New York: W. W. Norton, 1968.

———. "Youth: Fidelity and Diversity." *Youth and Culture: A Human-Development Approach*. Ed. Hazel V. Kraemer. Monterey, California: Brooks/Cole Publishing Company, 1974.

———. *Identity and the Life Cycle*. New York: W. W. Norton, 1980.

Fiske, Edward B. "Colleges Playing Larger Role in Guiding Lives of College Students." *The New York Times*. February 22, 1987: 1.

———. "Student Debt is Reshaping College and Careers." Education Life, *The New York Times*. August 3, 1986: 34.

———. *Selective Guide to Colleges*. 1986–87. New York: Times Books, 1986.

Fiske, Edward B. and Joseph M. Michalak. *The Best Buys in College Education,* New York Times Books, 1985.

Fleming, Jacqueline. *Blacks in College: A Comparative Study of Students' Success in Black and White Institutions*. San Francisco: Jossey Bass, 1984.

"The Freshman Year at Harvard College." (Booklet mailed by the Freshman Dean's Office to parents of entering students), March 1984.

Friends and Lovers in the College Years. Formulated by the Committee on the College Student Group for the Advancement of Psychiatry. New York: Mental Health Materials Center, 1983.

Gilligan, Carol. *In a Different Voide: Psychological Theory and Women's Development*. Cambridge, Massachusetts: Harvard University Press, 1982.

Goethals, George W., and Dennis S. Klos. *Experiencing Youth: First Person Accounts*. 2nd Ed. Boston: Little, Brown and Company, 1976.

Goleman, Daniel. "What Colleges Have Learned about Suicide." *New York Times*. February 23, 1986.

Goodman, Ellen. "When Students Fly from the Empty Nest." *The Philadelphia Inquirer*. September 17, 1986.

Gordinier, Jeff. "Sophomore Slump." *Princeton Parents*, February 1987.

Greene, Elizabeth. "Conservative Activists Eye Politics; Leftists Focus on Campus Issues." *The Chronicle of Higher Education,* September 2, 1987: 84.

Green, Madeleine F., ed. *Minorities on Campus: A Handbook for Enhancing Diversity*. Washington D.C.: American Council on Education, 1989.

Griffin, Carolyn Welch, Marian J. Wirth, and Arthur G. Wirth. *Beyond Acceptance: Parents of Lesbians and Gays Talk About Their Experiences*. Englewood Cliffs, New Jersey: Prentice-Hall, Inc., 1986.

Halpern, Howard M. *Cutting Loose: An Adult Guide to Coming to Terms with Parents*. New York: Simon and Schuster, 1976.

Hassan, Steven. *Combatting Cult Mind Control*. Rochester, Vermont: Park Street Press, 1988.

Heller, Scott. "Teaching Assistants Get Increased Training: Problems Arise in Foreign Student Programs." *The Chronicle of Higher Education*. October 29, 1986: 9.

Heston, Jos. C., and Willard B. Frick., eds. "The Role of Alienation in Identity Formation in College Students." Address by Edward S. Bordin of University of Michigan. *Counseling for the Liberal Arts Campus: The Albion Symposium*. Antioch Press, 1968.

Hodgkinson, Harold L. *All One System: Demographics of Education, Kindergarten through Graduate School*. Washington, D.C.: Institute for Educational Leadership, Inc., 1985.

Horowitz, Helen Lefkowitz. *Campus Life*. New York: Alfred A. Knopf, 1987.

Hughes, Jean O'Gorman, and Bernice Sandler. "Friends Raping Friends: Could It Happen to You?" Washington, D.C. Project on the Status and Education of Women, Association of American Colleges, April 1987.

Institute of International Education. "Basic Facts on Foreign Study." New York: 1982.

Johnston, Lloyd D., Patrick N. O'Malley, and Jerald G. Bachman. *Drug Use Among American High School Students, College Students, and Other Young Adults: National Trends through 1985*. Rockville, Maryland: National Institute on Drug Abuse, 1986.

Johnston, Lloyd D., Jerald F. Bachman, and Patrick O'Malley. *Monitoring the Future: A Continuing Study of the Lifestyles and*

Values of Youth. Ann Arbor, Michigan: The University of Michigan Institute for Social Research, 1991.

Jones, Thomas B., ed. *The Educated Person: A Collection of Contemporary American Essays.* St. Paul: Metropolitan State University, 1983.

Josselson, Ruthellen. *Finding Herself: Pathways to Identity Development in Women.* San Francisco: Jossey-Bass Publishers, 1990.

Judkins, David. *Study Abroad: The Astute Student's Guide.* Charlotte, Vermont: Williamson Publishing Co., 1989.

Kaplan, Louise. *Oneness and Separateness: From Infant to Individual.* New York: Simon and Shuster, 1978.

———. *Adolescence: The Farewell to Childhood.* New York: Simon and Schuster, 1984.

Katchadourian, Herant A., and John Boli. *Careerism and Intellectualism Among College Students.* San Francisco: Jossey-Bass, 1985.

Katz, Montana, and Veronica Vieland. *Get Smart! A Woman's Guide to Equality on Campus.* New York: The Feminist Press at The City University of New York, 1988.

Keniston, Kenneth. "Youth: A 'New' Stage of Life." *Readings in Adult Psychology: Contemporary Perspectives.* Ed. Lawrence R. Allman and Dennis T. Jaffe. New York: Harper & Row, 1977.

Lamont, Lansing. *Campus Shock.* New York: E. P. Dutton, 1979.

Ledray, Linda E. *Recovering from Rape.* New York: Henry Holt and Company, 1986.

Leo, John, "When the Date Turns into Rape." *Time.* March 23, 1987.

Levine, Arthur. *When Dreams and Heroes Died: A Portrait of Today's College Student.* San Francisco: Josey-Bass, 1980.

———. "Riding First Class on the Titanic: A Portrait of Today's College Student." *National Association of Student Personnel Association Jounal.* 20 (Spring, 1983).

———. "Hearts and Minds: The Freshman Challenge." *American Association of Higher Education Bulletin,* 1986: 3–6.

Littwin, Susan. *The Postponed Generation: Why American Youth Are Growing Up Later.* New York: William Morrow and Company, Inc., 1986.

Mahler, Margaret S., Fred Pine, and Anni Bergman. *The Psychological Birth of the Human Infant.* New York: Basic Books, 1975.

Mayner, Denise K. "Amid the Diversity, Racial Isolation Remains at Berkeley." *The Chronicle of Higher Education* (November 19, 1990): 37–39.

Minorities in Higher Education: Fourth Annual Status Report. Washington D.C.: American Council on Education, 1985.

Moll, Richard. *The Public Ivys.* New York: Penguin Books, 1986.

Morrill, Weston, and James Hurst with E.R. Oetting *et al. Dimensions of Intervention for Student Development.* New York: John Wiley and Sons, Inc., 1980.

National On-Campus Report. Vol. 14, No. 9. Madison, Wisconsin: Magna Publications, Inc., May 5, 1986.

Offer, Daniel, and Judith Baskin Offer. *From Teenage to Young Manhood.* New York: Basic Books, 1975.

Park, Clara Claiborne, and Leon N. Shapiro, M.D. *You are Not Alone: Understanding and Dealing with Mental Illness.* Boston: Little, Brown and Company, 1976.

Parrot, Andrea, ed. *Acquaintance Rape: The Hidden Crime.* New York: John Wiley & Sons, Inc., 1991.

Perry, William G., Jr. *Forms of Intellectual and Ethical Development in the College Years.* New York: Holt, Rinehart and Winston Inc., 1968.

Powell, Elizabeth, M.S., M.A. *Talking Back to Sexual Pressure.* Minneapolis, Minnesota: CompCare Publishers, 1991.

Reese, Deborah Frankel. "The Children Are Gone." *The New York Times.* December 1985.

Reiz, Fred. "When Your Child Goes to College . . . Don't Make the Bed." (Pamphlet for parents at Wittenberg University), 1974.

Reschke, Wayne, and Karen H. Knierim. "How Parents Influence Career Choice." *Journal of Career Planning and Employment.* Spring, 1987.

Rockwell, W. J., M.D. "Brief Psychotherapy with University Students." *Psychiatric Annals,* 14 (September 1984): 9.

Rudin, Marcia. *Cults on Campus: Continuing Challenge.* New York: International Cult Education Program, 1991.

Sanford, Nevitt. *Where Colleges Fail.* San Francisco: Jossey-Bass Inc., 1967.

———. *The American College.* New York: John Wiley & Sons, Inc., 1962.

Schumer, Fran. "A Return to Religion." *The New York Times Magazine.* April 22, 1984: 90–94, 98.

Schwartzm John. "Doing Good." *Newsweek on Campus.* November 1986: 27–31.

Sheehy, Gail. *Spirit of Survival.* New York: William Morrow and Company, Inc., 1986.

Smith, Michael Clay, and Dr. Margaret D. Smith. *Wide Awake: A Guide to Safe Campus Living in the 90s.* Princeton, New Jersey: Peterson's Guides, Inc., 1990.

Springan, Karen. "Broader Horizons." *Newsweek on Campus.* September 1986.

Stein, Sandra. "Parents' Guide, Cornell University." 1985–1986.

Sweet, Ellen. "Date Rape: The Story of An Epidemic and Those Who Deny It." *Ms/Campus Times.* October 1985: 56–85.

Taylor, Charles. "Black Students on Predominantly White College Campuses in the 1980's." *Journal of College Student Personnel 27* (May 1986): 196–202.

Toth, Susan Allen. *Ivy Days: Making My Way Out East.* New York: Ballantine Books, 1984.

Viorst, Judith. *Necessary Losses.* New York: Simon and Schuster, 1986.

Warshaw, Robin. *I Never Called It Rape: The Ms. Report on Recognizing, Fighting & Surviving Date Rape.* Scranton, Pennsylvania: Harper Collins Publishers, Inc., 1989.

Whiteley, John. *Character Development in College Students: The Freshman Year.* Volume I. Schenectady: Character Research Press, 1982.

Williams College: Handbook for Parents (Published and distributed by Williams College, Williamstown, Mass.)

Wolensky, Robert. "College Students in the Fifties: The Silent Generation Revisited." *Adolescent Psychiatry: Developmental and Clinical Studies.* Vol. V, Ed. Sherman C. Feinstein and Peter Giovacchini. New York: Jason Aronson, Inc., 1977.

Zikopoulos, Marianthi, ed. *Open Doors 1989/90: Report on International Educational Exchange.* New York: Institute of International Education, 1990.

Zuker, R. Fred. *Peterson's Guide to College Admissions.* Princeton, New Jersey: Peterson's Guide, 1990.

INDEX

Academic assistance, 174–75
Academic expectations, in advance of starting college, 118–22
Academic life, 63–68
  freshman, 161–78
Academic standing
  of entering freshmen, 32
  in freshman classes, 119–20
  and identity, 170
Acceptance, to college, reactions to, 87–90
Accidents, at college, 211
Ackerman, Mary, 198
Acquaintance rape. *See* Date rape
Admission
  competition for, 72–73, 79–81
  marathon process of, 75–87
  students' procrastination about, 78
Adolescent
  intellectual development, 17–20
  separation from parents, 12–13
Adolescent development, 8–9, 17–20, 291–92
Advisors, 176
AIDS, 55, 61, 196
Alcohol
  freshman's encounter with, 190–96
  and parental values communicated to student, 123
  use, abuse, and college policies about, 31–32, 50–52, 212
Allowance, student's, 116–17
The American Freshman: Twenty Year Trends (Astin, Green, Korn), 29
Anorexia. *See* Eating disorders
Anxiety, student's, 213. *See also* Stress
Arnstein, Robert, 214
Astin, Alexander, 29, 33, 62

BACCHUS, 51
Beede, Laurence, 114
Beyond Acceptance (Griffin, Wirth), 229
Blacks, scholarship on, 63
Blacks in College (Fleming), 58
Black students, groups for, 57–59
Blos, Peter, 292
Borhek, Mary, 229
Boyer, Ernest, 29, 31, 43, 67, 248
Buckley Amendment, 174
Bulimia, 207. *See also* Eating disorders

Campus groups, 56. *See also* *specific group*
Campus life
  as reflection of society, 9
  today's, 38–68

Campus Life (Horowitz), 37

Career centers, 45–47

Careerism, among today's students, 33, 36

Care packages, 204

Case, Jim, 280

Change
during college career, 231–33
as college experience, 26–27

Chodorow, Nancy, 292

Classes, freshman, 163–72

Coed living in dorms, 38–39, 188
off-campus, 260

College
anticipation about, by prospective freshmen, 95–96
expectations about, 6–7, 71–75
out-of-the-classroom facilities, 39–41
selection of, 90–93
reaction to, 93–95
as time of transition, 8
today's experience of, 74–75
withdrawal from, 209–10

College: The Undergraduate Experience in America (Boyer), 29–30

College applications, 81–83. *See also* Admission
parents' attitudes about, 82–83
students' ambivalence about, 79–82

Coming Out to Parents (Borhek), 229

Communication
importance of, 204
and open-ended questions, 227–28
between student and family, 109–14, 202–204

Community service, students' participation in, 34

Computers on campus, pervasiveness of, 40–41

Control, as issue for students, 242

Counseling services, 47

Courses, introductory, 165–66

Cox, Harvey, 65

Credit card, student's, 117

Cult Awareness Network, 60

Cults, 59–60

Curriculum reform, 66–68

Date rape, 48–49, **216-18**
and substance abuse, 50–52

Departure, for college, 97–128
last days before, 127–28
last months before, 98–106
last weeks before, 106–109
by student alone or with parents, decision about, 107–108

Depression, student's, 213–16

Development. *See also* Adolescent development; Intellectual development
intellectual and ethical, theories about, 292
psychosocial, theories about, 291–92

Disorientation
of first days on campus, 136–45
of first weeks away from home, 145–50

Divorced parents
financial arrangements

made by, 117

at graduation ceremony, 287–88

student's allegiances to, 221–22

Donovan, Bruce, 123

Dormitories. *See* Residence halls

Drugs

freshman's encounter with, 190–98

and parental values communicated to student, 123–24

and social life, 185

use, abuse, and college policies about, 31, 50–52, 212

use, signs of, 81

and values held by students, 125–26

Drum, Alice, 101–102, 137

Eating disorders, 32, 212

campus services for intervention with, 49–50

Eckert, Charles, 36

Edmiston, Andrew J., 124–26

Ehrlich, Thomas, 63

Empty nest, 147

Engram, Barbara, 180–81

Erikson, Erik, 292

Exercise, students' participation in, 32

Extracurricular activities

on college campuses, 62

of upper classmen, 272

Family characteristics, and student characteristics, 31

Family dynamics, when

student returns for vacation, 223–27

Family Educational Rights and Privacy Act of 1974, 174

Felson, Ethan J., 61

Final exams, freshman year, 156

Finances

family pressures from, 85–86

issues for graduates, 283

numbers of students needing help with, 30–31

planning for, by student and family, 115–19

and sophomore slump, 239

Financial aid, 86, 115

Fiske, Edward B., 42–43, 66–67, 89

Fleming, Jacqueline, 58

Foreign languages, in curriculum, 64–65

Foreign students, numbers in US colleges, 30

Foreign study, 264–70

Fraternities, 61–62

Freedom, in freshman year, 178

Freshman year, rhythm of, 151–61

Freshmen

academic performance, 172–73

factors affecting, 172–73

today's, attitudes and values of, 33–34

Friends

changing, in sophomore year, 241

in first days on campus, 138–39

in freshman year, 153–54, 179–90, 184–87

and graduation, 283–84
and intimacy, 194
student's attachment to, 217–18
Friends and Lovers in the College Years, 54
Futter, Ellen, 19–20

Gardner, John, 192
Gay and lesbian students. *See also* Homosexuality support groups for, 60
coming out, to parents, 228–29.
Geographic distance
and choice of college, 86–87
problems created by, 202–203
of selected college, and separation issues, 92
Gilligan, Carol, 292–93
Ginsberg, Paul, 37
Goodman, Ellen, 147
Gott v. Berea College, 42
Grade point average, 121, 172
Grades. *See also* Academic expectations
as barometer, 173
freshman, 170–71
parents' access to, 174
parents' concerns about, 62, 171–72
view of extracurricular activity, 62
Graduate school, 278
Graduation
attitudes toward, 288–89
disorientation of, 286–87
Griffin, Carolyn, 229

Hallie, Philip, 36

Hedrick, Robert, 85
Homesickness, 153, 158, 161, 209
Homophobia, 61
Homosexuality, 60–61, 197. *See also* Gay and lesbian students
Honors thesis, 275
Horowitz, Helen Lefkowitz, 37–38
Hospitalization, of student, 211–212
Housing, 101–103
Hyson, Marion, 242, 249

Identity, 293
and college admissions process, 79–80
and college choice, 91
of college graduate, 281–82
formation of, 8
and friends, 184–85
and independent decision making, 141
and intimacy, 23
for freshmen, 141–45
for men vs. women, 292
search for, 11–12, 13–17
sophomore's definition of, 241
Illness, student, 210–11
Independence
and academic life, 162
ambivalence about, 207–208
and fears, 22
after freshman year's end, 160
struggle for, 8, 20–23
vs. asking for help, 22
Individuation
definition of, 291

second, 292
In loco parentis, current status
    of colleges as, 42–43
Intellectual development,
    adolescents', 17–20
Intimacy
    establishing, children's ef-
        forts at, 8
    issues for sophomores, 241
    search for, 23–25, 194, 293

Job hunt, in senior year, 278–80
Junior year, 271–72
Junior year abroad, 264–70

Keniston, Kenneth, 243
Kennedy, Delores, 107
Kisker, Harry, 36
Kohm, Barbara, 146
Koss, Mary P., 48

Lachman, Seymour, 60
Latin American studies, 65
Letters, between student and
    family, 109–112, 201
    importance of, 204
Levine, Arthur E., 32
Liberal arts
    enrollments in, 33, 65
    and job success, 249
Loneliness, freshman, 187–88
Lovers. *See* Sexual relation-
    ships
Loxley, Janet, 180, 215–16

Mahler, Margaret, 291–92
Major(s)
    combined, 250
    popular, and economic con-
        siderations, 33–34
    selection of, 122, 243–51

pressures about, 257–58
    and stereotyping, 245
Materialism, of today's
    students, 36–37
McPherson, Mary Patterson,
    248
Midterms, 154–55
    freshman year, 158
Minority students
    groups for, 56–59
    percentage entering college,
        30
Money management, student's
    learning about, 21, 116–17
Moving, while student is at
    college, 222–23
Multiculturalism on campus,
    56–59

OAs. *See* Orientation assistants
Off-campus residence, 259–62
Older students, in college, 30
On Adolescence (Blos), 291
Orientation assistants, 132
Orientation programs, 130–36
    for parents, 131
    summer, 105

Packing, as indication of
    student's attitude toward
    leaving home, 127–28
Parents
    and academic problems, 176–
        77
    accompanying child to
        school, 107–108
    and admissions process, 76–
        79
    anticipation of child's
        college career, 95–96
    anxiety about children's

friends, 139
attitudes toward child's acceptance by college, 88
attitudes toward grades, 172
and bad news for student, 206
in college selection process, 92–93
and communication, 161–63
expectations and assumptions of, communication to child, 108–109
idealized views of college, 74–75
informing college about special needs of child, 101
and intellectual growth of child, 19–20
misunderstanding of children, 7
overreactions vs. underreactions to student's problems, 201–202
pressures put on students by, 7
reactions to child's rejection by college, 87–88
and residential life problems, 182–83
students' changing views of, 231–32
and student's choices, 252–53
as support system for student, 200
vists to campus by, 219–21
Parents and Friends of Lesbians and Gays, 229
Parents FLAG, 229
Park, Clara Claiborne, 216
Perry, William, 292–93
Phone calls, between student and family, 112–13, 201
importance of, 204
Politics, of today's students, 34–35
Premeds, 246–47
Preregistration, 105
Privacy, student's need for, 192
Procrastination, among students, 169–70
Professional school, 278
Psychological illness, of student, 212–16

Rape prevention, 48
RAs. *See* Resident advisors
Rassias, John, 64
Reese, Deborah Frankel, 127
Reiz, Fred, 118
Rejection, by college, handling, 87–90
Religion
on college campuses, 59–60
courses on, 65
Residence halls, parents' reactions to, 134
Resident advisors, 45–46, 132
Residential life, 44–46, 103
problems with, 179
Resources, on college campus, 39–41
Robinson, John M., 123
Roommate(s), 103–104, 137–38, 143, 154, 179–90
communication between, 180
future, contacting before freshman year starts, 104–105
The Roommate Negotiation Workbook (Engram), 180
Roommate questionnaires, 100–101

Salamon, Linda, 167, 249, 250, 275
SATs, 75
Schmitter, Barbara, 134, 184
Schroeder, Charles, 62
Schroer, Anne, 113, 211, 245
Sciences, in curriculum, 63
Security, on college campus, 40–41
Seminars, freshman, 164–65
Senior projects, 275
Senior year, 271, 274–89
Separation
    in adolescence, 13
    ambivalence about, 4–6, 13
    child's view of, 5
    and college selection, 93
    and communication, 114
    definition of, 291
    in early childhood, 12–13
    and identity, 198
    individual experience of, 9
    issues of, at winter break, 156
    during orientation, 133–34
    parents' view of, 4–6
    process, 3–4, 9–10
    as stress, 214–15
Services, for students, campus, 41–43
Sex roles, student attitudes toward, 35
Sexual behavior, on college campuses, 196
Sexual identity, issues of, 196–97
Sexuality, campus workshops and seminars on, 55
Sexual relationships, 190–98
    current practices on college campuses, 52–56
    and dependency, 188–89

freshman year, 179–90
future of, after graduation, 285–86
and identity, 25
and sophomores' search for identity, 241–42
and values held by students, 124
vs. intimacy, 25
Shapiro, Leon N., 216
Sheehy, Gail, 98
Siblings
    adjustment to student's leaving, 148–49
    older, as counsellors, 126
Single parents
    attitudes about separation from child, 84–85
    disorientation of child's leaving, 147–48
Sixties, courses about, 65
Smith, Kiki, 172–73
Smoking, among students, 32
Social life, freshman, 152, 185
Sophomores, decisions faced by, 251–53
Sophomore slump, 234–43
Sororities, 62, 140–41
Spahn, Stephen, 92
Special needs, informing college about, 101
Spring break, freshman year, 158
Stopping out, 253–59
Stress, 213
    and grades, 172
    of midterms, 154
    as part of college experience, 175
STS programs, 64
Student(s)

attitudes and values of, 35–37
conservative vs. liberal, 35
diversity of, 186
expectations and oppor-
  tunities, 32–33
generalizations about, 37–38
limitations of, 38
increasing power over their
  own lives, 42–43
intellectual and ethical
  development of, 292–93
today's, characteristics of,
  29–38
media portrayals of, vs.
  reality, 37
numbers of, today, 73
protection of parents, 201–
  202
stereotypes of, 37
unresponsive, 207–208
view of future, 32–33
Student activism, 35
  student activities, 187
  students' rights, 43
Substance abuse. *See* Alcohol;
  Drugs
Suicide, 218
Summer vacation
  after freshman year, 159–60
  decisions about, 253
  symbiosis, 291

TAs. *See* Teaching assistants
Teaching assistants, 164
Technology, on college cam-
  pus, 40–41
Thanksgiving holiday, fresh-
  man year, 155

Thirsk, Robert, 280
Tidmarsh, Karen, 43, 172
Time management, learning,
  169
Titanic ethic, 32–33
Transfers, 262–64

Vacations
  freshman year, 155–56
  students' behavior during,
    221–33
Valedictorian syndrome, 72
Values
  of departing freshman, 122–
    27
  establishment of, 190–92
  questioning of, by
    sophomores, 237–38
Vandalism, and substance
  abuse, 51
Visits home, students' behavior during, 221–33
Visits to campus, by parents,
  219–21

*When Dreams and Heroes
  Died* (Levine), 32–33
Winter break, freshman year,
  157–58
Wirth, Marian and Arthur, 229
Women
  major selection by, 246
  numbers entering college, 30
  scholarship on, 63

You Are Not Alone (Park,
  Shapiro), 216